"This inspiring and comprehensive volume written by esteemed experts in the fields of art, music, dance/movement, drama, and phototherapies successfully navigates the topic of the global crisis of depression. Through current research, evidence-based practice, case studies and clinical vignettes this book richly weaves together how creative arts disciplines address the challenge of working with a variety of populations with depression across the lifespan and across cultures. With the goal of demonstrating proof of effectiveness with this challenging crisis of depression, the authors present an engaging compilation of studies using a myriad of creative and diverse clinical approaches, research designs and methods, and perspectives. The study designs are well-suited to the arts therapies and clients and chapters provide both breadth as well as depth. Authors are self-reflective and culturally aware presenting a variety of work with individuals, groups, and short-term and long term treatment. The book as a whole is well organized, balanced, readable and well grounded in research. I anticipate that the impact of this book will be far-reaching and appreciated by arts therapy clinicians and researchers and anyone who works with individuals with depression."

Susan Loman, MA, BC-DMT, NCC, Certified KMP analyst, professor emerita, adjunct faculty was director of the Dance/Movement Therapy and Counseling Program, Department of Applied Psychology, Antioch University New England

Arts Therapies in the Treatment of Depression

Arts Therapies in the Treatment of Depression is a comprehensive compilation of expert knowledge on arts therapies' potential in successfully addressing depression. The book identifies ways of addressing the condition in therapy sessions, shares experience of tools and approaches which seem to work best and guides towards a conscious and confident evidence-based practice.

Including contributions from international experts in the field of arts therapies, the book presents some of the most recent, high-profile and methodologically diverse research, whether in the form of clinical trials, surveys or case studies. The three sections of this volume correspond to particular life stages and explore major topics in arts therapies practice and the nature of depression in children, adults and in later life. Individual chapters within the three sections represent all four arts therapies disciplines. The book hopes to improve existing arts therapies practice and research by encouraging researchers to use creativity in designing meaningful research projects and empowering practitioners to use evidence creatively for the benefit of their clients and the discipline.

Arts Therapies in the Treatment of Depression is an essential resource for arts therapies researchers, practitioners and arts therapists in training. It should also be of interest to other health researchers and health professionals, particularly those who work with clients experiencing depression and in multidisciplinary teams.

Ania Zubala, PhD, is a health researcher who explores the role of arts and arts therapies for holistically-understood wellbeing, particularly in the context of remote communities and aging populations. She is a research fellow in health psychology and digital health at the University of the Highlands and Islands, Scotland.

Vicky Karkou, PhD, is a professor at Edge Hill University leading the research theme of arts and wellbeing. She is an educator, researcher and dance movement psychotherapist, widely published in peer-reviewed journals and books, and a co-editor of the international journal *Body, Movement and Dance in Psychotherapy*

International Research in the Arts Therapies

A Routledge Book Series

Series Editors: Diane Waller and Sarah Scoble

This series consists of high-level monographs identifying areas of importance across all arts therapy modalities and highlighting international developments and concerns. It presents recent research from countries across the world and contributes to the evidence-base of the arts therapies. Papers which discuss and analyse current innovations and approaches in the arts therapies and arts therapy education are also included.

This series is accessible to practitioners of the arts therapies and to colleagues in a broad range of related professions, including those in countries where arts therapies are still emerging. The monographs should also provide a valuable source of reference to government departments and health services.

Diane Waller and Sarah Scoble

Titles in the Series

1 **International Arts Therapies Research**
Edited by Ditty Dokter and Margaret Hills de Zárate

2 **Arts Therapies and New Challenges in Psychiatry**
Edited by Karin Dannecker

3 **Arts Therapies in the Treatment of Depression**
Edited by Ania Zubala and Vicky Karkou

For more information about the series, please visit www.routledge.com.

Arts Therapies in the Treatment of Depression

Edited by Ania Zubala
and Vicky Karkou

Routledge
Taylor & Francis Group
LONDON AND NEW YORK

ECArTE
EUROPEAN CONSORTIUM FOR ARTS THERAPIES EDUCATION

ICRA
INTERNATIONAL CENTRE FOR RESEARCH IN ARTS THERAPIES

First published 2018 by Routledge

2 Park Square, Milton Park, Abingdon, Oxfordshire OX14 4RN
52 Vanderbilt Avenue, New York, NY 10017

Routledge is an imprint of the Taylor & Francis Group, an informa business

First issued in paperback 2020

British Library Cataloguing-in-Publication Data
A catalogue record for this book is available from the British Library

Library of Congress Cataloging-in-Publication Data
Names: Zubala, Ania, editor. | Karkou, Vassiliki, editor.
Title: Arts therapies in the treatment of depression / edited by Ania Zubala and Vicky Karkou.
Description: Abingdon, Oxon ; New York, NY : Routledge, 2018. | Series: International research in the arts therapies | Includes bibliographical references and index.
Identifiers: LCCN 2018003032 (print) | LCCN 2018004109 (ebook) | ISBN 9781315454412 (E-book) | ISBN 9781138210769 (hardback : alk. paper) | ISBN 9781315454412 (ebk)
Subjects: | MESH: Depression—therapy | Sensory Art Therapies
Classification: LCC RC489.A72 (ebook) | LCC RC489.A72 (print) | NLM WM 171.5 | DDC 616.89/1656—dc23
LC record available at https://lccn.loc.gov/2018003032

ISBN: 978-1-138-21076-9 (hbk)
ISBN: 978-0-367-48784-3 (pbk)

Typeset in Bembo
by Apex CoVantage, LLC

Contents

Contributors

Badr Alrazain, PhD, is originally from the Kingdom of Saudi Arabia. He graduated from King Saud University in Art Education in 1999. He later worked as an art education teacher in a secondary school in Riyadh and then as a lecturer at Qassim University. He obtained his Masters from King Saud University, focusing his work on learning difficulties. He completed his doctoral studies at the QMU, Edinburgh, in the area of arts therapies for children affected by ADHD. Badr currently works as an assistant professor at Qassim University and leads art therapy at the Mohammed bin Nayef Center in Riyadh.

Ashley Beck, MS, is a recent graduate from the Florida State University Master's of Art Therapy program. Ms. Beck graduated with a BA in pre-professional art therapy, where she developed an interest for marginalized forensic populations. She has had clinical experience in both male and female institutions and forensic psychiatric units. Her current research interests include promoting the field of art therapy in prison settings as well as art therapy and sustainability within an international context.

Iris Bräuninger, PhD, is a professor and researcher at the University of Applied Sciences of Special Needs Education Zurich. She also teaches at the DMT Program at Autonomous University Barcelona and works as a DMT supervisor and practitioner. Previously, she worked as deputy head of the DMT, Physio, Music Therapy Department, a researcher at the University Hospital of Psychiatry Zurich and post-doctoral researcher at the University of Deusto Bilbao. Iris teaches internationally in DMT, research and KMP. She is a registered Supervisor of the German (BTD) and Spanish (ADMTE) Association and holds the European Certificate of Psychotherapy (ECP).

Jane Burns, PhD, is a qualified art psychotherapist currently working at Queen Margaret University as a lecturer on the MSc art psychotherapy programme. Her research has been in the arts therapies with the older person, and her PhD research mapped how arts therapists work in practice with the person who has dementia. Jane is also interested in how the arts can support a

Contributors

Badr Alrazain, PhD, is originally from the Kingdom of Saudi Arabia. He graduated from King Saud University in Art Education in 1999. He later worked as an art education teacher in a secondary school in Riyadh and then as a lecturer at Qassim University. He obtained his Masters from King Saud University, focusing his work on learning difficulties. He completed his doctoral studies at the QMU, Edinburgh, in the area of arts therapies for children affected by ADHD. Badr currently works as an assistant professor at Qassim University and leads art therapy at the Mohammed bin Nayef Center in Riyadh.

Ashley Beck, MS, is a recent graduate from the Florida State University Master's of Art Therapy program. Ms. Beck graduated with a BA in pre-professional art therapy, where she developed an interest for marginalized forensic populations. She has had clinical experience in both male and female institutions and forensic psychiatric units. Her current research interests include promoting the field of art therapy in prison settings as well as art therapy and sustainability within an international context.

Iris Bräuninger, PhD, is a professor and researcher at the University of Applied Sciences of Special Needs Education Zurich. She also teaches at the DMT Program at Autonomous University Barcelona and works as a DMT supervisor and practitioner. Previously, she worked as deputy head of the DMT, Physio, Music Therapy Department, a researcher at the University Hospital of Psychiatry Zurich and post-doctoral researcher at the University of Deusto Bilbao. Iris teaches internationally in DMT, research and KMP. She is a registered Supervisor of the German (BTD) and Spanish (ADMTE) Association and holds the European Certificate of Psychotherapy (ECP).

Jane Burns, PhD, is a qualified art psychotherapist currently working at Queen Margaret University as a lecturer on the MSc art psychotherapy programme. Her research has been in the arts therapies with the older person, and her PhD research mapped how arts therapists work in practice with the person who has dementia. Jane is also interested in how the arts can support a person's wellbeing during periods of life transition such as retirement; she has completed an RBS funded project with colleagues looking at this topic. Jane has presented at conferences and has been a consultant on a variety of projects.

Aileen B. Cho, MA, RDT, LMFT, earned her MA in Counseling Psychology & Drama Therapy from the California Institute of Integral Studies (CIIS) Graduate School of Professional Psychology in San Francisco, CA. She currently has a private practice in San Francisco and is the program director and drama therapist at a residential treatment program for children, adolescents and teens ages 10–19 with eating disorders in Menlo Park, CA. Aileen is also a bilingual clinician and practitioner of Developmental Transformations (DvT) who provides psychotherapy and couples/family therapy in both Korean and English in her private practice and directs self-revelatory performances and social justice theater.

Jana Duhovska, MSc, MA, is a doctoral student at Rīga Stradiņš University in the "Medicine" study programme, assistant in the Department of Health Psychology and Pedagogy at the Faculty of Public Health and Social Welfare, and Head of Rīga Stradiņš University master's study programme "Arts therapies". She is a practicing music therapist; her field of scientific interest is assessment in music therapy and application of Expressive Therapies Continuum and awareness-informed music therapy to address the social and emotional functioning of cancer patients and survivors.

Jasmin Eickholt, music therapist and social worker, completed her music therapy training specializing in geropsychiatry at the University of Applied Sciences Würzburg-Schweinfurt (Germany). She works as music therapist in a geropsychiatric hospital, in a nursing home and with private clients. Furthermore, she works as a lecturer in music therapy and behavioral therapy at the University of Applied Sciences Würzburg-Schweinfurt and at the University of Augsburg. Her previous research addressed depressive symptoms of elderly nursing home residents. In further research, her aim is to examine specialized music therapy interventions for elderly nursing home residents with dementia and depression.

Jaakko Erkkilä, PhD, is Professor of Music Therapy at the University of Jyväskylä, Finland. For over 20 years, he worked with children and adults with psychiatric developmental and neurological disorders. He has initiated and collaborated with research networks including the Academy of Finland, the EU and the Finnish Centre of Excellence in Interdisciplinary Music Research. He serves on international editorial boards of music therapy-related journals, and he has published leading books, chapters and journal articles on music therapy. His particular recent interest is the theory, practice and research of improvisational music therapy, for which he has gained new funding.

Jörg Fachner, PhD, is Professor of Music, Health and the Brain at Anglia Ruskin University. He specialises in interdisciplinary research topics within the medical field, humanities and music sciences. Originating in Germany, he has worked worldwide, contributing to music therapy and brain research, including for NESTA, the EU and The Finnish Academy of Music. His research into music therapy process, treatment of depression, stroke, addiction, consciousness states and time perception, led to publications in high-ranking journals and books across the disciplines. His scientific output comprises over one hundred publications. Recent projects and collaborations focus on biomarkers and timing of the MT process.

Monika Geretsegger, PhD, is a music therapist and clinical and health psychologist based in Vienna, Austria, and senior researcher at GAMUT, Uni Research Health, Bergen, Norway. She received her PhD from Aalborg University, Denmark, where she explored music therapy for children on the autism spectrum. As a music therapy clinician, she specialises in adults with psychiatric conditions, including affective disorders and dementia, and in children and adolescents with autism. Her current research activities focus on effectiveness and applicability of music therapy in the fields of developmental disorders and mental health.

Christian Gold, PhD, is Principal Researcher at GAMUT, Uni Research Health, Bergen, Norway. He is also Adjunct Professor at the University of Bergen and at Aalborg University, Denmark. He serves as the Editor of the *Nordic Journal of Music Therapy* and as Associate Editor of the Cochrane Developmental, Psychosocial and Learning Problems Group. He received his music therapy degree at Vienna University of Music and Performing Arts and his PhD from Aalborg University. His research includes randomised trials and systematic reviews of music therapy in mental health, as well as process-outcome research and reviews of research methodology.

David E. Gussak, PhD, ATR-BC, is Professor of Art Therapy and Chairperson of the Department of Art Education at Florida State University. He is the author of *Art on Trial: Art Therapy in Capital Murder Cases*, and is co-editor and contributing author of *The Wiley Handbook of Art Therapy*, *Drawing Time: Art Therapy in Prisons and Other Correctional Settings* and *Art Education for Social Justice*. Dr Gussak is also the author of the *Psychology Today* blog, "Art on Trial: Confessions of a Serial Art Therapist", and he has published numerous articles and chapters and lectured widely both nationally and internationally.

Sue Jennings, PhD, is a specialist in Neuro-Dramatic-Play, creator of the EPR developmental model of Dramatherapy and the Creative Care model. She is a performer, storyteller, author, dramatherapist and play therapist. She is Honorary Professor in Expressive Therapies at the University of Derby and Honorary Fellow at the University of Roehampton. She is founder of the British Association of Dramatherapists and has developed play, drama and theatre therapy training in other countries, including Malaysia, Romania and Czech Republic. She has written over 40 books and has held academic appointments at UK Universities including Coleraine, Leeds Beckett and Exeter.

David Read Johnson, PhD, is Co-Director of the Post Traumatic Stress Center in New Haven Connecticut and Associate Clinical Professor in the Department of Psychiatry at Yale University School of Medicine, US. A leader in the creative arts therapies and drama therapy, he has written extensively about schizophrenia, dementia and trauma, and he conducted numerous quantitative and qualitative studies of the contribution of drama therapy and the creative arts therapies to the treatment of these conditions.

Vicky Karkou, PhD, is a professor at Edge Hill University leading the research theme of arts and wellbeing. An educator, researcher and dance movement psychotherapist, she has lengthy experience working with diverse clinical populations in different settings. She is widely published in peer-reviewed journals and books, and acts as the co-editor of the international journal *Body, Movement and Dance in Psychotherapy* published by Taylor and Francis. She travels extensively around the world for research and teaching purposes.

Heidi Landis, RDT-BCT, LCAT, TEP, CGP is in private practice in New York City where she sees clients and facilitates trainings. She has expertise with several populations including refugee children and adults, adults and youth on the autistic spectrum and youth in residential settings and therapeutic schools. In addition, Heidi is an adjunct professor at Lesley University, The College of New Rochelle and Concordia University. Her work has been published in *Trauma-Informed Drama Therapy* and the *Handbook of Child and Adolescent Group Therapy*. She is the past Associate Executive Director of the clinical and training program at Creative Alternatives of New York (CANY).

Vija Bergs Lusebrink, PhD, ATR, Professor Emerita, was born in Latvia. She has been an art therapist since 1969 and was a faculty member of the Expressive Therapies graduate programme at the University of Louisville, Kentucky, from 1974 to 1995 (as director from 1985 to 1995). She is an honorary life member of the American Art Therapy Association and has served on the Editorial Boards of art therapy journals. She is the author of *Imagery and Visual Expression in Therapy* (1990), as well as many book chapters and articles on art therapy, imagery and sandtray therapy.

Kristīne Mārtinsone, PhD, is a professor at Rīga Stradiņš University, Latvia, Head of the Department of Health Psychology and Pedagogy at the Faculty of Public Health and Social Welfare and an expert in psychology in the Latvian Science Council. She has authored/co-authored more than 200 scientific publications, including her work as a compiler and scientific editor of collective monographs, collections of articles and textbooks. Dr Martinsone is the key contributor for the establishment and development of arts therapies education and professions in Latvia.

Elizabeth McAdam, MA, RDT, is Associate Director of the ALIVE Program at the Post Traumatic Stress Center in New Haven, Connecticut, providing trauma-centered drama therapy services in both clinical and public school settings. She is also an adjunct faculty member at New York University. As a former educator-turned-drama therapist, she is interested in examining systems of power, privilege and oppression within educational settings and working with students to connect their lived experience to their learning process.

Helen Odell-Miller, PhD, OBE, is Professor of Music Therapy, and Director of the Cambridge Institute for Music Therapy Research at Anglia Ruskin University. As a therapist, and manager of the arts therapies services in mental health, she contributed to the development of music therapy in the UK and internationally. She has published and lectured widely and is a founder of the European Music Therapy Council. She is a Board Member for The Music Therapy Charity, and The International Consortium for Research in the Arts Therapies (ICRA). She is a pianist and violinist, and she primarily sings with Cambridge Voices, in the UK.

Amelia Oldfield, PhD, has worked as a music therapist with children and families in the UK for over 34 years. She currently practices as a clinician in Child and Family Psychiatry in Cambridge and is a professor and lectures at Anglia Ruskin University, where she co-initiated the MA Music Therapy Training in 1994. She has completed four music therapy research investigations and published six books and many articles in refereed journals. She has presented papers and run workshops at conferences and universities all over the world.

Unnur Ottarsdottir, PhD, has practiced art therapy in private practice and in a variety of organizations, including schools in Iceland, since 1990. She completed a PhD in art therapy at the University of Hertfordshire, in England, in 2006. Unnur conducts research on art therapy at the Reykjavik Academy, and she has written articles and book chapters about art therapy and the methodology of Grounded Theory. Unnur has taught art therapy at the Icelandic Academy of the Arts, University of Akureyri, University of Iceland (continuing education programme), the Art Therapy Association of Romania and the University of Hertfordshire in England.

Päivi Pylvänäinen is a clinical psychologist and a dance movement therapist. She completed DMT training in the US at the MCP Hahnemann University (Drexel University). She has done clinical work in occupational rehabilitation and psychiatric outpatient service, working with individuals and groups. She also contributes to the DMT training in Finland. Currently she

Introduction

Arts therapies' response to the global crisis of depression: current research and future developments

Ania Zubala and Vicky Karkou

We have known for a long time now that health is not simply a "lack of illness" but rather a constantly evolving condition of general wellbeing (WHO, 2017), enhanced by opportunities to be creative and form meaningful relationships. Holistic approaches to health and the need for humanising care are widely postulated (Todres, 2007), while pressures currently experienced in health and social care worldwide demand innovative solutions.

A recent major report demonstrated that arts can be enablers of connectedness and enhanced wellbeing on individual and community levels (All-Party Parliamentary Group on Arts, Health and Wellbeing, 2017). It is not surprising perhaps that researchers are increasingly more interested in exploring the nature of the long-established relationship between arts and health (Davies et al., 2014; Stuckey & Nobel, 2010) and, most importantly, the potential applications and relevance of this relationship in the modern context of fast-changing and ageing societies.

We know that arts may have powerful impacts on mood, actions and relationships and make important contributions to improved health, traversing treatment, recovery and maintenance (Karkou et al., 2017; MacDonald et al., 2012). We know this, as practitioners, from our daily experience. As researchers, we gather glimpses of the evidence, slowly painting a routinely patchy but evolving picture of the role of the arts therapies in enhancing global wellbeing. Developing excellent practice and research becomes, perhaps, an important support to our belief that arts therapies have the potential to improve health and wellbeing outcomes, can lead to reduced costs of healthcare, and contribute to more resilient and engaged communities.

Depression is the most common of the mental health problems one may face, exacerbated at times of crisis and global unrest. The socio-economic and political changes that are currently affecting us, as they have done throughout human history, create fear and pose a threat to what is known and familiar. In the face of a perceived inability to control the situation, anger, fear, and insecurity can be internalised, turning against oneself, resulting in helplessness and hopelessness (Seligman, 1974). Depression is one of the most likely, though destructive, responses to both global and individual challenges of the fast-changing and unpredictable modern world.

It is, thus, described as a "global burden" or a "global crisis" (WFMH, 2012; Cagney, 2015). To reflect its complex presentation, treatment of depression requires an appropriately holistic and individual approach, often combining pharmacological and psychosocial interventions. By responding to the universal human need for self-expression, not necessarily on a verbal level, arts therapies could potentially address the common withdrawal within depression and encourage sharing. For a more widespread access to arts therapies, we need to understand how arts therapies contribute to the treatment of the condition or to enhancing the lives of those who live with it.

In scoping literature reviews (Mala et al., 2012; Zubala, 2013), we found that, although numerous case studies have confirmed that arts therapies are used extensively to address depression, the effectiveness, and to some extent the nature of these interventions, remained unclear. There seemed to be a lack of robust research to support the wealth of anecdotal evidence or to explain what the active ingredients of therapy were. While health providers and policy makers seemed to need convincing scientific evidence to continue, or indeed, introduce arts therapies as part of health provision, we were aware that it was becoming increasingly difficult to provide this much-needed proof.

In general, quantitative research on primary depression is sparse, but there are significant studies that consider depression-related outcomes in people suffering from other conditions, like cancer, dementia, or substance misuse (Geue et al., 2010; Guetin et al., 2011). Two Cochrane reviews (Meekums et al.,2015, Maratos et al., 2008) confirmed methodological inadequacy of the majority of the research studies evaluating the effectiveness of dance movement therapy and music therapy for depression. However, both indicated potential benefits of arts therapies and highlighted urgent need for more high-quality research. The most recent Cochrane review (Aalbers et al., 2017) indicates that music therapy provides at least short-term benefits for people with depression but stresses the need of further research investigating mechanisms of this therapy for depression specifically. Another meta-analysis confirms the potential of music therapy interventions for not only successfully addressing the symptoms of this condition but also for improving the quality of life across many age groups for those who live with depression (Laubner & Hinterberger, 2017).

While evidence synthesis is crucial for the disciplines, we need to also remember that the sole focus on effectiveness does not always paint a full picture of the needs and complexities of modern practice and health culture where "does it work?" is perhaps not the most appropriate and certainly not the only question we should be asking. Arts therapies provision demands answers to more complex questions: for whom interventions work, in what contexts, and, as noted previously, what their active ingredients are, which are all questions already posed in psychotherapy by researchers such as Roth & Fonagy as early as 1996. It is argued that wider psychotherapy research on active ingredients of therapy (Yalom & Leszcz, 2005; Laurenceau et al., 2007), while being important and often providing a methodological base, does not focus on unique arts therapies ingredients (Sporild & Bonsaksen, 2014). A few attempts have been made on this front so far across arts therapies that need further attention and research support. For example, although Karkou and Sanderson (2006) (see also Karkou, 2012, 2017) in the survey of UK practitioners have identified shared therapeutic trends (namely humanistic, psychoanalytic/psychodynamic, developmental, active/directive, and artistic/creative and eclectic/integrative), the key features of arts therapies they describe emerge from a review of the literature. They name, for example, participatory definitions of the arts, creativity and playfulness, imagery, symbolism and metaphors, non-verbal communication, and the triangular therapeutic relationship between the client, the therapist, and the arts work; all are still to be tested through empirical data. Similarly, Koch (2017) attempts to articulate active factors across the different arts therapies, whilst there is a growing number of publications that refer to therapeutic factors specific to their discipline (Czamanski-Cohen & Weihs, 2016; Robb, 2016; Gabel & Robb, 2017). In many cases the evidence base of these factors demands further investigation. Thanks to the researchers from Sweden in particular, we have very recently learned more about the therapeutic factors in art therapy to address depression (Blomdahl et al., 2013). Nevertheless, to our best knowledge, no similar reviews are available in other arts therapies, and despite the above advances in recent years, the gap in knowledge remains.

While we are observing a slowly but steadily growing body of research, the still fragmented evidence does not (yet) paint a consistent picture of arts therapies' role in tackling depression. More in-depth insights into the mechanisms of practice are needed to initiate the process of evaluation, which could potentially place arts therapies among other well-recognised treatment options.

Inspired by the above questions and challenges, a few years ago we set out to find out how arts therapists work with depression in the UK context, with which we were most familiar. Our initial research involved a nationwide survey completed by nearly 400 practitioners of all arts therapies disciplines (Zubala et al., 2013,2014a; a follow up survey from Karkou, 1998). We learnt from them that over 91% therapists worked with depression in their daily practice and for 17% depression was the main focus of their work. Those therapists who specialised in depression tended to work with adults and older adults rather than children, which is not surprising given the growing reluctance to diagnose childhood depression. Our findings also seem to indicate that working with depression requires experience from the therapists, suggesting the level of challenge such work poses. Arts therapists who worked primarily with depression worked with groups significantly more often and agreed more strongly with psychoanalytic/psychodynamic principles than arts therapists who did not encounter depression among their clients. The respondents' practice was influenced primarily by attachment theory and group analysis, but it was often an eclectic/integrative approach responsive to the needs of individual clients or settings and reflecting the underlying problems, comorbidity, and the complex nature of depression. Main themes in this work included: a) motivation (mainly, how to attract clients to therapy, while they are likely to continue once they have started attending); b) reconnecting (in response to withdrawal, disconnection, and isolation); c) depression as "desired state" (consequence of therapy, indicating change, typically a "depression spike" (Hayes et al., 2007), following reconnection with self and/or emotions); and d) re-parenting (re-building trust and relationships) (Zubala et al., 2014b).

Following the survey, we designed a pilot clinical study (Zubala, 2013; Zubala et al., 2016), in which an art therapy group for adults suffering from depression was facilitated. Within the general quasi-experimental design, we attempted to include multiple methods in order to demonstrate how quantitative, qualitative, and arts-based methods could be creatively combined to offer multidimensional findings meaningful to a range of audiences and potentially achieving wider impact. We were able to observe not only positive changes in depression levels and self-reported wellbeing but also understand participant experience and identify benefits of therapy as described directly by the participants. We were also able to examine the therapeutic process taking place and draw more in-depth meaning of the journey through the therapy by using elements of artistic inquiry. Synthesising all findings led to a conclusion that the tension between the desire to withdraw and desire to connect prevailed in the group and created a place from where the therapeutic process could develop. Through therapy, this "creative tension" eventually enabled self-expression and connection in the group – and these had therapeutic effects in lowering anxiety levels and building stronger relationships (for details see Zubala, 2013).

While working on these projects, we were becoming increasingly aware of the developments in the area from research teams in other parts of the world. We wanted to capture this often fragmented but certainly growing evidence to support arts therapies' unique role in addressing the global burden of depression. We hoped for this research to be more visible, accessible, and inspirational for arts therapists, trainees, other health practitioners, researchers, and those shaping health provision.

And so, we were thrilled to be offered the opportunity to compile this work in a book as part of the International Research in the Arts Therapies series. We invited contributions from around the world including evidence of best research and accounts of diverse evidence-based practice, as well as discussion and critique of both existing practice and research methodologies. We were delighted and privileged to work with 26 authors, practitioners, and researchers, who contributed chapters diverse methodologically, often highly personal, and showcasing work from all arts therapies disciplines and with all age groups. In this volume, arts therapists from the UK, Finland, Norway, Iceland, Germany, Austria, and Latvia talk about their work next to arts therapists from the US, Canada, and Saudi Arabia, while examples of practice in Singapore and Malaysia are also included. Collaborations across countries are apparent, highlighting shared needs for collaborative and interdisciplinary research.

We are now presenting you with what we believe is a comprehensive (though by no means complete) compilation of expert knowledge on arts therapies' potential in addressing depression. The three sections correspond to particular life stages (children, adults, older people) and individual chapters within them represent the main four arts therapies disciplines (music therapy, art therapy, dance movement therapy, and dramatherapy) and less-known arts-based therapies, e.g. phototherapy.

Chapters 1 to 4 are dedicated to research and practice of arts therapies with children and young people. In the very first chapter in this volume, Amelia Oldfield introduces us to a music therapy assessment tool, discusses its use within the family psychiatric unit in the UK, and offers case vignettes, illustrating the mechanisms and benefits of music therapy for children with symptoms of depression. In Chapter 2, Unnur Ottarsdottir explains how art therapy was integrated within an educational setting in Iceland to address trauma-related depressive symptoms experienced by a particular young client, whom we meet again 17 years after his therapy. Chapter 3 again refers to trauma: using examples from two case studies from their practice in the US, Elizabeth McAdam and David Read Johnson propose how trauma-centred drama therapy could be used to reduce depression in adolescents. Final in this section is the chapter by Badr Alrazain and the editors of this volume, who describe the development and first application of a culturally sensitive movement-based arts therapy programme in primary schools in the Kingdom of Saudi Arabia.

Chapters 5 to 10 discuss ways of application and benefits of arts therapies for depression in adult population. In Chapter 5, Nisha Sajnani and co-authors from the US use the method of a collaborative discourse analysis to discuss the nature of their drama therapy work with adults experiencing depression and the therapeutic mechanisms that underpin their practice. In Chapter 6, Ania Zubala introduces her UK-based research on art therapy, highlighting the new method of visualising the moments of change, and guides us through the therapeutic process in an art therapy group for adults experiencing depression. Päivi Pylvänäinen from Finland in her Chapter 7 proposes a dance movement therapy model, which explains how DMT alleviates depression by promoting more flexible ways of relating with the environment and the self. In Chapter 8, David Gussak and Ashley Beck from the US discuss the nature of depression in a prison environment and demonstrate how art therapy assists inmates who suffer from depression in regaining purpose and identity. A collaborative and international Chapter 9, by Helen Odell-Miller (UK), Jörg Fachner (Germany), and Jaakko Erkkilä (Finland), explains the potential of music therapy to address depression from neurological, musical and psychological standpoints. Finally, in Chapter 10, Kathrin Seifert from Germany introduces us to phototherapy and the role it could play in alleviating the symptoms of depression.

Chapters 11–15 complete the life cycle mirrored within this volume and enhance our understanding of the role of arts therapies in addressing depression in later life. Initially, in Chapter 11, Jane Burns from the UK explores the potential of art therapy to support an older person to express and process loss, often underpinning depression in older age. In Chapter 12, Sue Jennings from the UK describes her work with people affected by dementia, including examples from Singapore and Malaysia, and highlights how dramatherapy responds to their need for playfulness and creativity – an antidote for depression. Chapter 13 invites us into the care home and the ballroom, and Iris Bräuninger, a German dance therapist based in Switzerland, discusses the emotional, psychosocial, and recreational roles that dance movement therapy plays in addressing depression in older adults. In Chapter 14 an international team, Jasmin Eickholt (Germany), Monika Geretsegger (Austria), and Christian Gold (Norway), introduce an evidence-based working model of music therapy for depression associated with later life and discuss its role in reducing isolation, improving mood, and increasing self-esteem. In the final chapter in this volume, Jana Duhovska, Vija Bergs Lusebrink, and Kristīne Mārtinsone from Latvia and the US present application of the Expressive Therapies Continuum in music therapy for cancer-related depression in older age.

As indicated above, particular contexts are explored in this book as uniquely influencing the type of arts therapies delivered. Chapters of work in schools or in prisons for example, remind us of the impact the setting has on how symptoms of depression are expressed and how the work is modified to address these needs. Working with staff in care homes is mentioned a few times as active support in caring for older people. Many authors talk about working with clients who do not have a formal diagnosis but do have symptoms of depression next to other conditions, such as ADHD, autism, trauma, eating disorders, and dementia. Diverse settings and client groups in this volume correspond to real life practice. Such complexity perhaps highlights potential methodological difficulties with designing robust and clinically-meaningful research in the area.

Since we believe that arts therapies research should reflect the essentially creative and non-linear character of the interventions (Gilroy, 2006), the book has become a compilation of examples of similarly diverse research designs and methods. Methodologies included range from case studies to randomised controlled trials, from experience-focused, arts-based research to neuroscience. Both process and outcome are equally important. Theoretical explanations of why certain practices may work add to the discussion around therapeutic factors and active ingredients responsible for therapeutic change. Models of practice enable us to identify and theoretically explain particular arts therapies perspectives that have been developed specifically for the treatment of depression. Focus on therapists' and clients' perspectives completes the picture of current practice and is an essential step towards further process and outcomes research.

We trust that arts therapies research needs to be courageous, bold, and innovative – and essentially responsive to the needs of highly individual communities and ways of providing services in different contexts. It needs both learning from the current models of health and developing new, more appropriate approaches. It should reflect the creative nature of the disciplines and focus equally on the outcomes and the process (Meldrum, 1999; Gilroy, 2006; McNiff, 2007). Creativity here is essential, while long-established research designs such as clinical trials may need to be adapted to remain relevant to the changing needs of societies. Nevertheless, responsiveness and flexibility does not have to compromise systematism and robustness – combining these qualities will ensure the success of arts therapies research and practice. Perhaps the future might see us undertaking more longitudinal studies, participatory research and developing arts-based methods appropriate for the field (Ledger & Edwards, 2011). We also believe that the future of research in arts therapies lies in interdisciplinary collaboration and openness towards novel ideas. Our field of practice and research naturally reaches across and beyond disciplines. Learning from, but extending beyond, the medical model is essential and could eventually bridge the current gaps between arts, science, and health.

As we were approaching the completion of this book, even more questions started to arise. Among them, how else can we, as researchers and practitioners, enrich study designs with methods more suited to our area of work, reflecting real life practice, and the needs of real clients we work with? Each research project and new method developed is a contribution to the emerging knowledge on arts therapies' current and future response to depression. It is absolutely crucial that we continue this work.

We hope that identifying the best possible ways of addressing depression, sharing experience of tools and approaches that work, and discussing particularly relevant methods of evaluation will inevitably lead to a conscious and confident evidence-based practice. We also hope that understanding the nature of depression itself and its response to arts therapies interventions will ensure that future practice is enriching and satisfying for the practitioners – empowered not only to work successfully with depression but also to share current research evidence with other professionals from health, education, and arts sectors.

We would like to welcome you on the journey towards uncovering some of the many faces of depression that our authors encountered in their practice and research. Ultimately, we hope that the journey will lead you to truly evidence-based, as opposed to purely intuitive, recognition of arts therapies' potential to address depression, reveal creativity, and promote empowering self-expression. In the end, arts therapies can simply help us all see beyond depression and into health and wellbeing for ourselves, our loved ones, and the communities we live in.

References

Aalbers, S., Fusar-Poli, L., Freeman, R. E., Spreen, M., Ket, J. C. F., Vink, A. C., Maratos, A., Crawford, M., Chen, X. J., & Gold, C. (2017). Music therapy for depression. *Cochrane Database of Systematic Reviews*, 2017(11). Art. No.: CD004517. Doi: 10.1002/14651858.CD004517.pub3.

All-Party Parliamentary Group on Arts, Health and Wellbeing (2017). Creative health: The arts for health and wellbeing. Retrieved from www.artshealthandwellbeing.org.uk/appg-inquiry/

Blomdahl, C., Gunnarsson, A. B., Guregård, S., & Björklund, A. (2013). A realist review of art therapy for clients with depression. *Arts in Psychotherapy*, 40(3), 322–330. Doi: 10.1016/j.aip.2013.05.009.

Cagney, H. (2015). Depression: An economic and moral case to tackle the crisis. *The Lancet Psychiatry*, 2(1), 20.

Czamanski-Cohen, J., & Weihs, K. L. (2016). The bodymind model: A platform for studying the mechanisms of change induced by art therapy. *The Arts in Psychotherapy*, 51, 63–73. Doi: 10.1016/j.aip.2016.08.006.

Davies, C. R., Knuiman, M., Wright, P., & Rosenberg, M. (2014). The art of being healthy: A qualitative study to develop a thematic framework for understanding the relationship between health and the arts. *British Medical Journal Open*, 4, e004790. Doi: 10.1136/bmjopen-2014–004790.

Gabel, A., & Robb, M. (2017). (Re)considering psychological constructs: A thematic synthesis defining five therapeutic factors in group art therapy. *The Arts in Psychotherapy*, 55, 126–135. Doi: 10.1016/j.aip.2017.05.005.

Geue, K., Goetze, H., Buttstaedt, M., Kleinert, E., Richter, D., & Singer, S. (2010). An overview of art therapy interventions for cancer patients and the results of research. *Complementary Therapies in Medicine*, 18(3–4), 160–170.

Gilroy, A. (2006). *Art therapy, research and evidence-based practice*. London: Sage Publications.

Guetin, S., Florence, P., Gabelle, A., Touchon, J., & Bonté, F. (2011). Effects of music therapy on anxiety and depression in patients with Alzheimer's disease: A randomized controlled trial. *Alzheimer's & Dementia*, 7(4, Supplement), e49. Doi: 10.1016/j.jalz.2011.09.204.

Hayes, A. M., Laurenceau, J.-P., Feldman, G., Strauss, J. L., & Cardaciotto, L. (2007). Change is not always linear: The study of nonlinear and discontinuous patterns of change in psychotherapy. *Clinical Psychology Review*, 27, 715–723. Doi: 10.1016/j.cpr.2007.01.008.

Karkou, V. (1998). A descriptive evaluation of the practice of arts therapists in the UK (Doctoral thesis). University of Manchester.

Karkou, V. (2012). Aspects of theory and practice in dance movement psychotherapy in the UK: Similarities and differences from Music Therapy. In R. A. R. MacDonald, G. Kreutz, & L. A. Mitchell (Eds.), *Music, health and wellbeing* (pp. 213–229). Oxford: Oxford University Press.

Karkou, V. (2017). Explainer: What is dance movement psychotherapy? *The Conversation*. Retrieved December 06, 2017 from https://theconversation.com/explainer-what-is-dance-movement-psychotherapy-79860.

Karkou, V., Oliver, S., & Lycouris, S. (2017). *The Oxford handbook of dance and wellbeing*. New York: Oxford University Press.

Karkou, V., & Sanderson, P. (2006). *Arts therapies: A research-based map of the field*. Edinburgh: Elsevier.

Koch, S. (2017). Arts and health: Active factors and a theory framework of embodied aesthetics. *The Arts in Psychotherapy*, 54, 85–91. Doi: 10.1016/j.aip.2017.02.002.

Laubner, D., & Hinterberger, T. (2017). Reviewing the effectiveness of music interventions in treating depression. *Frontiers in Psychology*. Doi: 10.3389/fpsyg.2017.01109.

Laurenceau, J.-P., Hayes, A. M., & Feldman, G. C. (2007). Some methodological and statistical issues in the study of change processes in psychotherapy. *Clinical Psychology Review*, 27, 682–695, Doi: 10.1016/j.cpr.2007.01.007.

Ledger, A., & Edwards, J. (2011). Arts-based research practices in music therapy research: Existing and potential developments. *The Arts in Psychotherapy*, 38(5), 312–317. Doi: 10.1016/j.aip.2011.09.001.

MacDonald, R. A. R., Kreutz, G., & Mitchell, L. A. (2012). What is music health and wellbeing and why is it important. In R. A. R. MacDonald, G. Kreutz, & L. A. Mitchell (Eds.), *Music, health and wellbeing* (pp. 3–12). Oxford: Oxford University Press.

Mala, A., Karkou, V., & Meekums, B. V. F. (2012). Dance/Movement Therapy (D/MT) for depression: A scoping review. *Arts in Psychotherapy*, 39 (4), 287–295. Doi: 10.1016/j.aip.2012.04.002.

Maratos, A., Gold, C., Wang, X., & Crawford, M. (2008). Music therapy for depression. *Cochrane Database Systematic Review*, 1. Doi: 10.1002/14651858.CD004517.pub2.

McNiff, S. (2007). Art-based research. In J. G. Knowles & A. L. Cole (Eds.), *Handbook of the arts in qualitative research: perspectives, methodologies, examples, and issues*. London: Sage Publications.

Meekums, B., Karkou, V., & Nelson, E. A. (2015). Dance movement therapy for depression. *Cochrane Database of Systematic Reviews*, 2015(2), CD009895. Doi: 10.1002/14651858.CD009895.pub2.

Meldrum, B. (1999). Research in the arts therapies. In A. Cattanach (Ed.), *Process in the arts therapies*. London: Jessica Kingsley.

Robb, M. A. (2016). Overview of historical and contemporary perspectives on art therapy research. In D. Gussak, & M. Rosal (Eds.), *The Wiley handbook of art therapy*. Chichester, UK: Wiley and Sons, Ltd.

Roth, A., & Fonagy, P. (1996). *What works for whom?: A critical review of psychotherapy research*. New York: Guilford Press.

Seligman, M. E. (1974). Depression and learned helplessness. In R. J. Friedman & M. M. Katz (Eds.), *The psychology of depression: Contemporary theory and research*. Oxford, England: John Wiley.

Sporild, I. A., & Bonsaksen, T. (2014). Therapeutic factors in expressive art therapy for persons with eating disorders. *Groupwork*, 24(3), 46–60. Doi: 10.1921/10201240104.

Stuckey, H. L., & Nobel, J. (2010). The connection between art, healing, and public health: A review of current literature. *American Journal of Public Health*, 100(2), 254–263.

Todres, L., Galvin, K., & Dahlberg, K. (2007). Lifeworld-led Healthcare: Revisiting a humanising philosophy that integrates emerging trends. *Medicine, Health Care and Philosophy*, 10, 53–63. Doi: 10.1007/s11019-006-9012-8.

World Federation for Mental Health (2012). Depression: A global crisis. Presentation for World Mental Health Day, 12th October 2012. Retrieved from http://wfmh.com/wpcontent/uploads/2013/11/2012_wmhday_english.pdf.

Yalom, I., & Leszcz, M. (2005). *Theory and practice of group psychotherapy* (5th ed.). New York, NY: Basic Books.

Zubala, A. (2013). Description and evaluation of arts therapies practice with depression in the UK (Doctoral thesis). Queen Margaret University. Retrieved from http://etheses.qmu.ac.uk/1775/

Zubala, A., MacIntyre, D. J., Gleeson, N., & Karkou, V. (2013). Description of arts therapies practice with adults suffering from depression in the UK: Quantitative results from the nationwide survey. *The Arts in Psychotherapy*, 40(5), 458–464. Doi: 10.1016/j.aip.2013.09.003.

Zubala, A., MacIntyre, D. J., Gleeson, N., & Karkou, V. (2014a). Description of arts therapies practice with adults suffering from depression in the UK: Qualitative findings from the nationwide survey. *The Arts in Psychotherapy*, 41(5), 535–544. Doi: 10.1016/j.aip.2014.10.005.

Zubala, A., MacIntyre, D. J., & Karkou, V. (2014b). Art psychotherapy practice with adults suffering from depression in the UK: Qualitative findings from depression-specific questionnaire. *The Arts in Psychotherapy*, 41(5), 563–569. Doi: 10.1016/j.aip.2014.10.007.

Zubala, A., MacIntyre, D. J., & Karkou, V. (2016). Evaluation of a brief art psychotherapy group for adults suffering from mild to moderate depression: Pilot pre, post and follow-up study. *International Journal of Art Therapy*, 22(3), 106–117. Doi: 10.1080/17454832.2016.1250797.

Part I

Arts therapies with children and adolescents experiencing depression

Chapter 1

Music therapy and prevention of depression in primary-aged children

Reflections on case work and assessment in a residential child and family psychiatric unit

Amelia Oldfield

Introduction

I have worked as a part-time music therapist (two days a week) in a National Health Service Unit for child and family psychiatry for nearly 30 years. In all this time, I remember only two children who have been given a diagnosis of depression as such, although many children appear to be sad or unhappy or may have specific mood disorders. These children may also have emotional problems and display disturbed behaviours. While depression in adolescents is more commonly discussed in the literature, there is less mention of depression when referring to primary-aged children. In the June 2013 NICE Evidence Update on depression in children and young people (NICE, 2013), only one of the five cited articles is about children under 12. Interestingly, this article (Weitz et al., 2012) talks about children with "multiple problems" and then goes on to describe interventions designed to treat anxiety, depression and disruptive conduct. It would appear, therefore, that young children are not seen to display symptoms of depression in the same way as adolescents or adults. Children under 12 will often be described as anxious, withdrawn or attention-seeking, but are more rarely labelled as being depressed. Nevertheless, it is important to address the symptoms that these children are showing, not only because the child needs help, but also because, if untreated, the child is at risk of acquiring a full diagnosis of depression as they move into adolescence.

In addition, most of the children at the Unit have complex needs and overlapping conditions and diagnoses, for example they may appear sad and low in mood, but also show some features of autistic spectrum disorder, some aspects of hyperactivity and some aspects of obsessional compulsive disorder, without convincingly fitting into one diagnostic category. This is one of the reasons why it has been useful to develop Music Therapy Diagnostic Assessments (MTDAs) at the Unit, which can provide the multi-disciplinary team with an additional and sometimes different perspective on children's diagnoses. Over a period of two weekly music therapy sessions, the music therapist will observe behaviours that are symptomatic of autism, attention deficit disorder, emotional difficulties and mild learning disabilities. A simple and quick scoring sheet with cut-off points for each of the categories has been devised which is completed by the music therapist after the two diagnostic sessions (Oldfield, 2006b).

The other feature, which sets young children aside from adolescents and adults, is that they are dependent on their parents or carers and will be more strongly affected by these adults. There is evidence to suggest that one of the predictors for mental health problems in children is maternal depression (Seiner & Gelfand, 1995; Bassuk et al., 1997). The child will therefore need to be treated within the context of their family, as it is highly probable that the behaviours of the parents (or carers) influence the behaviours of the child, just as the child's behaviours and difficulties will affect the parents. As we will see in this chapter the Unit, I will refer to works with children AND their families.

In this chapter I will also reflect on short-term music therapy work at the Unit with children with some aspects of depression. I will focus on how the MTDAs were created, how I have used the MTDAs with some of these children, and how music therapy has fitted in with the multi-disciplinary approach on the unit.

The child and family psychiatric unit

The Unit is a residential centre that aims to assess and provide short-term treatment for children (usually up to 12 years old) who are troubled by emotional and behavioural disturbance. Children are admitted with their families from Mondays to Fridays and go home at the weekend. This is the only psychiatric unit in the UK that admits families on a residential basis. Families usually stay eight weeks, but in some cases, may be admitted for longer (three to six months). The family approach at the Unit is based on the idea that in order to help the children, we need to understand and support both them and their families (Holmes et al., 2011).

Children and their families will only be admitted when other out-patient work has failed. Children will often have been excluded from several schools and nurseries, and some may have been absent from school for many months. Families often arrive at the Unit in a state of crisis where, for example, sleeping and meal-time routines are non-existent and where family life revolves around dealing with the child's problem behaviours (Holmes et al., 2011). The parents will often have had difficult childhoods and may be affected by having been emotionally or physically abused themselves. They may also be struggling with their own mental health issues, such as depression or obsessive compulsive disorders.

Children admitted to the Unit may come with a diagnosis or receive a new diagnosis during their admission. Common diagnoses include: attention deficit disorder (with or without hyperactivity); autistic spectrum disorder; Giles de la

Tourette Syndrome; eating disorders; mild developmental delay; specific language disorders; and attachment disorders. However, as indicated earlier, most of the children do not have typical symptoms of a single condition but rather aspects of several disorders which often makes it harder both to diagnose the problems and to provide help for the children and support for their families.

The staff team on the Unit is multi-disciplinary and works closely together, discussing each family in detail at a two-to-three-hour meeting at the end of each week. The team includes: psychiatrists, specialist nurses, teaching staff, a clinical psychologist, a psychotherapist, family therapists, a social worker and a music therapist. The opinions of the entire team are valued and listened to and although the consultant psychiatrist may be the person who finally decides what diagnosis should or should not be given, her decision is informed by the team. The observations made by the night nurses, for example, will be valued and considered just as much as the family therapist's view, and the reports from the classroom and the playground. In addition, the team works closely with health visitors, as well as previous therapists and teachers who have been and continue to be involved with the children and their families while they are on the Unit.

Music therapy at the unit

I would describe my music therapy work at the Unit by saying that I have a positive, interactive approach which involves live and mostly improvised music making. Like Juliette Alvin (1975), with whom I trained at the Guildhall School of Music and Drama in 1979, I use music as a means to an end. My objectives are non-musical and will fit in with individual children and family's Unit care plans, often being the same as those of my multi-disciplinary colleagues. Like Alvin (1975), I use my first instrument in my sessions which for me is the clarinet, and for Alvin was the cello. However, I use less performance than she did, and I have a definite positive stance, identifying and celebrating strengths in the children and the adults I work with before addressing and working on difficulties. Another characteristic of my approach is that I involve parents in my work, which is becoming more usual now, but was more uncommon ten years ago (Oldfield, 2006a, 2006b, 2016a, 2016b, 2016c). The work that I describe in this chapter is short-term, which is very different from the longer-term work which was more typical during my training.

I think the two main reasons that music therapy is effective at the Unit are that the music making is motivating for the children and they generally are keen to come into the room and play, and that I can interact with the children without having to use words. I have written in more detail elsewhere (Oldfield, 2016c) how my approach is not clearly allied to one psychological model but informed by developmental theorists, behavioural approaches and psychodynamic writers. In this same chapter (Oldfield, 2016c), I outline how there are overlaps and many parallels between Winnicott's (1971) theories of "holding",

Bowlby's (1988) attachment theory, Stern's (1987) writing on "affect attunement" and my music therapy work at the Unit.

I have three different types of input at the Unit: a) I run a music therapy group; b) I do music therapy diagnostic assessments (MTDAs) for individual children at the beginning of their admission; and c) I do short-term treatment for individual children or families. During the MTDAs and sometimes during individual sessions and family sessions I include "song stories", which is a specific technique that I have developed with a psychotherapist, Christine Franke (Oldfield & Franke, 2005). I will describe each of these types of treatment/techniques and will illustrate these different interventions by including some vignettes with children who show signs and/or symptoms of depression. I have permission from the children and the families to write about this work, but have changed names and details for the sake of anonymity.

The music therapy group

The music therapy group is an open group for all the children on the Unit. It is run at the same time every week and lasts 45 minutes. As most of the children are only admitted to the Unit for eight weeks, there are often children arriving or leaving, and these events form an important feature of the group, as new children are welcomed, and we say good-bye to children who are about to leave. I run the group with a member of the nursing team, and we plan and review the session together every week (Carter & Oldfield, 2002). For the first two weeks, we will make general observations on a child's strengths and weaknesses within the group situation. We will then determine two or three aims for that child within the music therapy group, which will be different for each child depending on their individual needs.

Case vignette: Gemma's presence in the music therapy group

Gemma was admitted to the Unit when she was 12 years old. She was low in mood, had an eating disorder and was underweight. She often looked sad, lacked spontaneity and tended only to speak when spoken to. Her younger brother had a life-threatening condition and had been in and out of hospital since he was born. Her parents were concerned about Gemma's difficulties but too pre-occupied by her younger brother's ill health to attend sufficiently to Gemma's needs. They had been at the Unit for three months, but their attendance had been sporadic due to the brother's hospital admissions and the parents had not been able to attend therapy sessions on a regular basis. Although Gemma had not attended music therapy groups regularly she appeared more relaxed in these sessions than in other social situations at the Unit. Perhaps she was reassured and felt "held" (Winnicott, 1971) by the familiar beginning and ending of the group, and by the fact that it was easy to take part without having to speak. When we all played instruments together, Gemma would choose quiet instruments and blend in gently, avoiding being in the spotlight in any way. She joined in spontaneously though which she didn't usually do in other group situations with her peers. Gradually she gained confidence and I remember one particular group session, three months after she had been admitted, when she refused to have an "official" solo but allowed me to accompany her woodblock playing within the group by playing the tune of "horsey, horsey" to the rhythm of her playing. She looked at me and smiled, acknowledging that I had noticed she enjoyed the song and the sound of the woodblock. Children like Gemma who may have had to grow up too quickly and who have lost their "attachment figure" too soon (Bowlby, 1988) can be taken back to an earlier phase through songs associated with younger children. They can then allow themselves to enjoy this process without this needing to be acknowledged verbally.

Later on in this same session, Gemma was sitting next to a peer who was very outgoing and who was impatient when two boys took over the drum in the centre of the room. This girl then dramatically put her head on Gemma's lap and said loudly "I'm bored". With her peer's head on her lap, Gemma gestured to the adults in the group, smiled and said loudly "she's bored!", speaking up and volunteering information in a way that she had not done previously. In our next activity, she spontaneously encouraged one of her peers to take part when we were playing in two groups, and then, at the end of the session, she responded when we asked her what she would remember about a peer who was leaving the unit at the end of the week. This music group seemed to enable Gemma to take part at her own pace. She was reassured by the familiar structures and was more confident than usual to engage with her peers. After this session, she appeared a little less withdrawn with her peers and started a few art activities with the two other girls attending the Unit. When she left the Unit, I liaised with the head of music at her mainstream school and with a little encouragement from one of the music teachers, Gemma was confident enough to join the girls' choir. The conductor told me that Gemma still generally attempted to fade into the background, but she came every week, appeared slightly less troubled and looked a little less unhappy.

The music therapy diagnostic assessments (MTDAs)

All the children at the Unit come for two Music Therapy Diagnostic Assessments (MTDAs), which last half an hour each and usually take place on a weekly basis at the beginning of the children's admissions. After these two sessions, I will discuss the results of the assessments with the parent(s) of the child and further short-term music therapy treatment either for the child, or the family may then be arranged, depending on what the parents, the child and the multi-disciplinary team feel would be helpful.

The MTDAs gradually evolved as I worked at this psychiatric unit in the 1990s. During my first two individual music therapy sessions I not only tried to determine whether or not a child might benefit from further music therapy sessions, but I also tried to focus on strengths and difficulties that might be indicative of autism, hyperactivity, emotional difficulties and learning difficulties.

A new consultant psychiatrist took over at the time and there was a shift in emphasis from long-term admissions to short-term work with more attention paid to diagnosis and family work. I had already noticed that when I reported back on my first two individual music therapy sessions to the multi-disciplinary team, I often disagreed with observations made by other professionals in other contexts, or I had different things to say. I remember reporting, for example, that a usually passive and withdrawn child was playing the drum-kit in an aggressive and excited way, and this enabled the team to consider the child in a slightly different light. So, when the opportunity to pursue a music therapy research investigation arose in 2000, I developed and formalized the autism section of the MTDA, and then compared the results of 30 children receiving the MTDA and the Autistic Diagnostic Observation Schedule (ADOS). I devised a scoring system for the MTDA which was similar to that of the ADOS so that the results of the two tests could be compared. The research showed that there was a high level of agreement between the diagnostic categories in the MTDA and the ADOS indicating that the MTDA was providing similar information as a recognised diagnostic test. The results also showed that the two tests showed significantly different scores in individual questions, which showed that there was support for my original "hunch". Music therapy assessments were providing the multi-disciplinary team with different information which would help them in the diagnostic process (Oldfield, 2006b: 123–158).

I have continued to use the MTDA with the scoring system developed for the research over the past 12 years, and the MTDA now forms part of the standard assessment procedure at the Unit. The latest version of my MTDA is included in Box 1.1.

Box 1.1 Music therapy diagnostic assessment (MTDA)

Autism spectrum disorder

a) Child's playing seems to be independent of therapist's playing. Therapist has to work hard to "remain" with child and child often seems to be doing his/her own thing.
b) Child is not facially or physically engaged in playing process, or unusual eye contact (too little or too much).
c) Child doesn't make any spontaneous suggestions (musical or verbal) with communicative intent/or story is excessively simple showing inability to

be creative or imaginative. (This should not be caused by a general learning disability but appear untypical of the child's overall ability.)

d) Child is unusually interested in structure of instruments/lines instruments or beaters up/ "twiddles" with beaters or shakers/uses beaters in unexpected ways e.g. puts them in holes, sticks them on head.
e) Child becomes self-absorbed and difficult to distract from certain instruments such as the wind chimes or the ocean drum. (Not boredom or distractibility but a more isolated, engrossed type of playing, with possible repetitive playing.)
f) Child's tone of voice/intonation has an unusual or repetitive quality.
g) Child is unable/unwilling to make up a story where we both contribute to the story line. Child may be unwilling to make up a new story rather than telling a well-known story, or child may refuse to allow the therapist to contribute in any way.
h) Child develops obsessive/repetitive types of playing or obsessive repetitive patterns in story.
i) Child is unable to have more than one/immediate copying response. The exchanges don't develop into a dialogue.
j) Child is unable to have any playful or humorous exchange with the therapist.
k) Child wants entire session to be on his/her terms and can't accept any ideas or suggestions from the therapist. (Not in a calculated manipulative way but rather in an "own world" way.)
l) Child does not show a response to therapist's singing. No embarrassment or smile or communicative response. (Do not score if child is choosing to reject or ignore the therapist and showing a negative response.)

Attention deficit disorder

a) Child has difficulties remaining engaged in any one activity for more than a few minutes.
b) Child is very distractible.
c) Child fiddles with beaters or knobs on percussion Instruments.
d) Child has difficulty remaining in one place.
e) Child fidgets.
f) Child is impulsive.
g) Child has difficulties playing quietly.
h) Child has difficulties listening (or seems not to hear therapist's music or talking).
i) Child interrupts through playing or talking.
j) Child has difficulties or is uncomfortable waiting to play or waiting for their turn.

k) Child has difficulties finishing activities.
l) Child has difficulties remembering even simple phrases.

Emotional difficulties

a) Child is very anxious/or child finds it difficult making own choices/ child seems to lack a sense of self.
b) Child seems desperate for adult attention/reassurance.
c) Child seems over-anxious to please or be liked.
d) Child has difficulties moving from one activity to another/child has difficulties coming to the session or leaving the session.
e) Child seems to need to be in control of session and therapist in a "powerful" way rather than in order to be reassured about the session.
f) Child is defiant and seems to want to draw therapist into a conflict.
g) Child is impulsive and unpredictable.

Language/learning disabilities

a) Child is difficult to understand/has pronunciation difficulties/speaks in an ungrammatical way, (more so than age of child would lead you to expect).
b) Child speaks very little or not at all/or child seems very anxious about speaking. (Do not score when therapist feels child is making a point of not speaking but only if it is felt that child has real difficulties in this area.)
c) Child has difficulties understanding the therapist.
d) Child is clumsy or awkward/uncoordinated.

Scoring

0 = None of this behaviour was noted
1 = Some of this behaviour was noticed
2 = A lot of this behaviour was noticed
NB: Only score if you are certain you noticed some of the behaviour. If in any doubt do not score.

Cut off points

Autism: 10
Autism Spectrum: 6
Attention Deficit Disorder: 10
Emotional/Behaviour difficulties: 5
Language/Learning difficulties: 4

Case Vignette: Josh's MTDA

Josh was admitted to the Unit when he was eight years old because of outbreaks of violence at school and at home with his younger brother. He already had a diagnosis of autism, but the family wanted this diagnosis to be reviewed. He generally got on well with adults but spoke with a very strange "robot-like" voice, and was often made fun of and bullied by his peers. His way of retaliating was to lash out physically and then withdraw, avoiding his peers as much as possible. By the time he came to the Unit he was very angry with both the schools he had been expelled from and unwilling to go back to another school. His self-esteem was low, and he was very sensitive to any comments made about him, easily taking offence and quickly becoming angry and aggressive. If he thought he might not succeed at a task he would often refuse to attempt it and become sullen and bad tempered. Although he had not yet started to show signs of being low in mood, Josh was beginning to withdraw from his peers, and it was felt that unless his self-esteem improved he was at high risk of developing depression in adolescence.

Josh was very happy to come to the music therapy room with me, saying he liked music and was good at it. He accepted my "Hello" song, smiled and did not appear to be embarrassed by my singing. He was willing to take turns choosing what we were going to play, tolerating and accepting my choices although he clearly preferred to be the person choosing what we should do himself. Our improvisations flowed easily as he had a strong sense of pulse and enjoyed my piano accompaniment to his drum-kit playing. He appeared delighted to play freely and loudly, he felt happy and confident doing something where an adult played with him as an equal, but allowed him to lead. When I attempted to get him to follow my musical changes, he could do this eventually, but I had to work hard to gain his attention as he so enjoyed, and clearly preferred being in control of the way the music was evolving himself. This spontaneous and creative music making was in stark contrast to his voice when he spoke. Although we mainly played and did not speak very much, when he told me which instruments he wanted to choose his voice was monotone and robotic, with a strange repetitive intonation to the words. Interestingly, when we played the kazoos together, where you have to make a vocal sound into the instruments to produce a sound, our improvisation was stuck and did not flow in the same way as our previous instrumental exchanges. I tried to make our playing like a conversation making questioning vocal sounds, but he ignored my playing and sung tunes into the kazoos. Even when I joined in with these songs and tried to modify the tempi and the dynamics a little, he remained in his own rhythm and style, not listening or reacting to my musical suggestions. I wondered whether Joshua had struggled to have vocal exchanges with his parents as a baby and found out from his mother that he had missed out on the babbling stage altogether. He started speaking quite late, coming out suddenly with three-word sentences when he was four years old. It seemed to me that although he wasn't able to have spontaneous vocal exchanges with me, he was replacing the affect attunement exchanges he had missed as a baby (Stern, 1987) with spontaneous instrumental dialogues.

When scoring the MTDA after the sessions, Josh scored seven for the autistic spectrum section of the test, which meant his score was just above the cut-off point of six for autistic spectrum disorder, but below the cut-off point of ten which he would have needed to score for a diagnosis of autism. With Josh's and his parent's permission I showed DVD excerpts of this session to the multi-disciplinary team during our management meeting at the end of the week. Everyone was completely astounded by how engaged and interactive Josh was during our instrumental, non-verbal improvisations. As a result, we decided to change his diagnosis to being on the autistic spectrum, rather than being typically autistic. We also agreed that I would do six more individual music therapy sessions with Josh while he attended the Unit. During these sessions I focused on our free playing and instrumental improvisations, helping Josh to continue to enjoy these interactions where he could be free and at ease with another adult without having to use spoken language. During the last few sessions we started to incorporate vocal sound effects into our improvisations to help Josh to feel less stuck when using his voice. When Joshua left the Unit, he was more confident about communicating freely with adults and peers. His parents and adults around him had begun to expect him to be more free and spontaneous in his interactions with them. As a result, his risk of being isolated and developing depression had decreased.

Song stories

Song stories are included in some of the children's MTDAs and may then also be part of short-term music therapy individual or family treatment (Oldfield & Franke, 2005; Oldfield, 2006b).

I offer the children some instruments such as the large wooden xylophone and a cymbal and then go to the piano myself. If the child starts playing I will match their playing on the piano and then stop and say: "once upon the time there was a . . ." Sometimes the child will immediately respond, but if not I might say: "would you like this story to be about an animal or a person? Once a character has been chosen I will ask, where the person goes, who they go with, what happens next . . . at some point I usually insert a character or an event that might be threatening or dangerous, such as a crocodile, or a hurricane. I always give the child the opportunity to resolve conflicts without suggesting or insisting that this should happen, and I support the child to make a clear ending to the story. Often, once the child gets going, I simply echo back what has been said as I accompany the words on the piano. If the child starts telling a well-known story such as "Red Riding Hood" I will insert a new character such as a bear or a dragon to try and help the child imagine a new story line. While reflecting on the song stories that children tell and play, I have found it useful to consider the musical aspects, the non-verbal aspects and the text itself.

I usually start by including a "bland" introduction where the music does not convey an emotion or a feeling. I will then sometimes consciously match or imitate the child's music, or possibly interrupt or challenge the way they are playing. At other times, perhaps while I am waiting for the child to decide what will happen next, I will provide "neutral musical filler", or incorporate sound effects, atmospheric music or "associative" music such as "Happy Birthday" or a wedding march, to match the events taking place in the story.

In addition to improvising music and contributing to the text of the story I take non-verbal cues from the child's body language and try to remain aware of my own non-verbal body language as well. I note how the child is making us feel as we make up the story together and am aware of our tone of voice, noting whether it appears bored, emotional or non-confrontational. I make use of silence and observe changes in voice quality and speed.

While I originally found it quite easy to draw conclusions and significance from the children's music and non-verbal communication, the text of the stories that the children came up with was often confusing and baffling to me. When the psychotherapist, Christine Franke, came to the Unit to study the emotional world of children with autistic spectrum disorder for her PhD between 2002–2005, she helped me to study a number of these stories and find a way to make some sense of what was being said (Oldfield & Franke, 2005).

After studying and discussing a number of the song stories that had occurred in the music therapy sessions, we concluded that the musical context can provide "safety" for storytelling and made it possible for the child and therapist to be 'equal'. The stories gave the therapist some idea of the child's inner world and determined whether the child had the ability (or not) to talk about/think about emotions. The stories enabled the children to think about different worlds and revealed whether or not the children could think about themselves in metaphor.

Several years later, I was planning a joint lecture on music therapy and dramatherapy in child and family psychiatry with my dramatherapy colleague Amanda Carr. I realised then that there were many similarities between these song stories that had evolved out of clinical practice and diagnostic assessments through stories such as the one described in dramatherapy practice by Lahad (1992). Although the clinical setting was slightly different (Lahad's work was developed for children who had suffered trauma), in both situations the stories had a main character, the character had a mission or task, the main character often had a helper or friend and there were obstacles to be overcome. However, song stories are different because the improvised music and the words are combined so the role of the music and the non-verbal communication can be as important as the text itself.

Case vignette: David's song story

David was eight years old when he was admitted to the Unit. He was referred because of concern over hyperactivity and stereotyped behaviours. He had had a previous diagnosis of autism, but his parents wanted his diagnosis reassessed and wondered whether he might have attention deficit disorder and could benefit from medication for this.

On the Unit, David presented as a quiet, shy boy who would only speak when spoken to. He appeared troubled and sad and was often heard muttering under his breath. He was compliant and did what was asked of him, but rarely smiled or appeared to enjoy himself. He was referred for a short-term six-week individual music therapy intervention to give him an opportunity to express himself non-verbally. In the first two sessions, he had appeared compliant and self-effacing, but was more engaged and spontaneous in playing the instruments than he had appeared to be in other settings on the unit. In the MTDA he had scored as being on the autistic spectrum because he showed some repetitive behaviours and could get quite self-absorbed in his playing. The following description is taken from his fourth session where I introduced a song story for the first time. I had not done this previously because he seemed so quiet and reluctant to speak on the Unit that I had felt it was more important to focus on non-verbal improvisations.

David quietly came to the music therapy room with me, and looked a little surprised when I sang "Hello" to him, but he did not smile. When I asked him what he wanted to choose in the music room, he said he wanted to sing a song with me, and after some deliberation chose the rainbow song which he said he had previously sung in his school. He sang very quietly, and I accompanied him on the piano. I then suggested he sang louder, and he surprised me by singing at the top of his voice, so loudly that the tune became unrecognisable. I suggested a volume in between the barely audible version and the shouted version, but he went back to the extremely quiet singing, appearing not to be able to find a middle ground.

When I gave him the large bass xylophone and the cymbal and started the story at the piano, he immediately told the story of a boy who went to school and annoyed his teacher. The boy then went home and started smashing plates. David very quickly became excited and loud, appearing aroused by the violence of the boy in the story, and accompanying each new smashing of plates by loud cymbal crashes. I was surprised and a little shocked to see this completely different side to David and anxious to allow him to express himself as much as he wanted. I therefore mainly supported his suggestions by repeating them and making an accompanying musical response on the piano at the same time. I made very few contributions to the story myself, not wanting to interrupt the flow of his creation. The story then became darker, with the boy smashing the television and being told off by his parents. This was followed by the boy locking himself in his room, throwing away the key and turning off the electricity. When I eventually suggested that we needed to find an end to the story, his voice changed and became very quiet again and he brought in Father Christmas who restored order into the home. The transcribed text of the story is included in Box 1.2.

Box 1.2 Text to David's song story

- Amelia: Once upon a time there was a . . .
- David: a boy
- Amelia: a boy . . . Where did the boy go?
- David: um . . . to school.
- Amelia: the boy went to school, the boy went to school
- David: he smashed a plate
- Amelia: he smashed a plate . . . What happened?
- David: the teacher drove him up the wall
- Amelia: the teacher drove him up the wall
- David: he went home
- Amelia: he went home
- David: what did you do?
- Amelia: what did I do?
- David: naughty boy!
- Amelia: naughty boy! Naughty boy!
- David: sent him to his bedroom
- Amelia: sent him to his bedroom
- David: went downstairs
- Amelia: went downstairs
- David: smashed a plate
- Amelia: smashed a plate
- David: Mum came
- Amelia: Mum came
- David: She . . . he . . . she was very cross
- Amelia: she was very cross, very cross
- David: sent him back to his bedroom
- Amelia: sent him back to his bedroom
- David: went downstairs
- Amelia: went downstairs
- David: smashed another plate
- Amelia: smashed another plate
- David: Mum came in
- Amelia: Mum came in

- David: she was very cross
- Amelia: she was very cross
- David: she sent him up to his bedroom
- Amelia: she sent, she sent him up to his bedroom
- David: she locked the door
- Amelia: she locked the door
- David: she kept the key
- Amelia: she kept the key
- David: the boy got the . . . the boy got out of the window
- Amelia: the boy got out of the window
- David: got the key
- Amelia: got the key
- David: shut down the door and smashed another plate
- Amelia: Oh no, the boy smashed another plate
- David: Mum sent him back to his bedroom
- Amelia: Mum sent him back to his bedroom
- David: she locked the door, she locked the window
- Amelia: she locked the door, she locked the window
- David: he smashed the television on the floor
- Amelia: he smashed the television on the floor
- David: Mum came up
- Amelia: Mum came up
- David: brought Dad up
- Amelia: brought Dad up
- David: and told him off
- Amelia: and told him off
- David: he went downstairs
- Amelia: he went downstairs
- David: he smashed another . . . Mum came up . . . Dad came up . . . They were very cross . . . Throwed the clock on the floor
- Amelia: Sorry?
- David: throwed the clock on the floor . . . Smashed . . . Smashed another clock . . . Smashed . . .
- Amelia: . . . how is it going to finish?
- David: Mum came up
- Amelia: Mum came up
- David: Dad came up
- Amelia: Dad came up
- David: they were very cross
- Amelia: they were very cross . . . and how does this story finish?
- David: sent him up to his bedroom, locked everything, throw the keys away

- Amelia: sent him up to his bedroom, locked everything, threw the keys away
- David: smashed another window
- Amelia: we've got to find an end to this . . . he smashed a window
- David: went downstairs
- Amelia: went downstairs
- David: frightened Mum and Dad
- Amelia: sorry?
- David: frightened Mum and Dad
- Amelia: frightened Mum and Dad
- David: turned off the electricity
- Amelia: turned off the electricity
- David: in came Father Christmas
- Amelia: then came Father Christmas
- David: he told him off
- Amelia: he told him off
- David: that's the end of the story

From a musical point of view, David was quick to become engaged in playing the musical instruments, particularly the cymbal. He was easily engaged in a musical turn-taking structure where he waited for my imitative response. This response also served to encourage and support his contribution. His words were spoken in a sing-song voice with definite rhythmic phrasing, and he appeared to associate the cymbal with the smashing of plates in the story. His playing was mainly excited and loud, but he was also affected by and able to respond to my occasional changes of mood in the accompanying piano chords.

Non-verbally, David laughed excitedly, and his cymbal crashes were accompanied by big movements as the story became more violent and destructive. There was a sudden change of tone of voice when I suggested we must find an ending to the story, and Father Christmas appeared.

When reflecting on David's story it was clear that he was very engaged and expressive. He was able to tell a fairly coherent story and incorporate my suggestions. At times the story appeared repetitive, stuck and a little obsessive with plates being smashed again and again. What troubled me was David's excitement and enjoyment about the violence in the story. I felt uncomfortable and ill at ease, wondering what this might mean.

David and his parents allowed me to show a DVD of this song story to the psychiatric team. They were very surprised to see this new side of David, who remained quiet and meek and compliant with his peers on the Unit. Like me, they also felt concerned about his interest and excitement in violence. A few days later after liaising with social services and his family, it was revealed that he had witnessed violent behaviour at home. Counselling sessions were arranged for both David and his parents. His parents gradually were able to accept that some of David's behaviours were caused by past traumatic events, that he did not have attention deficit disorder and that he had only borderline ASD rather than autism.

Conclusion

The three case vignettes I have described in this chapter have illustrated different types of music therapy interventions with three children with symptoms of depression. Gemma was motivated to be involved in improvised group music making and was able to have a voice in her peer group. Musical improvisation allowed a childlike Gemma with very low self-esteem to take part because there was no risk of playing in the wrong way or failing. Once the child was engaged, as the therapist I could pick up on the way the child was playing in her own improvised musical responses, and in this way I could accept and validate the child's contribution. Josh found new spontaneity and expression when improvising on the instruments with me, and David became stimulated and excited when telling a song-story which then shed new light on his difficulties. I have also written about how two research investigations (Oldfield, 2006a, 2006b) informed the clinical approaches that I have outlined.

As explained in my introduction, the diagnosis of depression is rarely given for primary-aged children. Nevertheless, I believe that the music therapy interventions, combined with the input by the multi-disciplinary team at the psychiatric Unit, were instrumental in stopping these three children from developing depression in adolescence and/or later life.

References

Alvin, J. (1975). *Music therapy*. New York: Basic Books.

Bassuk, E., Weinreb, L., Dawson, R., Perloff, J., & Buckherr, J. (1997). Determinants of behaviour in homeless and low-income housed pre-school children. *Pediatrics*, 100, 92–100.

Bowlby, J. (1988). *A secure base: Clinical applications of attachment theory*. London: Routledge.

Carter, C., & Oldfield, A. (2002). A music therapy group to assist clinical diagnoses in child and family psychiatry. In A. Davies & E. Richards (Eds.), *Group work in music therapy* (pp. 149–163). London: Jessica Kingsley.

Holmes, J., Oldfield, A., & Polichroniadis, M. (2011). *Creating change for complex children and their families; A multi-disciplinary approach to multi-family work*. London: Jessica Kingsley.

Lahad, M. (1992). Storymaking in assessment method for coping with stress. *Dramatherapy Theory and Practice II*, 150–163.

NICE (2013). Depression in children and young people, evidence update 42 (June 2013), National Institute for Health and Care Excellence. Retrieved from www.nice.org.uk.

Oldfield, A. (2006a). *Interactive music therapy, a positive approach – Music therapy at a child development centre*. London: Jessica Kingsley.

Oldfield, A. (2006b). *Interactive music therapy in child and family psychiatry – Clinical practice, research and teaching*. London: Jessica Kingsley.

Oldfield, A. (2016a). Family approaches in music therapy with young children. In J. Edwards (Ed.), *The Oxford handbook of music therapy* (pp. 158–175). Oxford: Oxford University Press.
Oldfield, A. (2016b). Emotional expression in family music therapy. In L. Konieczna (Ed.), *Emotional expression and music therapy* (pp. 115–128). Katowice: The Karol Szymanowski Academy of Music Press.
Oldfield, A. (2016c). Music therapy with families in a psychiatric children's unit. In S. Lindahl & G. Thompson (Eds.), *Models of music therapy with families*. London: Jessica Kingsley.
Oldfield, A., & Franke, C. (2005). Improvised songs and stories in music therapy diagnostic assessments at a unit for child and family psychiatry – A music therapist's and a psychotherapist's perspective. In T. Wigram & F. Baker (Eds.), *Songwriting, methods, techniques and clinical applications for music therapy clinicians, educators and students*. London: Jessica Kingsley.
Seiner, S., & Gelfand, D. (1995). Effects of mother's simulated withdrawal and depressed affect on mother-toddler interactions. *Child Development*, 1519–1528.
Stern, D. (1987). *The interpersonal world of the infant*. New York, NY: Basic Books.
Weitz, J. R., Chorpita, B. F., Palinkas, L. A. et al. (2012). Testing standard and modular designs for psychotherapy treating depression, anxiety and conduct disorders in youth. *Archives of General Psychiatry*, 69, 274–282.
Winnicott, D.W. (1971). *The child the family and the outside world*. London, UK: Penguin.

Chapter 2

Art therapy to address emotional wellbeing of children who have experienced stress and/or trauma

Unnur Ottarsdottir

Introduction

Prior to the research presented in this chapter I worked as a special education teacher at a secondary school in Iceland where art therapy methods and theories were integrated into educational work. During that time, I observed the children from both an art therapeutic and an educational point of view. Following that preliminary work, I conducted the research presented in this chapter, which focuses on an art therapeutic method where the two perspectives of art therapy and education meet. The children who took part in the research had experienced emotional trauma and/or stress and had specific learning difficulties.

As a result of the research, the Art Educational Therapy (AET) method was created, whereby coursework learning is integrated into art therapy with the aim of enhancing emotional wellbeing and facilitating coursework learning. Art therapy and educational psychotherapy theories (Best, 2014) contribute to the conceptual framework of AET. Emotional factors which may get in the way of learning are explored in educational psychotherapy and within that theoretical framework the term 'symptomatic learning', emerged in the present research, referring to specific learning difficulties as symptomatic of emotional difficulties. The clients are free to choose art material and/or coursework learning to work with in AET and integrated emotional and intellectual processes are worked with simultaneously (Ottarsdottir, 2005, 2010a, 2010b).

One individual case study from the research project will be presented in this chapter, concerning a boy, here called Oli, who was depressed and had a mother who had been depressed. Oli had experienced stress and trauma and he had a specific learning difficulty, which related partly to his difficulty with learning math. 'Specific learning difficulty', is a term used in this chapter as an umbrella term for difficulties with coursework learning in a variety of subjects including math.

Art-making, integrated with writing, was applied both in therapy with the children and in the researcher's own process in terms of the research methodology. The 'writing-image' concept emerged through a grounded theory analysis referring to integrated drawing and writing (Ottarsdottir, 2010b). Oli made some drawings in therapy and he also drew in relation to learning math which, in combination with the therapeutic relationship, appeared to help him connect with his feelings, processing them and talking about the trauma he had experienced. Subjects, concepts, connections, emotions and conflicts relating to the research were also processed and clarified through the writing-image processes of the researcher.

Literature review

Depression can be caused by stress and trauma among other reasons. Depression is one of the likely consequences of traumatic experiences and stressful events (La Greca et al., 2013). Terms applied to describe the effects of trauma can also describe a depressive state, such as helplessness, hopelessness, emptiness and the loss of an 'internal other' – which is a term referring to loss of internal communication with the 'other' within, as a consequence of trauma (Laub & Podell, 1995). In AET attention is paid to whether the children have experienced stress and/or trauma, which has not been integrated and worked through and consequently it may affect the child's emotional wellbeing and coursework learning.

Art therapy has been reported to bring positive effects for people who experience trauma or stress (i.e. Appleton, 2001; Eaton et al., 2007; Hass-Cohen et al., 2014; Kaimal et al., 2016; Rowe et al., 2017; van Westrhenen et al., 2017). However, the challenges of art-making in relation to traumatized clients are not widely discussed in the art therapy literature. One exception is Johnson's (2009) claim that many clinicians worry that art therapies can be: '... too "stimulating", "unstructured", or "re-traumatizing"' (p. 115) when working with clients who have experienced serious trauma.

The psychoanalysts Laub and Podell (1995) agreed with the general art therapeutic claim that artwork is an important medium for representations of trauma, but they also claimed that art-making can have a certain limitation. Laub and Podell (1995) claimed that a consequence of trauma can be a loss of the 'internal other'. Although artistic expression can repair the loss of the internal other, emptiness may also emerge. It is possible, they claimed, that trauma-related pain may become overwhelming if allowed to surface in excessive quantities through art-making within too short a period of time. Laub and Podell's (1995) caution may be especially important to keep in mind when working in a setting where the duration of therapy is limited, like in the case study presented in this chapter, because there may be insufficient time to integrate the trauma-related material brought to the surface through the art-making.

Johnson (2009) recommended that creative arts therapists explore hybridized methods when working with clients who have experienced trauma. Rankin (2003) discussed a task-oriented art therapy approach which increased both the traumatized client's and the therapist's sense of control. The educational psychotherapist Geddes (1999) also stated that learning tasks can help in alleviating anxiety. Integrating the logical, cognitive function of coursework learning task as in AET may be an important approach when emptiness, feelings of hopelessness and helplessness become overwhelming, in order to increase a sense of control and facilitate feelings of hope.

The emptiness discussed by Laub and Podell (1995) may be linked to depression as in both cases there is often limited personal drive and motivation for continuing to create and live a meaningful life. When emptiness is too overwhelming, possibly resulting in a lack of motivation to draw, the dimension of coursework learning offers an additional therapeutic approach for clients to come to terms with and work with their emotions.

It is generally implied in the art therapy literature that specific learning difficulties can be caused by emotional conflict, although this is not explored in great depth (Dalley, 1987; Glassman & Prasad, 2013; Grossman, 1990). Partly, to compensate for the weakness of this general implication, educational psychotherapy theory was incorporated into the conceptual framework of AET because of its in-depth exploration of how emotional difficulties can affect coursework learning (Best, 2014).

Similarly to educational psychotherapy, direct teaching is incorporated into AET and everything the child says and does is considered as a form of symbolic communication. The children often choose to solely create art during the AET sessions. At times the therapist suggests ways of working with coursework material integrated with image-making. On many occasions the children spontaneously work with their coursework material while integrating image-making in their own creative way. In the same way as in art therapy and educational psychotherapy the therapeutic relationship is important in AET in terms of containing emotional and intellectual processes.

Research methodology

The participants in the research project were five children aged eleven to fourteen. The main body of the research data was derived from case notes from 123 individual therapy sessions. The data was collected and described in detail using the case-study method (Yin, 2014) in order to study in depth the complex therapeutic process of each individual child. Grounded theory (Óttarsdóttir, 2010, 2013; Strauss & Corbin, 1998) was applied in the research analysis in order to organize the data, draw up categories for investigation and create an initial theory of the therapeutic method.

In order to observe the emotional wellbeing of the participating children and the effect of therapy, a Child Behaviour Checklist (Achenback, 1991) was also completed by the children's parents before and after therapy. The scores indicated whether the children were anxious and depressed, among other difficulties they might have had. School grades from before and after therapy, in comparison to the average student, were compared in order to evaluate coursework learning progress.

Along with the above mentioned research methods, creative methods were also employed in the present research. Art therapists have applied art creation in relation to research in a variety of ways (Chilton & Scotti, 2014; Kapitan, 2010; McNiff, 1998; Moon & Hoffman, 2014). Drawn diagrams, one of the analytical tools used in grounded theory, were employed in the present study (Óttarsdóttir, 2010, 2013). Writing-images, which are a part of the AET method, were also adapted as a research methodology whereby the researcher´s intellectual and emotional functions were integrated. The researcher made writing-images in the present study for: conceptualizing, knowledge forming, exploring subjects, investigating connections between concepts/categories/phenomena, coming to terms creatively with the research as well as for processing and reflecting on her emotions and conflicts. In that way, art-making served as a creative and self-reflective research methodology in a variety of ways and contexts at all stages of the research project.

As a researcher, I generally found conducting the research project interesting, especially when new insights emerged while discovering and understanding new perspectives. However, at certain stages in the research process feelings of hopelessness emerged due to being stuck or not knowing what to turn to next, not understanding the meanings of certain concepts and not knowing exactly what was taking place in the research. This sometimes led to decreased motivation to continue conducting the research, which felt like mild depression if it lasted for a long time. Throughout the research process I created a variety of images, often integrated with writing, which related to the topics of research and to my own often personal, associated emotions. During and following creation of these images, difficult emotions would often, to some degree, be replaced by increased curiosity, which fuelled a renewed motivation to continue conducting the research.

One way in which art-making was applied as a research methodology was when colors, brushes and paints were used, and I spontaneously worked with imagery relating to what was taking place and being studied, for example a specific concept. One example created at the beginning of the research process is shown in Figure 2.1.

When painting the letters shown in Figure 2.1, I somehow got into a space of understanding the phenomenon in question – in this case the phenomenon of 'research' – in a different dimension than when reading or writing about it. The kinesthetic of the fingers and the body through the application of brushstrokes, the use of color and the creation of forms in a large A1 format, created understanding and connection to the term and its application on a different level to writing about it in verbal concepts using pen or pencil. The painting process created an understanding where the emerging knowledge linked up with personal meaning. Consequently, understanding of the concept manifested in a wider and more meaningful dimension, in comparison to solely writing and reading about it, which tends to facilitate a more linear process and understanding.

Figure 2.1

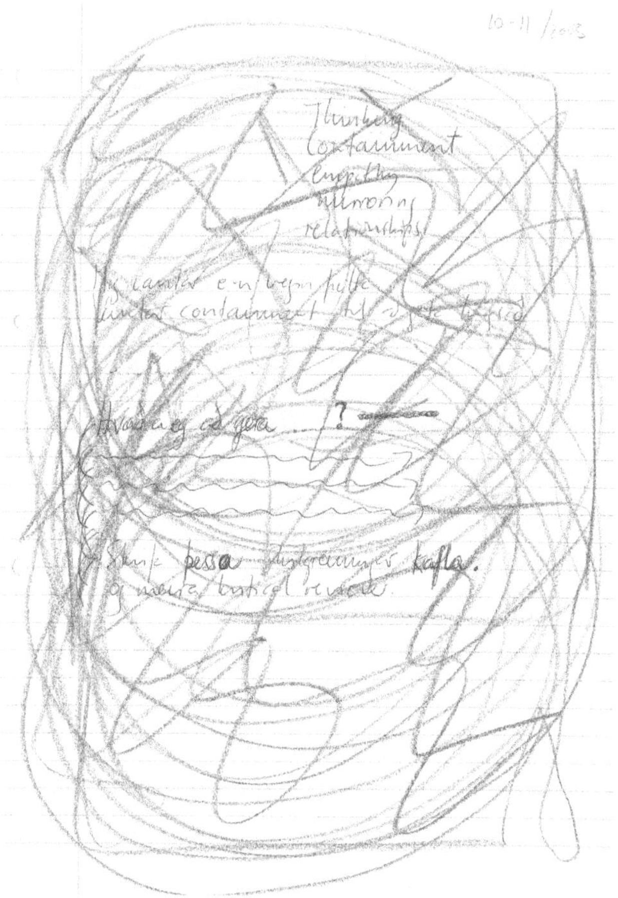

Figure 2.2

When being challenged by the unknown in the research, the feelings and thoughts evoked were in many cases brought into creative image-making, often integrated with writing. Throughout the whole research process countless images were created expressing such feelings and thoughts as exemplified in Figure 2.2.

Through making of such images, feelings and conflicts were to some degree expressed, processed and reflected on, and thereby energy to continue conducting the research was released. It was often found that the emerging emotions that had been evoked or tapped into by the subject of the research related to personal experiences. The visual expression helped them come to terms with those emotions, integrating, releasing and reflecting on them. The dual role of being both a therapist and researcher was at times challenging. Sorting out emotional responses through drawing and writing assisted the researcher in being reflexive and consequently increasingly subjective when conducting the therapy, gathering data, conducting the research analysis and creating the grounded theory.

The researcher's integrated drawing and writing process served as a creative and self-reflective research methodology in a variety of ways and contexts at all stages of the research project. The image-making provided a space for tolerating the unknown and clearing a pathway for new knowledge to emerge.

Findings

Oli's story

Oli attended therapy weekly for sixteen sessions at fourteen to fifteen years of age. He missed another two arranged sessions because of illness. Oli's mother was interviewed at the end of his therapy about Oli and his life, and his math teacher also reported on the boy´s progress at the end of therapy. Oli´s father was not interviewed, and no information was obtained directly from him.

Oli was referred to the school psychologist in the year prior to therapy because he was a victim of severe bullying, and he suffered from anxiety. The psychologist told me that when Oli was seven years old he preferred staying at school to going home. He also said he had some information on Oli that he could not tell me.

Oli's parents divorced when he was nine years old. His father was a recovering alcoholic who had been sober for a few years at the time of therapy. Oli's mother had been depressed but seemed able to provide support for the boy at the time of therapy. Oli himself was depressed at times. Other relatives also suffered from depression.

Oli´s grades were low, especially in math. Psychological reports on Oli at the age of six showed that his drawings were like those of a younger child, and that he did not fully comprehend numerical values. Before therapy, he did not come across as a troublemaker; he was rather quiet, and he did not disrupt others in his class. In therapy he showed willingness to work on his specific learning difficulties, and to some degree he was honest and open about his difficult experiences.

Oli initially told me that he did not like to draw. When I asked him what he would like to do, he tended to choose to study math. In some sessions he only talked. He spoke about the bullying, but rapidly dismissed it, saying that many of the boys who had bullied him were now his friends. He also mentioned that his father used to drink and that when he did he was moody. He also rapidly dismissed this topic by saying that his father had been sober for three years. Oli repeatedly told me he was doing well at school and had a lot of friends, which I later discovered was not altogether true.

Oli complained that he became depressed when he was ill. He also discussed being depressed when he was younger and said that his mother had also been depressed. When he was ten years old his mother isolated herself and did not go out due to depression.

Coursework learning

Oli began studying easy math exercises, such as drawing a number line, putting numbers on it (Figure 2.3a) and drawing percentage graphs (Figure 2.3b).

As time went on, Oli requested my assistance with more difficult coursework. I suggested that he include drawing as much as possible. When he struggled to understand the exercises, I realized how far away he was from mastering the material. Mastering the content of the math that was being taught in the classroom at that time appeared to be a hopeless task for Oli. Nevertheless, I let him choose what he wanted to study, which often was the math exercises presently worked with in his classroom. When he struggled to make sense of the math exercises, the atmosphere was heavy, and I found myself feeling hopeless and tired at the end of the sessions.

I questioned whether the hopelessness and helplessness I felt while assisting Oli with his math was a projection of his feelings or an echo of his helplessness in the wake of the trauma he had experienced, which I presumed at the time was the bullying, his mother's depression, his parents' divorce and his father's previous alcohol abuse. Oli's choice to study math that were too advanced for him and his failure to master the subject might have been a way of recreating the hopeless situation of the trauma, with the purpose of having me contain his feelings in order to help him integrate them.

As time went by, the situation seemed to grow more and more hopeless. Oli discussed the difficulties concerning his own depression and that of his mother, as well as the bullying. However, he did not work with the issues regarding his father, either through talking or drawing. Nevertheless, it seemed that an unexplained helplessness, had emerged through the coursework learning process and in the therapeutic relationship. This was manifested by his constant choice of

When the man recovered, he had no desire to be violent any more. After Oli had explained the film, he said with determination: 'I taped the movie and I'm going to let my mother watch it'.

I was not sure how best to approach this. There was only one session left: should I ask Oli about his childhood, which the film might have been symbolizing, or should I leave the topic alone because there was too little time left to process the available information? The fact that he had brought up the subject might have indicated that he was indeed ready to explore the issue to some degree. I therefore decided to ask him: 'Was your father ever violent when you were small?' Without hesitation he said: 'Yes, he hit my mother and my grandmother, but never me . . . I do not remember much of it, though'.

I attempted to show empathy by saying: 'It must have been difficult for a little boy to experience that'. He quickly closed the subject by saying: 'But my father is fine now. He is sober and has been through two treatments for alcoholism'.

After this session, I conjectured that the domestic violence, among other difficulties Oli had experienced as a young child, may have been interfering with his coursework learning. How could a child make sense of violence from a person he was supposed to trust? It similarly could have become impossible for Oli to make sense of mathematics.

Artwork

Oli made few drawings during therapy beyond the mathematical drawing exercises. He made two drawings at the beginning and end of therapy which were derived from a part of the Silver Drawing Test of Cognition and Emotion (SDT). The goals of SDT are partly to identify children who may be depressed and to provide a pre-post instrument for evaluating effectiveness of therapeutic and educational programs (Silver, 1996). At the beginning of therapy Oli chose to draw a bed and a television (Figure 2.5a). The image looks empty, as there is nothing on the television screen and no one in the bed. The bed and television seem to be floating because there is no ground line. The drawn lines seem fragile. There is a compositional balance between the text, the television, and the bed. The text Oli wrote says:

> *Mér þykir mjög gott að horfa á sjónvarp á kvöldin og hvíla mig.*
> [I really like to rest and watch television in the evenings.]

In a similar drawing made at the end of therapy (Figure 2.5b), Oli chose to draw a cat and a mouse. He chose a title and asked me to write it at the top of the page:

> *Köttur étur mús.*
> [A cat eats a mouse.]

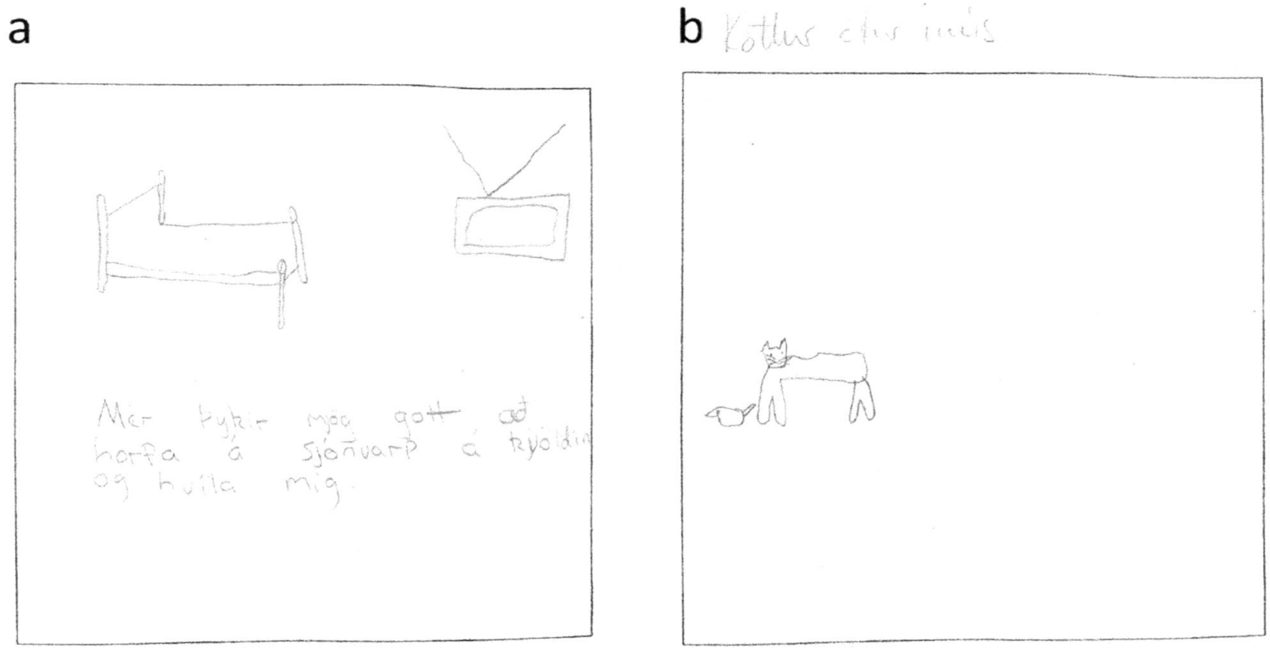
a
Mér þykir mjög gott að
horfa á sjónvarp á kvöldin
og hvíla mig.
b

Figure 2.5

This drawing appears even emptier than the earlier one, with a lot of empty space. The drawn lines are fragile, as in the earlier image, but they appear slightly better defined.

The slight difference in how Oli drew the lines in the later drawing could symbolize that he felt a little more definite and determined at the end of therapy. The lack of a ground line in both drawings may be evidence of how 'floating' and insecure he felt. Both drawings are empty, but there is even more emptiness in the later one. However, there is more life in it, with the presence of two living creatures, a cat and mouse (Figure 2.7), instead of an inanimate bed and television (Figure 2.6). This development could indicate that he had regained some of his 'internal other' through therapy.

As discussed earlier, Laub and Podell (1995) explained that trauma can result in loss of the internal other and a feeling of emptiness. In their view, creating artwork may be the only way to repair the loss of the internal other and to represent the emptiness of trauma. However, they cautioned that artwork can sometimes reach too far in recalling trauma. Oli did not enjoy drawing much, which could have been partly because he was experiencing unbearable emptiness due to his trauma.

Final part of therapy

As the therapy was coming to an end, I was concerned about leaving Oli unsupported. Had the therapeutic relationship, conducting the drawings and the coursework learning brought up too much for him to handle on his own? Information provided by Oli's math teacher at the end of therapy increased my concern. The teacher reported that since Oli commenced therapy he had become more careless and more talkative. The reason that Oli acted out more in class as the therapy unfolded might have been that memories and emotions relating to his difficult experience, including the domestic violence, were emerging.

It is possible that Oli experienced more emptiness at the end of therapy than at the beginning, although there was some gain in the internal other, as symbolized by a living cat and mouse and the emptiness in the drawing (Figure 2.7). By bringing his problems to the surface in therapy, Oli might have felt emptier but nevertheless he seemed to be more able to connect with his internal other which may have provided greater possibility of facing and mastering his difficulties.

In an interview with Oli's mother at the end of therapy, she reported that Oli lived in insecure circumstances when he was a baby. According to her, the father drank a lot, sometimes for a week without stopping, and he was verbally and physically abusive to her when drinking. The mother said that she often left home with the boy for several days at a time while the father was drinking. When Oli was seven years old he became absolutely wild with terror when he twice witnessed domestic violence. The mother reported that Oli was not doing any better in terms of coursework learning, but he appeared to be feeling better as a consequence of the therapy.

Grades and psychological testing

The scores on the Child Behaviour Checklist completed by Oli's mother indicated that, among other difficulties, he was severely anxious/depressed at the beginning of therapy. Scores on the four sub-scales on which Oli scored high before therapy – somatic complaints (SC), anxious/depressed (AD), attention problems (AP) and internal feelings (IF) – improved after therapy (Table 2.1). This indicated that Oli was feeling better at the end of therapy and that his anxious/depressed feelings and somatic complaints had diminished.

School grades from before and after therapy were observed in order to study Oli's progress in coursework learning. Oli's grades in math did not improve after therapy. All five children who participated in the study felt better following therapy, but for some of the children a larger number of sessions seemed to be needed in order to positively affect their coursework. It may have been that additional therapeutic sessions would have been needed for Oli in order to further integrate and process his emotions, which might in turn have had a positive effect on his math learning.

Symptomatic learning

Educational psychotherapy theories were found to be useful in contributing to explaining and working with the underlying emotional difficulties which were possibly causing specific learning difficulties (Best, 2014). 'Symptomatic learning' is a concept and a category which emerged through the grounded

Table 2.1 Child Behaviour Checklist for Oli. Scores over 70 indicate clinical significance.

	Before therapy	*After therapy*
Withdrawn (W)	62	62
Somatic complaints (SC)	**75**	59
Anxious/depressed (AD)	**76**	70
Social problems (SP)	59	63
Thought problems (TP)	64	64
Attention problems (AP)	70	65
Delinquent behaviour (DB)	50	50
Aggressive behaviour (AB)	58	50
Internal feelings (IF)	**74**	68
External behaviour (EB)	56	49
Total (T)	**67**	**60**

theory analysis, referring to specific learning difficulties which are symptom of emotional difficulties as stated in the introduction of this chapter.

One of the principles of educational psychotherapy theory is that children need a secure attachment in order to feel safe enough to learn (Barrett & Trevitt, 1991; Bowlby, 1999). Oli had experienced depressed mother, alcoholic father, domestic violence and bullying, which were likely to have created insecurity in his attachments and consequently limited his safety to explore and learn.

The educational psychotherapist Beaumont (1991) proposed that some children who are put into the role of a partner to one parent adopt an infantile omnipotent defense. This may have been one of the reasons for Oli's specific learning difficulties, since he lived alone with a depressed mother, which may have resulted in Oli taking on a partner´s role. In therapy Oli often gave the impression that his studies were going well, but when looking at this closely in one-to-one sessions he often did not know exactly how to approach the tasks. His unrealistic confidence about how to approach his coursework could have been an indicator of an omnipotent defense.

According to McKeever (1999), adolescents who have been treated badly may have difficulties with logical thinking and learning at school. If they think logically, they understand the reality of the abuse. Briere (1992) argued that abused children attempt to make sense of the abuse by blaming it on themselves. I argue that when a child illogically takes on responsibility for abuse or other traumatic events, the child's thinking may consequently become illogical in other areas, such as in relation to coursework learning, which may result in increased specific learning difficulties. It is possible that Oli´s specific learning difficulties was partly due to illogical self-blame as a consequence of his stress and trauma.

Barrett and Trevitt (1991) suggested that children who do not experience predictability or containment in their lives feel as if they are in an 'impossible calculation'. This may have been the way Oli felt in relation to his life and mathematical study.

In therapy, Oli repeatedly chose to work on overly advanced mathematical exercises. Through being unable to master his math coursework, Oli may have come to terms with how he felt about the domestic violence and other difficult events in his life. His hopeless attempt to try to master the math was possibly partly his way of repeating emotions relating to trauma, in order to master them. While assisting Oli with his mathematics, I felt heavy and hopeless, as if I was containing his feelings. These emotions may have arisen from his trauma, regarding the bullying, the domestic violence, his mother´s depression, his father's alcohol abuse and his parents' divorce, which he then projected onto his coursework learning. In a way, his hopeless attempts at learning mathematics, while being contained within the therapeutic relationship, may have served Oli well in coming to terms with his feelings and consequently moving toward mastering them. Through his hopeless math exercises, he may have moved away from being depressed and out of touch with his emotions to connecting with his feelings and internal other, which appeared to facilitate his emotional wellbeing.

Oli seventeen years after therapy

At the time of writing this chapter, Oli is thirty-one years old and lives with his wife and son. He carries a lot of responsibility at work and is well known in his career field. Oli has also competed successfully in organized sports.

When I met Oli in order to obtain consent to discuss his case in this publication, I interviewed him informally, asking about his life and what he remembered about the therapy. He remembered the location in the school where the therapy took place and that he was happy to go to the sessions. Prior to our meeting, knowing he was going to meet me, he had asked his mother about her experience of him being in therapy. His mother told him that he had changed in a positive way following the sessions we had together.

Oli said that when he was seventeen years old he had made a conscious decision to change his life for the better. As we talked and he looked back in time, he speculated that the therapy may have set off those positive changes.

My impression in our conversation was that Oli had the willpower to face difficulties and improve his life. He told me that the bullying at school had stopped in the year following therapy. He completed three further years of education after therapy and then commenced working life. Oli told me that he enjoyed a good relationship with both his parents at the present time. He also told me that he is successful in his career and happily married and had a healthy social life. Although I was aware that he might not be telling me the whole story, like he did when he was a child in therapy, I nevertheless observed that Oli had grown into a successful, charming, energetic and outgoing man.

Oli completed the Adult Behavior Checklist (Achenback, 1991) again, seventeen years after therapy. The scores fell outside the clinical range in all areas except for problems of an intrusive nature which relate to, for example, bragging, teasing, being loud and showing off. The scores indicate that he is emotionally well and that he is not anxious or depressed. Although the Child Behavior Checklist that his mother completed after therapy did not indicate intrusive nature, the present scores are in line with what his mathematics teacher said about him being disruptive in class seventeen years earlier. The intrusive scores raised may indicate that although Oli has come a long way, he may still have some work to do in terms of integrating emotions relating to the difficulties he experienced as a child.

Conclusion

Different stages and degrees of depression appeared at various levels of this research project. Oli was depressed at the beginning of the study but became less so following therapy. His mother had also been depressed as well as other relatives. As a therapist I sometimes felt hopeless, which to some degree felt like depression, during and after the therapy sessions, especially when Oli repeatedly requested help with mathematical exercises which were too advanced for him to master. As a researcher, I sometimes lacked motivation, which at times felt like mild depression, when faced with the unknown for too long and when I was not sure where to turn next in the research process.

I found image-making in combination with writing helpful in processing my own feelings and thoughts relating to the therapy and research as well as in coping with the uncertainty in the research process which lead to finding a way to move forward towards forming new knowledge. Oli made few drawings in therapy, some of which related to learning math, while others related more directly to his emotions. The math drawings (Figures 2.3–2.5) may have tapped into some of his feelings of hopelessness and helplessness toward his math learning, which could have helped him come to terms with his internal other and feelings relating to his stress and trauma. Also, Oli's artistic expression within the therapeutic relationship, including the emptiness and increased liveliness expressed in Figures 2.6 and 2.7, in combination with his verbal expression, seemed to have enhanced his emotional wellbeing.

Through the hopeless attempts to master too advanced mathematical coursework, Oli seemed to come to terms with and repeat emotions which appeared to relate to the stress and trauma he had experienced. Integrating the coursework material into therapy created a space where he was able to come to terms with and bring up such feelings of hopelessness and helplessness. Through working with difficult mathematical material and drawing within the therapeutic relationship seemed to eventually have led Oli to being able to talk about the context of some of those emotions which consequently appeared to facilitate his emotional wellbeing.

Emotional wellbeing is in the foreground in AET. In the case of Oli, his emotional difficulties were seen and approached through the lens of his specific learning difficulty. The shift between education and art therapy and the space between those two areas in AET offers an additional dimension to approach and work therapeutically with increased number of people.

References

Achenback, T. M. (1991). *Manual for the child behaviour checklist/4–18 and 1991 profile*. Burlington: University ofVermont, Department of Psychiatry.

Appleton, V. (2001). Avenues of hope: Art therapy and the resolution of trauma. ARTherapy; *Journal of the American Art Therapy Association*, 18(1), 6–13.

Barrett, M., & Trevitt, J. (1991). *Attachment behaviour and the schoolchild: An introduction to educational therapy*. London: Routledge.

Beaumont, M. (1991). Reading between the lines: the child's fear of meaning. *Psychoanalytic Psychotherapy*, 5(2), 261–269.

Best, R. (2014). Educational psychotherapy: an approach to working with children whose learning is impeded by emotional problems. *Support for Learning*, 29(3), 201–216. Retrieved from https://doi.org/10.1111/1467-9604.12058.

Bowlby, J. (1999). *Attachment and loss* (2nd ed). New York: Basic Books.

Briere, J. N. (1992). *Child abuse trauma: Theory and treatment of the lasting effects*. London: Sage Publications.

Chilton, G., & Scotti, V. (2014). Snipping, gluing, writing: The properties of collage as an arts-based research practice in art therapy. *Art Therapy*, 31(4), 163–171. Retrieved from https://doi.org/10.1080/07421656.2015.963484.

Dalley, T. (1987). Art therapy and education. *Presented at the image and enactment in childhood* (pp. 18–23). St Albans: Hertfordshire College of Art and Design.

Eaton, L. G., Doherty, K. L., & Widrick, R. M. (2007). A review of research and methods used to establish art therapy as an effective treatment method for traumatized children. *The Arts in Psychotherapy*, 34(3), 256–262. Retrieved from https://doi.org/10.1016/j.aip.2007.03.001.

Geddes, H. (1999). Attachment Behaviour and Learning: Implications for the Pupil, the Teacher and the Tas. *Educational Therapy and Therapeutic Teaching*, April(8), 20–34.

Glassman, E. L., & Prasad, S. (2013). Art therapy in schools: Its variety and benefits. In S. Prasad & P. Howie (Eds.), *Using art therapy with diverse populations: crossing cultures and abilities* (pp. 126–133). London and Philadelphia: Jessica Kingsley.

Grossman, G. S. (1990). Spontaneous art: Its role in education. *The Canadian Art Therapy Association Journal*, 5(2), 18–27.

Hass-Cohen, N., Clyde Findlay, J., Carr, R., & Vanderlan, J. (2014). "Check, change what you need to change and/or keep what you want": An art therapy neurobiological-based trauma protocol. *Art Therapy*, 31(2), 69–78. Retrieved from https://doi.org/10.1080/07421656.2014.903825.

Johnson, D. R. (2009). Commentary: Examining underlying paradigms in the creative arts therapies of trauma. *The Arts in Psychotherapy*, 36(2), 114–120. Retrieved from https://doi.org/10.1016/j.aip.2009.01.011.

Kaimal, G., Ray, K., & Muniz, J. (2016). Reduction of cortisol levels and participants' responses following art making. *Art Therapy*, 33(2), 74–80. Retrieved from https://doi.org/10.1080/07421656.2016.1166832.

Kapitan, L. (2010). *Introduction to art therapy research*. New York: Brunner-Routledge.

La Greca, A. M., Lai, B. S., Joormann, J., Auslander, B. B., & Short, M. A. (2013). Children's risk and resilience following a natural disaster: Genetic vulnerability, posttraumatic stress, and depression. *Journal of Affective Disorders*, 151(3), 860–867. Retrieved from https://doi.org/10.1016/j.jad.2013.07.024.

Laub, D., & Podell, D. (1995). Art and trauma. *International Journal of Psychoanalysis*, 76(5), 991–1005.

McKeever, P. (1999). Taking children seriously: Applications of counselling and therapy in education. In *When learning is a dangerous thing* (pp. 3–12). London: Cassell.

McNiff, S. (1998). *Art-based research*. London and Philadelphia: Jessica Kingsley.

Moon, B. L., & Hoffman, N. (2014). Performing art-based research: Innovation in graduate art therapy education. *Art Therapy*, 31(4), 172–178. Retrieved from https://doi.org/10.1080/07421656.2015.963485.

Ottarsdottir, U. (2005). Art therapy in education: For children with specific learning difficulties who have experienced stress and/or trauma (Unpublished PhD thesis). University of Hertfordshire, Hatfield.

Ottarsdottir, U. (2010a). Art therapy in education for children with specific learning difficulties who have experienced stress and/or trauma. In V. Karkou (Ed.), *Arts therapies in schools: Research and practice* (pp. 145–160). London: Jessica Kingsley.

Ottarsdottir, U. (2010b). Writing-images. *Art Therapy*, 27(1), 32–39. Retrieved from https://doi.org/10.1080/07421656.2010.10129566.

Óttarsdóttir, U. (2010). Grunduð kenning sem rannsóknaraðferð. Presented at the Fjórða samræðuþingið um eigindlegar rannsóknir við Háskólann á Akureyri, Akureyri: Unpublished.

Óttarsdóttir, U. (2013). Grunduð kenning og teiknaðar skýringarmyndir. In S. Halldórsdóttir (Ed.), *Handbók í aðferðafræði rannsókna* (pp. 361–375). Akureyri: University of Akureyri.

Rankin, A. B. (2003). A task-oriented approach to art therapy in trauma treatment: AR therapy: *Journal of the American Art Therapy Association*, 20(3), 138–147.

Rowe, C., Watson-Ormond, R., English, L., Rubesin, H., Marshall, A., Linton, K., . . . Eng, E. (2017). Evaluating art therapy to heal the effects of trauma among refugee youth: The Burma art therapy program evaluation. *Health Promotion Practice*, 18(1), 26–33. Retrieved from https://doi.org/10.1177/1524839915626413.

Silver, R. (1996). *Silver drawing test of cognition and emotion*. Sarasota: Albin Press Distributors.

Strauss, A. L., & Corbin, J. M. (1998). *Basics of qualitative research: Techniques and procedures for developing grounded theory* (2nd ed). Thousand Oaks: Sage Publications.

van Westrhenen, N., Fritz, E., Oosthuizen, H., Lemont, S., Vermeer, A., & Kleber, R. J. (2017). Creative arts in psychotherapy treatment protocol for children after trauma. *The Arts in Psychotherapy*, 54, 128–135. Retrieved from https://doi.org/10.1016/j.aip.2017.04.013.

Yin, R. K. (2014). *Case study research: Design and methods* (5th ed). Los Angeles: SAGE.

Chapter 3

Reducing depressive symptoms in adolescents with posttraumatic stress disorder using drama therapy

Elizabeth McAdam and David Read Johnson

Depressive symptoms are common among adolescents; indeed, mood variability may be at the center of developmental challenges of this age which centers around consolidation of identity, differentiation from one's caregivers and family, making initial choices regarding career and relationships, and learning to stand on one's own (Karkou & Joseph, 2017). Some adolescents develop severe levels of sadness, fatigue, problems concentrating, sleeplessness, self-criticism, worthlessness, and thoughts of dying (National Institute of Mental Health, 2016). These adolescents are often diagnosed with Major Depressive Disorder (MDD) or, if manic symptoms are present, Bipolar Disorder, and treated with medications and psychotherapy when available.

Youth with depressive symptoms report feeling hopeless about their future, trapped in their current circumstances, and not confident about their skills (Saluja et al., 2004; Meekums et al., 2015). They report having frequent episodes of sadness and worry, even in the absence of current stressors. Many have lost interest in activities previously enjoyed, and have a hard time avoiding boredom and fatigue. They are easily distracted, and have a hard time concentrating on their schoolwork even for brief periods of time. Many are among the most functional members of their family and are burdened with responsibilities of taking care of other members who are ill or in trouble.

A significant number of adolescents who develop depressive symptoms have previously experienced highly stressful or traumatic experiences, such as maltreatment, exposure to violence and death, natural disasters, sexual molestation, or assault. The frequency with which traumatic events occur in the lives of adolescents has been estimated at around 10% for all adolescents, and substantially higher among youth from low income, urban, and minority populations (DHHS, 2003). Studies have shown that when these events occur, depression is one of the most likely outcomes (Felitti, 2009). It is known that even in the absence of a mood disorder diagnosis, 50% of people who have Posttraumatic Stress Disorder (PTSD) from a traumatic event show depressive symptoms (Kessler et al., 1995). Research has also shown that increased exposure to violence and trauma is associated with more self-reported PTSD and depression symptoms (Ozer & Weinstein, 2010). Therefore, among adolescents who may have experienced what Shonkoff et al. (2012) describe as "toxic stress," the etiology of the disorder and thus the treatment of choice (i.e., for depression or PTSD) may not be clear (p. e236).

This chapter will attempt to lay out the conceptual basis for understanding the overlap in symptoms between the diagnoses of MDD and PTSD, and we raise the question of whether a trauma history assessment should be completed for all adolescents presenting with depressive symptomatology in order to determine the best treatment course. We will then illustrate the impact of a trauma-centered drama therapy treatment on depressive symptoms in two cases of adolescents with depression.

The overlap between PTSD and MDD

Diagnostically, PTSD and MDD, as described in the DSM-V, have seven overlapping symptoms, notably negative beliefs about self, self-blame, negative mood, loss of interest, problems concentrating, sleep disturbance, and lack of positive emotions (DSM-V). Thus seven out of 20 PTSD symptoms are also depression symptoms, and seven out of 12 depression symptoms are also PTSD symptoms. The Beck Depression Inventory-II (Beck et al., 1996), which is the most common standardized measure for diagnosing Depression, includes two more PTSD symptoms: irritability and loss of interest in sex. Table 3.1 outlines this overlap.

The importance of this information is that structurally and formally, PTSD and depression overlap in significant ways. This goes beyond co-morbidity, in which two separate conditions tend to co-exist, and raises questions about the prevalence and relationship between these two diagnoses, including the ways in which they develop and inform one another. The result is that clinicians must be discerning in their diagnosis of these two conditions.

Table 3.1 Overlap of symptoms among DSM-V diagnoses of PTSD, depression, and BDI-II

Symptoms	*PTSD*	*Depression*	*BDI-II*
Intrusive Memories	√		
Distressing Dreams	√		
Dissociative Reactions	√		
Psychological Distress	√		
Physiological Distress	√		
Avoidance of Thoughts	√		
Avoidance of Situations	√		
Psychogenic Amnesia	√		
Detachment	√		
Reckless Behavior	√		

(Continued)

Table 3.1 (Continued)

Symptoms	*PTSD*	*Depression*	*BDI-II*
Hypervigilance	√		
Startle Response	√		
Irritability	√		√
Negative Beliefs about Oneself	√	√	√
Distorted Cognitions Blaming Self	√	√	√
Negative Emotional State	√	√	√
Loss of Interest	√	√	√
Problems Concentrating	√	√	√
Sleep Disturbance	√	√	√
Lack of Positive Emotions	√	√	√
Depressed Mood		√	√
Weight Loss		√	√*
Psychomotor Agitation		√	√
Fatigue		√	√
Thoughts of Death		√	√
Crying			√
Loss of Interest in Sex			√

(*Listed as *loss of appetite* in the BDI-II).

Treatment for depression

The primary treatment for depression is medication (Gaynes et al., 2012). Over 10% of adult Americans are currently taking antidepressants (Pratt et al., 2011). Unfortunately, recent empirical studies have shown that in comparison to placebo, medication makes little significant difference except perhaps in the short-term course of treatment (Kirsch et al., 2008). Furthermore, cognitive psychotherapy interventions have been shown to be as effective as medication for treating depression and may even reduce the risk of relapse (DeRubeis et al., 2008).

Typical psychotherapeutic interventions for the treatment of depression include Cognitive Behavior Therapy (CBT) and Interpersonal Psychotherapy. In CBT, the client's distorted ideas and beliefs are challenged in ways that foster a more positive, open, and resilient mindset that is in turn reinforced with coping strategies (Beck & Beck, 2011; Kennard et al., 2016; Seligman, 2006). Due to the structured nature of CBT, however, clients must have a high level of motivation to commit to this form of treatment, which is often at odds with the symptomology of depression itself. CBT also requires clients to engage in logical reasoning and verbalization – which clients who have experienced trauma may struggle with (Johnson & Lubin, 2016). Furthermore, CBT focuses on current disruptions in a client's life, possibly bypassing systemic and complex underlying causes of depression such as traumatic life events and toxic stress.

Interpersonal Psychotherapy examines the client's relationships and how they have been influenced to maintain the clients' depressive symptoms; interventions are designed to disrupt and shift these maladaptive patterns of behavior (Klerman & Weissman, 1984; Weissman et al., 2000). This form of therapy relies on the client's ability to maintain the full course of treatment with fidelity. This may be especially challenging for clients who may be blocked from accessing ongoing or long-term treatment due to poor healthcare, lack of transportation, need for child care, or other factors that result from systemic oppression that lead to toxic stress.

Drama therapy for depression

Many published works on drama therapy suggest that their methodologies are effective with depressive symptoms, though rarely are depressive symptoms targeted, leaving the reader with the sense that drama therapy interventions may be a generalized way of helping people feel better about themselves. Thus, for clients entering drama therapy who are diagnosed with depression, a specifically designed treatment format for their condition may not be currently available.

Several chapters on the use of drama therapy and depression were included in Brooke and Myers' book, *The Use of the Creative Arts Therapies in Treating Depression* (2015). Gheorghe's (2015) approach is more closely aligned with cognitive behavior therapy in aiming to reduce the maladaptive and cyclical thinking characteristic of depression. Balancing aesthetic distance and catharsis, he uses "a more subtle and nuanced approach, in which enactment is complemented by intellectual explorations" (p. 216). Role-plays, film, and projective exercises explore the main themes of depression.

Rubin (2015) utilizes psychodrama, psychoeducation, and attachment work to combat shame and negative thoughts about the self. Her work aims to help the client externalize, process, and heal their depression through embodying new roles, reversing roles, and creating symbols. She combines the intensity of physical enactment with the distancing of symbolization to lower the client's core sense of shame and guilt.

Senroy (2015) employs the Sesame Approach (Pearson, 1996) which utilizes mask work, role-play, and therapeutic theater to engage clients in transforming the illness of depression into a creative process characterized by aesthetic distance, which is the "ability to express feeling without the fear of becoming overwhelmed, and to reflect upon an experience without the fear of completely shutting down emotionally" (Landy, 2009: 72–73). Through this work, clients were able to use the metaphor and distance of the mask to explore different emotions in depth, and it provided opportunities for both verbal and nonverbal communication and reflection. The mask work allowed the women to consider their depression from a distanced perspective, and also challenged the larger community to consider the many myths surrounding mental health in the South Asian community. The result was an increase in the clients' "understanding, identification, and empathy toward depression" (p. 255). While this work helped group members engage with their peers and express themselves more fully, what remains unclear is whether or not this work allowed the group members gain insight into the direct links between their symptoms and their personal history that led to these symptoms so that maladaptive thought and behavior patterns could be challenged and reformed.

Over the past eight years Johnson and his colleagues have developed a form of trauma-centered drama therapy to address the symptoms of PTSD called Trauma-Centered Developmental Transformations, or TC-DvT (Johnson, 2009, 2014; Pitre et al., 2014; Pitre, 2014). This method centers on improvised, mutual, embodied play between the therapist and client that helps rigid behavioral patterns become more flexible, lowering the client's fears around life's inherent instability. This exposure method helps reduce the symptoms of PTSD, as well as the avoidance that many clients understandably feel towards upsetting material, helping them differentiate between past harm and present circumstances.

For adolescents who have experienced traumatic life events, their depression and PTSD-related symptoms are inherently linked to their history. Confronting the symptoms alone without addressing the underlying cause may not help loosen what Johnson & Lubin (2016) describe as the trauma schemas, or ideas that often trap clients in their shame, self-loathing, and blame. We hypothesize that when working with this population, a trauma-centered treatment plan using TC-DvT will address the avoidance to the underlying history and might in turn lead to an abatement of the accompanying depressive symptoms.

Methodology

Background

In surveying high school students in New Haven, Connecticut, an urban area with a large under-resourced minority population (mostly Black and Latino students), we have found that 80% are exposed to at least one adverse childhood event and 50% are exposed to three or more events (Johnson et al., 2015). Depressive symptoms, especially sadness, hopelessness, self-blame, and problems concentrating, are reported by almost 40% of all students. We suspect that the high rate of depressive symptomatology in urban low-income adolescents is due largely to the sequelae of toxic stress from trauma, abuse, neglect, lack of resources, and systemic oppression, rather than being caused by an independent biological disease.

Screening of high school students

We conducted an assessment of this population in October-November 2015. A total of 711 public high school students across three schools in New Haven, Connecticut were administered a questionnaire that asked them whether they had experienced instances of maltreatment, neglect, or conflict at home; a list of common psychological symptoms, and a list of stressful events such as illness, death, divorce, hospitalization, homelessness, prostitution, pregnancy, or arrest. The questionnaire was optional as was including their names on it.

Table 3.2 lists the results. 88% of the students included their names on the questionnaire despite the highly sensitive information being asked. The results show a high level of strife in these students' families' homes, including severe arguments (50%), witnessing violence or abuse (34%), emotional abuse (28%), or physical fights (22%). Neglect, physical abuse, and being made to work followed, with 4% reporting sexual abuse. Also striking are high levels of experiencing death of loved ones, by disease (19%) or violence (14%), followed by hospitalizations. Significant levels of depression, anxiety, and anger symptoms were reported.

Table 3.2 High school students' self-reports of stressful events and symptoms (N = 711).

Item	*Percent Reporting*
Placed Name on Questionnaire	88%
Experienced in Last Six Months?	
Abuse:	
Severe arguments in home	50%
Witness abuse/violence	34%
Emotional abuse	28%
Physical fights in home	22%
Physical abuse	15%
Made to work when others do not work	14%
Neglect	12%
Sexual abuse or assault	4%
Stressful Event:	
Someone close die of disease	19%
Someone close die of violence	14%
Hospitalized for psychological reason	8%
Hospitalized for medical reason	6%
Became pregnant (girls only)	4%
Child Protection referral made on family	3%
Fired from job	2%
Arrested	2%
Homeless for more than a week	2%
Paid money for sex	1%
Symptoms:	
Worries about others	60%
Problems concentrating	55%
Anger	39%
Depression	31%
Feel you won't succeed	31%
Anxiety	29%

(*Continued*)

Table 3.2 (Continued)

Item	*Percent Reporting*
Feel like giving up	24%
Hopelessness	17%
Fear	17%
Not eating enough	16%
Lost a lot of weight	13%
Use drugs to deal with pain	9%
Use alcohol to deal with pain	8%

Sample

To examine whether or not TC-DvT might reduce symptoms of MDD, a focused case-study method was employed. Two high school students who had experienced traumatic life events and who were currently demonstrating depressive symptoms were selected to participate in a series of individual TC-DvT sessions over a period of two months.

The students were selected from a public high school made up of predominantly Black and Latino populations. Both students had participated in verbal counseling sessions throughout their lives both in and outside of school but had never participated in drama therapy. These sessions were conducted by the same drama therapist (EM), and they took place in a high school classroom.

Data sources

Multiple sources of quantitative and qualitative data were collected in order to be able to identify a thorough history of traumatic life events and current symptoms for each student. The quantitative data included the Beck Depression Inventory (BDI-II; Beck et al., 1996) and the traumatic life events questionnaire. The BDI-II was administered as a pre- and post-test to measure the depressive symptoms over time.

The traumatic life events questionnaire was administered prior to starting the sessions, and a correlated one-time Adverse Childhood Experiences (ACEs) score was calculated (Felitti, 2009). The ACEs score includes ten categories across three topics: Abuse (physical, emotional, and sexual), Neglect (physical and emotional), and Household dysfunction (mental illness, incarcerated relative, primary caregiver treated violently, substance abuse, and divorce).

Qualitative data included teacher and administrator reports of student behaviors in class and therapist observations from each TC-DvT session.

The intervention: trauma-centered developmental transformations

The method we used was Trauma-Centered Developmental Transformations, or TC-DvT, an application of Developmental Transformations with traumatized people (Johnson, 2009, 2014; Pitre, 2014; Pitre et al., 2015). This work involves an improvisational play session with the client in which the therapist actively participates, engaging in a variety of roles that are transformed gradually into images or scenes reminiscent of the traumatic situations the client has experienced. The client is allowed to react to these reminders by enacting defensive or assertive behavior that was not allowed in the original event, adapting to the challenge presented by the therapist. The client is invited to enact a moment of empowerment over a portrayal of their perpetrator. This helps clients to de-sensitize themselves to the traumatic triggers and propel them toward a state of mourning over the losses that the event caused in their lives. These sessions take place during the school day and may be as short as 15 minutes or as long as 30 minutes.

The critical aspect of TC-DvT is the therapist's focus on the youth's traumatic experiences, not their symptoms of depression or anxiety. The intention is to unearth and play out, within the restraints imposed by a dramatic portrayal, their fears from the past in order to desensitize them to these reminders. An assumption is made that once these shadows have been lifted, the depressive and anxiety symptoms will decrease. Thus, the method is based on the therapeutic component of exposure, rather than challenging distorted beliefs or teaching new coping strategies. In TC-DvT sessions with students ages 5–13 years old, rapid and dramatic decreases in their levels of experienced stress, worry, and sadness have been observed after even one session. In this study, we were interested in the effects of DvT in an older population of adolescents ages 14–18 years old.

TC-DvT was conducted within the context of a larger program called ALIVE, which applies a public health approach to addressing toxic stress among urban youth, ages 5–18 in the public schools. ALIVE provides targeted stress reduction interventions for youth who have experienced traumatic events such as maltreatment (abuse, neglect), exposure to neighborhood violence, or other events such as death, divorce, incarceration of the parents, medical illnesses, or homelessness. At the time of writing this chapter, ALIVE counselors were working with 2,500 youths each week in New Haven, Bridgeport, and New Britain, Connecticut, and in Minneapolis, Minnesota. A fuller description of the ALIVE program is available (Johnson et al., 2015; Sajnani et al., 2014; www.traumainformedschools.org).

Procedure

The traumatic life events questionnaire with correlated ACEs score and the BDI-II were administered prior to beginning the drama therapy sessions. Qualitative observations of each student from teachers and administrators were collected to gain a picture of each student's symptomatology. Individual TC-DvT sessions were then conducted once weekly with each participant over a two-month period. Each session was 15–20 minutes long, with a total of eight sessions for one client ("Jamal") and six sessions for the second client ("Maria"). At the end of the two-month period the BDI-II was administered as a post-test to measure the change in depressive symptoms.

Case examples

Examples from the treatment of each student are included below. Pseudonyms for each student are used throughout.

Case 1: Jamal

Jamal is a 15-year-old second generation Caribbean-American male who is currently a freshman in high school. Throughout his entire childhood he was subject to verbal, physical and emotional abuse by his mother. She often beat him with objects, and he witnessed his mother physically abuse his older sister. His father was incarcerated for domestic violence toward Jamal's mother early in his life, and Jamal has not been in contact with him since he was released. His mother remarried several years ago, and his stepfather was also verbally and emotionally abusive towards Jamal. One year prior to starting these sessions, Jamal was removed from his mother's care by the Department of Children and Family Services and placed in the care of his paternal grandmother. His grandmother had a history of verbally abusing him and had often ignored the mother's abuse of Jamal as a child.

Jamal's current symptoms, as reported by his teachers and himself, included nightmares, intrusive memories of the abuse, negative beliefs about himself, loss of interest in academic work, withdrawal from social activities, depressed mood, tearfulness, fatigue, loss of pleasure and interest in daily activities, blaming himself for some of the abuse, irritability, and problems concentrating in class. Teachers reported that he often distracted his peers by talking, and then when redirected he argued or left the classroom. He was often accused by school staff of starting fights with peers as a way to avoid doing work in class. Jamal's ACEs score was an 8 out of 10, very severe, and his Beck score was 32, indicating severe depression.

Jamal participated in eight trauma-centered DvT sessions over a two-month period of time, with one session per week. The following excerpts illustrate some of the ways in which Jamal's trauma was named and played with in the course of the sessions.

Box 3.1 Jamal's therapy: example sessions

First session

The therapist (EM) and client move around the room, pretending to play basketball. They are circling each other, checking each other out as the competition.

Therapist: Can I trust you?
Jamal: Can I trust YOU?
Therapist: Probably not. You've been hurt before.
Jamal: I'm still going to beat you.
Therapist: Oh yeah? We'll see about that.

A game of basketball plays out, with Jamal dunking the pretend ball again and again over the therapist's head, refusing to let the therapist make any shots.

Therapist: You always win, huh?
Jamal: Yup.
Therapist: You still look a little soft to me. I need to whip you into shape. Drop down and give me 20!

Jamal, surprised, does so.

Therapist: That's right, you're never going to amount to anything if you don't work at it! Train, harder, harder you little worm! You're never going to make it in this life!
Jamal: *Jamal* pauses, as if all energy drains out of him, and collapses on the ground. I'm tired. I don't want to play anymore. Crosses his arms over his chest.
Therapist: Oh, no! things got too real, I killed him! Or maybe he's only dreaming. . .?
Jamal: This is all a nightmare. He moves towards the door, playing with the doorknob.
Therapist: Pre*tending to wake up.* Where am I? Am I dreaming? Why is it so dark?
Jamal: *Becoming re-energized and moving away from the door.* I'm going to get you and you'll never see me coming.

A nightmare scene plays out, where he becomes a monster and chases after the therapist, trying to eat her.

Therapist: Help! Help! I bet this is what it feels like in real life! Like a nightmare that will never end!
Jamal: Yeah, that's right, and you're never going to escape.
Therapist: How horrible!

Jamal laughs, and corners the therapist.

Second session

Prior to this session Jamal told the therapist about a time when his mother beat him with a telephone cord that left scars on his back and neck. At Jamal's suggestion, he began in a dream sequence again. He wanted to be the monster who runs after the therapist.

Jamal: I'm the biggest and baddest you've ever seen. I'm going to eat you! I'll never stop chasing you ever ever EVER!
Therapist: Where will I go? I live here!
Jamal: You can't get away!
Therapist: Help! Is this how it always goes, on and on with no escape? This is horrible! I have nowhere else to go!
Jamal: Yes! Laughing.
Therapist: Well, mom, you might as well get you-know-what and get to it.
Jamal: You mean my cord?
Therapist: Yeah but if you hit me with that, I might tell someone.
Jamal: You'll never tell anyone. It's our business. You can't take it outside [the family].
Therapist: Is this all I have to look forward to? Don't you love me?
Jamal: Stops suddenly. Begins to cry. Turns his back to therapist so she can't see him.
Therapist: This stops you in your tracks, huh?
Jamal: Nodding his head in agreement, wiping his eyes.
Therapist: You can't stop thinking about her?
Jamal: She turns into the monster in my dreams.
Therapist: Your mom becomes the monster.
Jamal: Yeah.
Therapist: That's terrible. No wonder you feel upset.
Jamal: You won't tell anyone [that I cried]?
Therapist: Jamal, all of your feelings are important and what you went through with your mom was terrible. Yet your tears tell me that you still love her despite what she did to you.
Jamal: Nods quietly.

Eighth (last) session

Jamal: We're in the nightmare again!
Therapist: Again? How do we always end up back here? I'm going to find a way out.
Jamal: No you can't, it doesn't exist.

Therapist: You may be in control but this place is terrible. We're stuck here forever . . . hiding, running for our lives . . . slowly starving to death. . .

Jamal: I'm so hungry. But you look delicious!

Therapist: Ahh no! Please don't eat me! I thought we were in this together!

Jamal: *Laughing, pretends to eat therapist in one gulp.*

Therapist: It's survival of the fittest out here, you have to eat the ones you love to stay alive.

Jamal: Laughing, making crunching sounds. Your bones are delicious!

Therapist: Be careful, once you eat my bones you'll become infected too. You'll become tired, not care about life anymore. . .

Jamal: Hisssssssssssss! Begins making noises like he is possessed: Rolling around on the floor, eyes rolled back, gurgling and hissing.

Therapist: You see, he's possessed!

Jamal: Still rolling around, hissing, eyes rolling back.

Therapist: I cast you out, demons! In the name of all that is holy I cast you out!

Jamal: Hissing at me, looking at me.

Therapist: We need to exorcise these demons or they'll take him for good! We need to get our Jamal back! Therapist moves forward and pretends to strap him down, dumping water on him. This is going to hurt tremendously.

Jamal: Through his hissing *and growling* – You'll never get me out!

Therapist: That's what you think! Out demons! Give us our Jamal back! You have controlled him for too long! Out! Out! Ouuuuuuuutttttttttt!

On the last "out," therapist is yelling while Jamal screams as if the demon is leaving him. He collapses in a limp pile, laying perfectly still with his body relaxed. After a few seconds, his eyes pop back open and he sits up. They look at each other in silence for a while, smiling at each other.

Jamal: Phew.

Therapist: That was something.

Jamal: Yeah. Long *pause. He smiles.*

Therapist: Ready to go back to class?

Jamal progressed rapidly through the eight weeks in being able to bring his anxieties and past experiences into the play with the therapist. The therapist, following the principles of TC-DvT (Johnson, 2014), tended to play a challenging figure, increasingly reminiscent of the perpetrating figures in Jamal's family, and then allowed Jamal to overcome or outwit these figures through his physical strength, intelligence, and willpower. Rather than providing a model of caring parents, the treatment instead provided Jamal with exposure to reminders of his trauma so that he could further process his experience and become empowered to do something about it in the play as Pitre (2015) discusses. When this process had been completed, Jamal demonstrated evidence of physical release through tears or bodily relaxation. Like all exposure treatments, the goal is not to avoid or cover up the nightmare of the memory, but rather to make it through to the other side; to wake up in a world now more benign and caring, often symbolized by the caring look or smile of the therapist at the end of a DvT session.

During the time of this treatment, Jamal's depressive symptoms and mood dramatically improved, and his teacher observed significant progress in his classroom behavior. The BDI-II post-test measure indicated a score of 17, within the mild range. His teachers reported that he was more engaged in his classwork and was able to stay in class for longer periods of time without being triggered. He completed his work with more consistency, and his grades improved.

Case 2: Maria

Maria is a 16-year-old, first-generation Latina female whose family immigrated from Puerto Rico; she frequently travels home to visit family there. Maria has a complex trauma history: She was raped at age four by two strangers, and since then she has fought off attackers who have attempted to rape her several other times throughout her life. Her mother, whom Maria describes as cold and distant, is severely ill with diabetes and heart disease. Her father, whom Maria identifies with and feels protective toward, has suffered from drug and alcohol addiction throughout her life. She has witnessed domestic violence between her father and mother many times; her father has been arrested and served jail time for both domestic violence and drug possession. Her grandmother, who raised her for part of her childhood and who Maria describes as her "actual mother," passed away several years ago. She has many friends in the school who often come to her for advice.

Maria appears bright, vivacious and social, but underneath she struggles to sustain the energy to support herself, her friends, and her family. In counseling sessions, she becomes tearful and speaks about how tired she is of her facade. She loves school and is a high achiever; often starting out the year with high grades that slip down to C's and D's by the end of the year due to poor attendance.

Her teachers report that she is smart and could easily be an honor roll student if her family burdens were not weighing so heavily on her. They note her emotional volatility – seemingly fine one moment but then becoming sad or angry and leaving the class because she cannot sit still. She reports losing interest in activities that are important to her, feeling fatigued, sleeping more than usual, feeling irritable, and having difficulty concentrating. Maria's ACES score was 9 out of 10, very severe, and her Beck score was 20, indicating moderate depression.

Maria participated in six trauma-informed DvT sessions over a two-month period of time, with one session per week. She missed two weeks due to not attending school on the day of the scheduled session. The following three session excerpts illustrate the themes of Maria's play and the ways in which the therapist directly addressed the trauma history.

Box 3.2 Maria's therapy: example sessions

First session

Therapist and client start by moving around the room, looking at each other, shrugging their shoulders and sighing. This transforms into Maria pretending to float up into the air while saying "finally."

Maria: Finally. . . *Breathes a sigh of relief.*
Therapist: You can't stay up there forever you know. *Starts to pull her down.*
Maria: Leave me alone. *Waves therapist away.*
Therapist: We need you here. There's so much to do, so many people to take care of.
Maria: *Laughing, pushing me away.* Just let me go!
Therapist: Oh so now you want to *leave* me?
Maria: You have plenty of people to help you.
Therapist: Honey, please come help me. *Grabbing at her shirt.*
Maria: *Pushes therapist off, seems upset, tears come to her eyes, her body tenses.* Get away from me. *Pretends to lock the therapist up.* There. Now you can't bother anyone.
Therapist: Okay so, be free to float for a little while, enjoy yourself while I suffer in here! Go ahead. I'll be waiting here, all alone.
Maria: *Looks at therapist, not sure what to do. Smiles.*

Third session

Maria shared with the therapist at the beginning of this session that her father had started smoking crack cocaine again and she was very worried about him. They begin by walking around the room arm in arm.

Therapist: Honey, I love you.
Maria: *Enrolling therapist as her father.* You have to be careful, Dad.

Therapist: *Pretending to smoke and drink.* I am being careful. I'm so careful and I love you.
Maria: No, you need to stop that! *Grabbing the pretend blunt out of therapist's hand, throwing it on the ground, crushing it.*
Therapist: Hey! You better give that back, I need it!
Maria: *Becoming the police.* Uh, excuse me sir? You're going to have to come with us.
Therapist: What? No I didn't do anything wrong. What did I do? My daughter, where is she? Maria?
Maria: You have been disrupting the peace. Your wife called. We're gonna take you in.
Therapist: You won't get away with this! That damn wife! Where's my daughter? Hey, honey! If you can hear me I'm sorry and please come visit me! You're the only one who understands me.
Maria: *Becoming tearful.* Yeah, it's exactly like that. That's how he is.
Therapist: Oh man, for real? He calls for you, he apologizes?
Maria: Yeah.
Therapist: I'll bet he really means it.
Maria: *Looks hard at the therapist.* Uh, yeah, what do you mean?
Therapist: That he is really regretful, not manipulating you.
Maria: *Looks worried.* He might be messing with me.
Therapist: That's really hard.
Maria: Yeah, that's why I'd rather float.
Therapist: I see.

Sixth (last) session

On the way to the room, Maria tells the therapist that her mother has recently gone into the hospital with kidney problems and the doctors have informed her that it is terminal. It is unclear if her mother will return home or not. Maria says she feels angry and numb at the same time. The session starts out with them running around the room at top speed, trying to knock each other out of the way. This becomes more aggressive until they start to fight.

Maria: I'm gonna kill you!

They are fighting – pretending to punch, bite, and choke each other. She pretends to put her hands around the therapist's throat and choke her.

Therapist: I know you're angry with me for being sick! Do it, then!
Maria: Ahhhhhhhhh! *Choking therapist until she falls on the ground, pretending to die. Maria appears relieved, dancing around the therapist's body.*

Therapist:	Well, now you don't have to play the waiting game.
Maria:	*Glaring at therapist.* I know what you're trying to do.
Therapist:	What? What am I trying to do?
Maria:	Talk about the real stuff.
Therapist:	You want me to avoid it like the rest of your family?
Maria:	*She shakes her head no, keeps dancing.*
Therapist:	*Coming back as a ghost.* I'm baaaaaaaack!
Maria:	I thought I got rid of you!
Therapist:	It's not that easy. You can't get rid of me.
Maria:	Ugh I don't really want you to go. *Becoming tearful.*
Therapist:	*Thinking of her grandmother, who had died three years earlier.* But also I'm not the only one you are missing, am I?
Maria:	*Crying.* No, grandma.
Therapist:	Come here honey, I miss you too. *They embrace.*
Maria:	It's just not fair that I have to live without her. She was my real mother. Now my real mom. . . .*becomes tearful.*
Therapist:	It isn't fair.
Maria:	I miss her. I don't want to be alone.
Therapist:	I know. *Long pause.*

In this trauma-centered treatment, Maria was given the opportunity to play out several scenarios relevant to the stresses she has experienced, again with the therapist playing out the challenging or perpetrating figures within the safety of the mutually created playspace (Johnson, 2009). As Maria's responses were given full expression, the underlying depressive emotions were expressed, and some of the energy they contained was released. Much of the internally-held conflict appeared to be negative feelings about her family that were not expressed, and therefore were redirected to herself, forming a depressive constellation of thought that propelled her negative behaviors in school. The BDI-II post-test measure indicated a score of 9, within the normal range. Teachers noted that she was much less irritable, her attendance improved, and she was able to make up a lot of her missing work. Maria benefited greatly from these sessions, and soon her energy and optimism returned, allowing her to become much more alert and functional in her academic work.

Pre-post testing

As illustrated in Figure 3.1, both students experienced dramatic reductions in their scores on the Beck Depression Inventory, Jamal dropping from a 32 (severe range) to 17 (mild range); and Maria from a 20 (moderate) to 9 (normal).

We created two subscales on the BDI-II, one consisting of the seven PTSD-related symptoms (specifically item numbers 2, 4, 11, 12, 16, 17, and 19) and

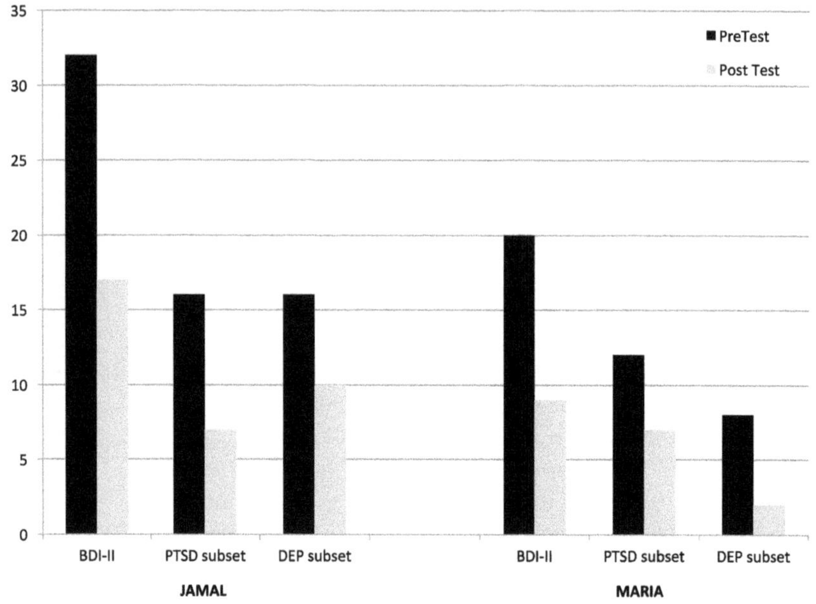

Figure 3.1 Results of the Beck Depression Inventory with two students, before and after drama therapy treatment.

the other consisting of 14 depression-only symptoms (specifically item numbers 1, 3, 5–10, 13–15, 18, 20, and 21), in order to determine whether the improvement on the BDI-II was predominantly due to the PTSD-related depressive symptoms. Both the trauma-related and primary depressive symptom subscales decreased, showing a general effect of the treatment on all depressive symptoms. Thus, the trauma-centered treatment appears to have had a strong effect in treating depressive symptoms across the board in these two students. Notably, for both students, the levels of symptom severity on the PTSD-related items were more than double those on the depression-only items.

Discussion

This study utilizes two brief cases and therefore cannot be used to establish any claim that trauma-centered drama therapy treatment is preferable over other treatments for depression among adolescents. However, it does illustrate that a trauma-centered treatment, which utilized exposure work through improvised play and directly confronting with emotions that arise out of traumatic life events, did result in a substantial abatement of depressive symptoms for the two young people described here.

The overlap in diagnostic criteria for depression and PTSD serves as our conceptual challenge: when are a young person's depressive symptoms caused by traumatic experiences, and when by other causes? As Karkou and Joseph (2017) point out, adolescence is a "complex phase" in and of itself, but for clients who have experienced "significant unresolved past issues, attachment issues or environmental adversity, it can become a time of real vulnerability" (p. 235). The case study findings suggest that for adolescents showing depressive symptoms (and possibly clients in other age groups), a thorough trauma assessment should be conducted upon intake to determine the presence or absence of toxic stress. If present, then the clinician can make a determination whether to proceed with a standard treatment for depression (medication or psychotherapy) or a trauma-centered treatment.

Further, the empirical evidence of poor response to antidepressant medication (Kirsch et al., 2008) and modest effects of psychotherapies for depression (Weissman & Markovitz, 2000) may possibly be due to the fact that a certain proportion of clients with depressive symptoms do not suffer from a depressive illness and are instead suffering from trauma-related conditions. In such cases, trauma-based treatments may have a higher degree of success.

Conclusions

This case study demonstrates the potential positive effects on depressive symptoms of adolescents when treated with a trauma-centered approach to drama therapy. It is proposed that both the trauma focus and the embodied method attend to areas of distress not targeted by either medications or psychotherapy for depression.

With these results in mind, we intend to collect data on a much larger sample of the responses of adolescents with depression to trauma-centered drama therapy, to establish whether such treatment is effective in reducing depressive symptoms. This work is underway. Additionally, we recommend future studies be conducted that compare standard psychotherapeutic treatment for depression with trauma-centered treatment for this population. We encourage drama therapy investigators to explore this area further due to the high prevalence of depression and the potential for drama therapy to contribute new forms of treatment.

References

Beck, J., & Beck, A. (2011). *Cognitive behavioral therapy*. New York: Guilford Press.

Beck, A., Steer, R., & Brown, G. (1996). *The Beck depression inventory-II*. San Antonio: Pearson.

Brooke, S., & Myers, C. (2015). *The use of the creative arts therapies in treating depression*. Springfield, IL: Charles C Thomas.

Department of Health and Human Services (2003). *National survey of child and adolescent well being*. Washington, DC: Dept. of HHS.

DeRubeis, R. J., Siegle, G. J., & Hollon, S. D. (2008). Cognitive therapy vs. medications for depression: Treatment outcomes and neural mechanisms. *Nature Reviews Neuroscience*, 9, 788–796.

Felitti, V. (2009). Adverse childhood experiences and adult health. *Academic Pediatrics*, 9, 131–132.

Gaynes, B., Lux, L., & Galtlehener, G. (2012). *Primary care guidelines for the treatment of depression*. Rockville, MD: National Guideline Clearinghouse, US Department of Health and Human Services.

Gheorghe, C. (2015). The angel who was not: Drama therapy and clinical depression. In S. Brooke & C. Myers (Eds.), *The use of the creative arts therapies in treating depression* (pp. 214–230). Springfield, IL: Charles C Thomas.

Johnson, D. (2009). Developmental transformations: Towards the body as presence. In D. Johnson & R. Emunah (Eds.), *Current approaches in drama therapy* (2nd edition), (pp. 89–116). Springfield, IL: Charles C Thomas.

Johnson, D. (2014). Trauma-centered developmental transformations. In N. Sajnani & D. Johnson (Eds.), *Trauma-informed drama therapy: Transforming clinics, classrooms, and communities* (pp. 68–92). Springfield, IL: Charles C Thomas.

Johnson, D. R., & Lubin, H. (2016). *Principles and techniques of trauma-centered psychotherapy*. Arlington, VA: American Psychiatric Association Publishing.

Johnson, D., Lubin, H., & Jewers-Dailley, K. (2015). *Annual report: Animating learning by integrating and validating experience*. New Haven, CT: Foundation for the Arts and Trauma (available from the authors).

Karkou, V., & Joseph, J. (2017). The moving and movement identities of adolescents: Lessons from dance movement psychotherapy in a mainstream secondary school. In D. Miell, R. MacDonald & D. J. Hargreaves (Eds.), *Handbook of musical identities* (pp. 232–244). Oxford: Oxford University Press.

Kennard, B., Hughes, J., & Foxwell, A. (2016). *Cognitive behavioral therapy for depression in children and adolescents*. New York: Guilford Press.

Kessler, R., Sonnega, A., Bromet, E., Hughes, M., & Nelson, C. (1995). Posttraumatic stress disorder in the National Comorbidity Study. *Archives of General Psychiatry*, 52, 1048–1060.

Kirsch, I., Deacon, B., Huedo-Medina, T., Scoboria, A., Moore, T., & Johnson, B. (2008). Initial severity and antidepressant benefits: A meta-analysis of data submitted to the Food and Drug Administration. *Plos Medicine*, 5(2), e45. Doi: 10.1371/journal.pmed.0050045.

Klerman, G., & Weissman, M. (1984). *Interpersonal psychotherapy of depression*. New York: Basic Books.

Landy, R. (2009). Role theory and the role method of drama therapy. In D. R. Johnson & R. Emunah's (Eds.), *Current approaches in drama therapy* (2nd Ed.) (pp. 65–88). Springfield, IL: Charles C. Thomas.

Meekums, B., Karkou, V., Nelson, E. A. (2015). Dance movement therapy for depression. *Cochrane Database of Systematic Reviews*, 2. Art. No.: CD009895.

National Institute of Mental Health (2016). Major depression among adolescents. Retrieved from www.nimh.nih.gov/health/statistics/prevalence/major-depression-among-adolescents.shtml.

Ozer, E. J., & Weinstein, R. S. (2010). Urban adolescents' exposure to community violence: The role of support, school safety, and social constraints in a school-based sample of boys and girls. *Journal of Clinical Child & Adolescent Psychology*, 33(3), 463–476.

Pearson, J. (Ed.) (1996). *Discovering the self through drama and movement: The Sesame approach*. London: Jessica Kingsley.

Pitre, R. (2014). Extracting the perpetrator: Fostering parent/child attachment with developmental transformations. In N. Sajnani & D. Johnson (Eds.), *Trauma-informed drama therapy: Transforming clinics, classrooms, and communities* (pp. 243–269). Springfield, IL: Charles C Thomas.

Pitre, R., Sajnani, N., & Johnson, D. (2015). Trauma-centered developmental transformations as exposure treatment for young children. *Drama Therapy Review*, 1, 41–54.

Pratt, L., Brody, D., & Gu, Q. (2011). *Antidepressant use in persons aged 12 and over: US, 2005–2008*. Washington, DC: National Center for Health Statistics.

Rubin, S. (2015). Almost magic: Working with the shame that underlies depression using drama therapy in the imaginal realm. In S. Brooke & C. Myers (Eds.), *The use of the creative arts therapies in treating depression* (pp. 231–244). Springfield, IL: Charles C Thomas.

Sajnani, N., Jewers-Dailley, K., Brillante, A., Puglisi, J., & Johnson, D. (2014). Animating learning by integrating and validating experience. In N. Sajnani & D. Johnson (Eds.), *Trauma-informed drama therapy: Transforming clinics, classrooms, and communities* (pp. 206–242). Springfield, IL: Charles C Thomas.

Saluja, G., Iachan, R., Scheidt, P., Overpeck, M. D., Sun, W., & Giedd, J. N. (2004). Prevalence of and risk factors for depressive symptoms among young adolescents. *Archives of Pediatrics and Adolescent Medicine*, 158(8), 760–765.

Seligman, M. (2006). *Learned optimism: How to change your mind and your life*. New York: Vintage Books.

Senroy, P. (2015). Inside out: A case study using masks and the sesame approach of drama therapy with South Asian women recovering from depression. In S. Brooke & C. Myers (Eds.), *The use of the creative arts therapies in treating depression* (pp. 245–257). Springfield, IL: Charles C Thomas.

Shonkoff, J. P., Garner, A. S., The Committee on Psychosocial Aspects of Child and Family Health, Committee on Early Childhood, Adoption, and Dependent Care, and Section on Developmental and Behavioral Pediatrics, Siegel, B. S., Dobbins, M. I., Earls, M. F., Garner, A. S., McGuinn, L., Pascoe, J., Wood, D. L. (2012). The lifelong effects of early childhood adversity and toxic stress. *Pediatrics*, 129 (1), e232–e246.

Weissman, M., Markovitz, J. & Klerman, G. L. (2000). *Comprehensive guide to interpersonal psychotherapy*. New York: Basic Books.

Chapter 4

Movement-based arts therapy for children with attention deficit hyperactivity disorder (ADHD) in the Kingdom of Saudi Arabia

Badr Alrazain, Ania Zubala and Vicky Karkou

Introduction

Children with attention deficit hyperactivity disorder (ADHD) are at risk of developing a broad range of difficulties such as cognitive, emotional, educational and social issues (Tsal et al., 2005), while adolescents with ADHD are at risk of substance abuse, underachievement, demoralisation and low self-esteem (Waite & Ivey, 2009). If unaddressed, both the particular disorder as well as associated difficulties increase the risk of developing depression in later life (Orth et al., 2008; Sowislo & Orth, 2013). Moreover, Biederman et al. (2008) argue that ADHD is often directly linked with depression and anxiety, which can easily remain undiagnosed.

In the United Kingdom, ADHD affects approximately 2–5% of children and teenagers (NHS Choices, 2016), while great variations are observed globally (Skounti et al., 2007). The prevalence of ADHD in the Kingdom of Saudi Arabia (KSA) is high (Al-Haidar, 2003; Al-Habeeb et al., 2012) and, according to various estimates, affects between 11.6% and 16.4% children (Abu Taleb & Farheen, 2013; Homidi et al., 2013; Al-Hamed et al., 2008).

Despite the evident need, there is a nationwide lack of treatment for children with ADHD in KSA; there is only one specialist school in the country and as a private school, access to it is limited by financial factors. In addition, teachers are commonly unaware of symptoms of ADHD and the need for early diagnosis, and often ill-equipped to support children with ADHD within mainstream education.

The situation becomes even further complicated by the fact that there is no universally recommended intervention procedure to follow when addressing the needs of children with ADHD. However, since deficient self-regulation and poor inhibition are regarded as characteristics of the disorder, research studies (e.g. Grönlund et al., 2005) argue for the need to shift from medication as a first port of call, towards therapies which aim to achieve rebalancing and emotional regulation. Furthermore, Erfer and Ziv (2006) add that, in order to meet the challenges of ADHD, modes of treatment must be adapted towards not only the individual needs of the child but also the environment within which the child lives. Paediatric and adolescent psychiatry are therefore beginning to use multidisciplinary approaches, where medical treatments are combined with various psychotherapy interventions (Bower et al., 2001). Arts therapies may constitute one such treatment option; their humanistic and creative ethos has indeed led to a growth of interest in their application in treating ADHD (Remschmidt, 2005).

Arts therapies provision for ADHD in KSA is currently very limited (Eisa & Abdulrashed, 2010). Interventions for ADHD tend to be in the form of medication, rather than the child-centred therapies which are more widely available in the UK. In particular, the cultural sensitivities of the KSA impose significant constraints on the use of arts therapies with this client population, despite the value that they can have in moving beyond behavioural symptoms to counter the underlying emotional dysregulation and anxiety associated with ADHD.

In this chapter, we look at relevant English publications by practitioners and researchers, and we discuss cultural adaptations needed to work with this client population in the school system in KSA. We describe a particular movement-based arts therapies programme developed as part of the doctoral studies of the first author to fit the work setting of a specialist school for children with ADHD and the overall cultural context of KSA. Summary of the evaluation of this programme will be included, presenting and discussing findings relating to its impact on emotional wellbeing and the development of social skills of young clients, as evidence of its preventive character to developing depression.

Arts therapies in the treatment of ADHD

Research on arts therapies with children shows positive effects on behavioural symptoms such as inattention, hyperactivity/impulsivity, anger management and sleep disorders, but also on wellbeing and social behaviour (Henley, 1998; Novy, 2003; Kearns, 2004; Majorek et al., 2004; Grönlund et al., 2005; Cope, 2009; Hamre et al., 2010) – all defining symptoms of ADHD, indicating the value that arts therapies may have in ameliorating the symptoms of the condition.

It is argued that arts therapies may provide particular benefits to children with ADHD (Reynolds et al., 2000) and may be a suitable medium through which children may exhibit their emotions and their struggle to deal with ADHD (Redman, 2007; Kennedy et al., 2014; Safran, 2002; Bower et al., 2001). Furthermore, there is evidence to suggest that dance movement therapy can be effective in improving emotional wellbeing and self-control in children who are at risk of developing anxiety and depression and those with lowered self-esteem (Bojner-Horwitz, 2003; Karkou, 2010).

There are indications that group work may be more successful than individual treatment (Safran, 2002) and can lead to increased social abilities (Chang & Liu, 2006). The importance of group therapy for practising interpersonal skills, cooperating toward a shared goal and alleviating isolation is particularly relevant to children with social and/or behavioural problems (Coholic et al., 2012).

The dominant focus in arts therapies practice and, limited, research with children with ADHD in the Arab world and beyond is on behaviour modification. For example, an art therapy programme for children with ADHD in Saudi primary schools was found to be successful in increasing students' attention and reducing hyperactivity (Eisa & Abdulrashed, 2010). Similarly, a study based in Dubai found that psychodrama helped to minimise hyperactivity among school children (Al Mulla, 2008). Moreover, music therapy has been reported to lead to improvements in restlessness and behavioural control (Rickson, 2006; Chen et al., 2012).

For children with communication and emotional issues, dance movement therapy has been considered to be a particularly suitable intervention (Karkou & Sanderson, 2006; Erfer & Ziv, 2006; Goodill, 2005; Van der Merwe, 2010). Furthermore, research has indicated the positive impact of dance movement therapy on self-awareness and group cohesion (Lanzillo, 2009), as well as ADHD symptoms and body related issues (Grönlund et al., 2005), including perceptual-motor abilities (Alotaibi, 2014).

In addition to direct benefits of arts therapies for symptoms associated with ADHD, their reported positive effects on children's emotional wellbeing, mood and self-esteem hold promise for a more balanced psychological wellbeing in later life and their preventative character might lower the risk of developing depression in adult life (Riley, 2003).

The cultural context of the KSA

The cultural and religious situation in the KSA presents challenges for the growth of arts therapies practice in the country. Activities such as dancing and playing musical instruments are not allowed to be practised in schools in the KSA (Van Nieuwkerk, 2008). As a result, the use of dance movement therapy, music therapy and, to an extent, dramatherapy, would raise questions around the exhibition of the body in a prohibited manner. Similarly, the limitations on artistic depiction constrain the activities which can be used in art therapy.

Arts therapies are not widely known in the KSA and there are no art therapists working in schools (Alkhenaini, 2013). Nevertheless, in 2000, the first therapeutic treatment clinic was granted permission to open, specifically to practise art therapy in Riyadh, the capital city of the KSA (Alyami, 2009). This step was a historical shift for art therapy in the Arab world. A few years later, the Saudi Ministry of Health (MOH) approved art therapy as a specialised field of psychotherapy (Saudi Ministry of Health, 2014).

However, as Alyami (2009) recounts, the process of founding art therapy in the KSA was highly challenging, and it involved a flexible and adaptive attitude. According to Alyami (2005), art therapy in the Arab world must be designed in line with the social and religious customs of the communities it serves. The need to offer interventions which are culturally relevant is also acknowledged outside the context of the KSA. For example, Koepfer (2000) recommended that arts therapists need to understand cultural and religious implications to increase the value of interventions offered, while Dokter and Hills de Zarate (2016) discuss this topic in an extensive way in a recent publication.

Evaluating the arts therapy programme

The purpose of the research study was to develop, conduct and evaluate a culturally sensitive programme of arts therapies for children with ADHD in the KSA. In its initial stages this research identified the current provision of support for children with ADHD in the KSA and learned from arts therapists practising in the UK with this group. Subsequently, a culturally sensitive programme of arts therapies was developed, with a primary aim to improve emotional wellbeing, social skills and emotional regulation. This programme was evaluated from the perspective of the children's parents and their teachers.

Methodology

In developing and evaluating a culturally sensitive arts therapies programme this research followed the recommendations of the Medical Research Council (MRC) framework for developing complex interventions (Craig et al., 2013) and it adopted a mixed-method approach (Creswell, 2009), using, mainly, semi-structured interviews and self-administered questionnaires. Observations also took place and provided the researcher with useful insights but were not explicitly included in the analysis of data.

A multi-phased mixed methods study was conducted. In the first stage, the researcher explored how experts in arts therapies describe arts therapies interventions. This stage was mainly conducted through qualitative methods, namely interviewing experts from both the UK and the KSA. The findings were used to develop a culturally-sensitive arts therapies programme. This intervention was subsequently piloted with a sample of twelve students with ADHD and evaluated.

In this chapter we will focus on this final phase of the research, which was conducted in a school in the KSA which specialises in supporting children with ADHD. The school setting was the most appropriate choice culturally and practically, giving good ecological validity for the intervention delivered in a natural environment. By not removing children from their familiar school setting, as little disruption as possible was caused to their normal school timetable.

The evaluation followed a pilot randomised control trial design. Some children were randomly assigned to receive the arts therapies intervention while others were observed during their normal classes.

Data collection and analysis

The quantitative data was collected using two instruments: the ADHD scale (Al-Khashrami & Ali, 2009) and Strengths and Difficulties Questionnaire (SDQ scale, Goodman, 1997), completed before and after the intervention by the participating children's parents and teachers. In this chapter, only results from the SDQ scale are presented, as more relevant for outcomes linked to depression. SDQ is recommended for use in studies to measure outcomes of mental health disorders and to assess emotional and behavioural difficulties (Goodman et al., 2000; Goodman & Goodman, 2009), and it has been used widely in research (e.g. Czamara et al., 2013; Classi et al., 2012; Papageorgiou et al., 2008).

Semi-structured interviews with parents and teachers were conducted to collect their accounts and perceptions of the programme. Initial interviews were designed to obtain information regarding children's behaviour and emotional wellbeing, relational/social skills, emotional regulation and potential value of the culturally sensitive arts therapies programme. Interviews following the intervention were aimed to gain insight into whether parents and teachers felt the therapy had any impact on the children's social skills, emotional wellbeing and emotional regulation, and to reassess their judgement of the value of arts therapies. A female research assistant was employed to assist with the data collection from the participating female parents who might have felt uneasy with being interviewed by the male researcher/therapist. In all other cases, the first author conducted the interviews.

Quantitative data was collected by another research assistant invited to support the first author. This enabled him to separate his research from his therapy role and thus, reduce bias and increase reliability of this study.

Descriptive and inferential statistics were used to describe and identify any differences before and after the intervention, both within each group and between the two groups. Due to the low number of participants, non-parametric testing was applied using the SPSS statistical software. Thematic analysis was used to analyse interview transcripts.

Participants

Participants in this study were children with ADHD, their parents and teachers, who met the following inclusion criteria:

1. Children with ADHD (n = 12): with diagnosis of ADHD for at least one year, between six and twelve[1] years old and willing to participate in the study. All participating children were boys.
2. One parent/guardian for each of the twelve participating children: living with the participating child for at least six months and available and willing to communicate with the arts therapist.
3. One teacher for each of the twelve participating children: working and having weekly contact with participating child for at least six months.

The head teacher of the school contacted the selected children and their parents and teachers by letter or email, providing them with the information sheet at least two weeks before the programme was due to start. The researcher made contact with the families one week thereafter, offering opportunity to ask questions and obtaining signed consent. Children were randomly allocated (using computer randomisation) to either the intervention or the control group, with six participants in each group.

Intervention

The arts therapies programme incorporated movement and art therapy elements. The programme consisted of twenty-four sessions, lasting between thirty and forty minutes, delivered three times a week over eight weeks.

The researcher also acted as therapist and worked with a male assistant. Therapy took place in an empty room, completely clear and painted in one colour. Mats were used as a sitting area and props were kept in a basket, including beach balls and balloons. Soft mats were used to cover the floor during more energetic activities.

Each session included two participating students and offered opportunities for social-skills learning with a large amount of one-to-one attention from the therapist and activities adapted from dance movement therapy literature. Activities, such as tossing balloons to each other using different body parts (Grönlund et al., 2005), tug of war (Curtis, cited in Karkou & Sanderson, 2006) and partner balances (Sherborne, 2001), were used to improve participants' social skills and trust. Koshland's (2010) use of fast-then-slow movement and Levy's (2005) division of the therapy room into 'energy zones' were among the exercises used to help children recognise and regulate their own emotions. Kestenberg's work on therapist-patient attunement was also used in the 'mirroring' activities which recurred in every session (Amighi et al., 1999).

Dance and music were not used due to the cultural context discussed earlier. Instead, rhythmic clapping and clicking were included. At some points, children were encouraged to add sounds to their movements. Where artwork was used, the children were asked to engage with tasks that did not include human or animal entities, in accordance with the Islamic stricture used in the KSA against the representation of living beings.

Based on insights coming from the interviews with UK-based therapists in phase one of this research, the programme adopted an integrative approach (Karkou & Sanderson, 2006), combining the principles of client-centred therapy (Rogers, 2003) with those of attachment theory (Bowlby, 1997) to meet the complex needs of children with ADHD. According to Rogerian principles, it aimed to respond to the needs and personality of the individual child, helping them to grow in self-confidence, emotional wellbeing and social skills by focusing on their strengths. Following Bowlby's ideas, the intervention was designed to provide a secure therapy space. Above all, it adopted unconditional positive regard. For example, throughout the programme, the therapist aimed to be warm and encouraging, accepting the child without judgement. Therefore, the therapist avoided praise, as this might have suggested to the child that the therapist expected him to behave 'correctly'. Further, the therapist adopted a client-centred approach in not challenging the child's chosen ways of expressing themselves, so long as no one in the room was endangered and the 'ground rules' were kept. Both attachment theory and client-centred therapy demand a high level of empathy and trust, from and in the therapist. In this programme, trust was developed through a variety of activities, such as 'rowing the boat' and drawing body outlines, designed to help the child trust the therapist, assistant and other participants.

The structure of session was an extremely important consideration, as research emphasises its significance for promoting group cohesion and providing a framework where children feel secure (Murphy et al., 2004; Rickson & Watkins, 2003). Ground rules, introduced in the beginning of the intervention by the therapist (see Alrazain, 2016), aimed to enable the development of a secure and inclusive therapy space. To ensure a degree of structure appropriate to the children's need for security and routine, stability and security was created by using a regular room and time and a predictable structure to the therapy session, particularly a routinely repeated beginning and ending. Knowing what to expect was hoped to help the children feel secure and relax into trusting the therapist. Nevertheless, children were free to leave this structure when they chose, and it was generally followed loosely to enable the therapist to respond to the child when he chose to diverge from the session's structure, focusing on the here-and-now of the session and adapting to the child's immediate needs. On a practical level, this meant that the therapist had to be prepared to adapt flexibly with little notice. Many activities on the programme were also based on responsiveness from the therapist and were centred on 'mirroring' and imitation, activities designed to help the child feel empathised with, understood and responded to.

Each session followed a similar structure: a) warm-up; b) main part of the session; c) closing activities. The course of therapy consisted of three phases:

- The beginning phase (three sessions) aimed to build trust in the children, increase their confidence and ensure they understand the ground rules and the purpose of therapy. The sessions in this phase were more directive, encouraging trust, with the therapist either interacting with both children at once or working with the assistant to demonstrate activities.
- The middle phase (eighteen sessions – six weeks) aimed to increase emotional wellbeing, emotional regulation and participants' social skills. The middle sessions, therefore, involved more pair work and were less directive, allowing the two children participating at one time to improvise more, while still remaining within a broad structure of the session.

- The end phase (three sessions) further increased participants' confidence by structuring sessions according to their choice of activities. Additionally, it focussed on acknowledging the upcoming end of the programme and, therefore, encouraged children to share feelings verbally and through movement, and to find concrete movement tasks and rituals that could signify the end of the work.

Quantitative results

The SDQ scores of parents and teachers of children in the control and the experimental group were compared using a non-parametric test of differences: Wilcoxon W test for paired groups. Neither parents nor teachers of children in the control group reported any statistically significant differences (see Table 4.1).

Table 4.1 Pre- and post-test SDQ scores of parents and teachers of children in the control group (Wilcoxon W test).

Factors	*Parents (control group)*				*Teachers (control group)*			
	Groups	*Mean Rank*	*Z*	*p*	*Groups*	*Mean Rank*	*Z*	*p*
Emotional problems	Negative Ranks	1.0 (1)	0.000	1.000	Negative Ranks	1.0 (2)	-1.342	.180
	Positive Ranks	3.0 (2)			Positive Ranks	4.0 (0)		
Conduct problems	Negative Ranks	1.0 (2)	-0.378	.705	Negative Ranks	1.0 (1)	.000	1.000
	Positive Ranks	2.0 (2)			Positive Ranks	4.0 (1)		
Hyperactivity/ inattention	Negative Ranks	0.0 (0)	1.857	.063	Negative Ranks	2.0 (2)	-1.414	.157
	Positive Ranks	2.0 (4)			Positive Ranks	4.0 (0)		
Peer problems	Negative Ranks	2.0 (3)	-0.368	.713	Negative Ranks	2.0 (3)	-1.633	.102
	Positive Ranks	2.0 (1)			Positive Ranks	3.0 (0)		
Prosocial	Negative Ranks	1.0 (2)	0.108	.854	Negative Ranks	1.0 (1)	-1.000	.317
	Positive Ranks	2.0 (2)			Positive Ranks	5.0 (0)		
Total difficulties	Negative Ranks	1.0 (2)	0.740	.459	Negative Ranks	1.0 (3)	-1.289	.197
	Positive Ranks	2.0 (4)			Positive Ranks	3.0 (1)		

In contrast, there were statistically significant differences between the pre- and post-tests in experimental group (see Table 4.2), including 'total difficulties' in both parents' ($Z = -2.21$; $P < 0.05$; $r = 0.85$) and teachers' groups ($Z = -2.23$; $P < 0.05$; $r = 0.91$). Similarly, the variables of 'emotional problems', 'conduct problems', 'hyperactivity/inattention' and 'prosocial' showed statistically significant differences between pre- and post-tests for both parents' ($Z = -2.04, -2.07, -2.21$ and 2.03 respectively; $P < 0.05$; $r = 0.83, 0.85, 0.90$ and 0.83 respectively) and teachers' ($Z = -2.04, -2.03, -2.21$ and 2.12 respectively; $P< 0.05$; $r = 0.83, 0.83, 0.90$ and 0.87 respectively) groups. However, there were no statistically significant differences between pre- and post-test regarding 'peer problems' in the parents' ($Z = -1.86$; $P > 0.05$) and the teachers' scores ($Z = -1.63$; $P > 0.05$).

Overall, while most variables, including 'total difficulties', revealed significant changes between the pre- and post-tests for the experimental group,

Table 4.2 Pre- and post-test SDQ scores of parents and teachers of children in the experimental group (Wilcoxon W test, * indicates statistically significant difference).

Factors	*Parents (experimental group)*				*Teachers (experimental group)*			
	Groups	*Mean Rank*	*Z*	*p*	*Groups*	*Mean Rank*	*Z*	*p*
Emotional problems	Negative Ranks	2.0 (5)	-2.041	.041*	Negative Ranks	2.0 (5)	-2.041	.041*
	Positive Ranks	1.0 (0)			Positive Ranks	1.0 (0)		
Conduct problems	Negative Ranks	3.0 (5)	-2.070	.038*	Negative Ranks	2.0 (5)	-2.032	.042*
	Positive Ranks	1.0 (0)			Positive Ranks	1.0 (0)		
Hyperactivity/ inattention	Negative Ranks	2.0 (6)	-2.207	.027*	Negative Ranks	2.0 (6)	-2.207	.027*
	Positive Ranks	0.0 (0)			Positive Ranks	0.0 (0)		
Peer problems	Negative Ranks	2.0 (4)	-1.857	.063	Negative Ranks	2.0 (3)	-1.633	.102
	Positive Ranks	2.0 (0)			Positive Ranks	3.0 (0)		
Prosocial	Negative Ranks	0.0 (0)	2.032	.042*	Negative Ranks	0.0 (0)	2.121	.034*
	Positive Ranks	2.0 (5)			Positive Ranks	4.0 (5)		
Total difficulties	Negative Ranks	2.0 (6)	-2.214	.027*	Negative Ranks	3.0 (6)	-2.226	.026*
	Positive Ranks	0.0 (0)			Positive Ranks	0.0 (0)		

peer problems were the sole variable which remained unchanged (in terms of statistical significance) in the quantitative responses of both parents and teachers.

Qualitative findings

Perception of change in emotional wellbeing

All parents in the experimental group felt that their child's emotional wellbeing had improved as a result of the programme, and several spoke about the changes in very animated language. The parents in the experimental group used a variety of terms to describe these changes: for instance, 'optimistic' and 'ambitious'. Several parents in this group noted a change in their child's confidence. One of the parents, for example, stated that his child used to be afraid of playing at the park with many children, which improved following therapy. Most notably, however, several parents talked about the changes in their child's happiness, improved relationships with their parents and their new willingness to open up and share their thoughts. For some children, previous avoidance and ambivalence towards parents and towards school was replaced with a greater sense of security and enthusiasm. None of the parents in the control group, however, noticed any changes in their child's emotional wellbeing, in terms of confidence, happiness or ability to trust. While around half of these parents felt their child was already happy, other parents in this group spoke clearly about their child's unhappiness. In stark contrast, only one parent in the experimental group felt there was no change in their child's emotional wellbeing.

A revealing difference between the pre- and post-intervention interviews of teachers became apparent while discussing the students' emotional wellbeing. In the pre-intervention interviews, teachers' comments on students' emotional needs were either monosyllabic or vague. In the post-intervention interviews, however, a couple of teachers implied that their students needed 'empathy', or 'attention and someone to listen'. Largely, though, children were still characterised as having no specific emotional needs, usually in extremely brief answers, while the teachers seemed to predominately focus on behavioural outcomes.

Perception of change in social relationships

Amongst the experimental group, every parent suggested that their child's ability to form functional social relationships had increased in some way, for example that their ability to share with others had improved (mostly in relationships with siblings). Changes were observed both in the quality of children's friendships and in their number. One exception to note was a parent of a child in the experimental group who noticed that their child's social relationships could be conflicted. This still, however, demonstrated progress towards the initial social interactions as opposed to none pre-therapy. While the control group parents also noted some changes in their child's social relationships, these tended to be described in terms such as 'very slight' and 'gradual'. Around half of the parents in the experimental group felt their child's activities had changed in some way due to the programme and that the skills learnt were internalised and used beyond the sessions themselves. There was a reported increased interest in physical movement, with one parent reporting that his child started to play the games that he had learned during the programme with his siblings. This implies an increase in physical exercise, especially as an aid to social relationships. One mother of a child in the treatment group perceived a shift away from isolation and an obsessive interest in technology towards a more outward-looking and social perspective.

A couple of teachers noted improvements in social relationships among children in the experimental group. One teacher noted that his student became more likely to share and help his friends. Discussions of social relationships differed strikingly between the control and experimental groups of teachers; while all children in the experimental group were described as getting on well with classmates at least to some extent, only around half of the teachers felt that the social relationships of children in the control group were positive. Teachers of students in the experimental group thought that their students played well together (all but one) and interacted easily.

Perception of change in emotional regulation

Most parents in the experimental group noted behavioural changes in their children. One parent told a story illustrating how her child had become more thoughtful and self-controlled. Another parent felt their child had become less hyperactive and his ability to control his movement had increased. On the whole, changes in self-regulation were described in terms of impulse control and understanding consequences. Aggression was an area in which parents described less of an improvement – one parent actually found that their child was getting angry quicker, though they attributed this to a change in medication halfway through the programme. Emotional regulation remained an issue for children in the control group, as anger, impulsiveness and difficulties with understanding consequences. All but one of the parents in the experimental group felt that their child's attention span had improved as a result of the intervention. Most parents discussed the change in concentration span in terms of their child's academic or intellectual performance. However, others reported on the impact that their child's improved concentration span had had on family life. Such changes were not noted by parents in the control group. The majority of parents in the control group expressed, in very definite terms that their child's inattention had not improved. The emphasis behind these answers may reflect a sense of disappointment and urgency, and perhaps shows how highly prized attentiveness is in this cultural context. There are perhaps underlying implications of the pedagogical expectations of children in the KSA culture, and the impact these might have on ADHD diagnoses, which are worthy of future research.

The teachers similarly noted improvements in impulsivity after the intervention. In contrast, children in the control group were almost universally described as impulsive. Two teachers felt that hyperactivity of their students had subsided following therapy; one child who habitually left the classroom was reported to now do it less than before. Most significantly, teachers noted a reduction in outbursts deriving from frustration. One teacher, for example, noted that their student's screaming had significantly decreased. Also, one teacher of a child in the control group noted a reduction in crying and stubbornness, but specified they are less now due to medication. A couple of teachers of children in the experimental group noted that their students had become more obedient, meaning less stubborn, less wilful and more understanding. Only three teachers mentioned changes in aggression. In the intervention group, one child's aggression was described as having reduced significantly in both intensity and duration, while another child was reported to still respond aggressively following therapy. The teacher of the child in the control group implied that his aggression continued to affect his social relationships. Almost all the teachers of the students in the experimental group specifically highlighted an improvement in attention, although the extent of the improvement varied. The enthusiastic feedback from the teachers confirms their focus on cognitive skills of their students. Improvements in this area have a direct impact on the child's performance in the classroom, which is obviously the main concern of the teachers.

Discussion

Improvements in children's confidence following the arts therapy are in line with findings from previous studies (Novy, 2003; Pratt, 2004; Lundy & Mcguffin, 2005), as are improvements in emotional wellbeing and social relationships (Pratt, 2004; Chong & Kim, 2010; Freilich & Shechtman, 2010; Karkou et al., 2010). According to Petruta-Maria (2015), arts therapies impact on the development of personal abilities of children with special needs, contributing to their social integration.

The current results also agree with previous literature, which suggests that arts therapies programmes have a positive influence on levels of inattention, hyperactivity and impulsivity for children with ADHD (Erfer & Ziv, 2006; Rickson, 2006; Eisa & Abdulrashed, 2010; Chen et al., 2012; Grönlund et al., 2005). While previous studies suggest that arts therapies can be successful in reducing anger in children (Grönlund et al., 2005; Koshland, 2010; Alavinezhad et al., 2014), the findings from this research study are inconclusive regarding the impact of the described arts therapy intervention on aggression.

Conclusions and recommendations

This study had small sample size hence it is not possible to draw robust and conclusive results on the effectiveness of arts therapies in the treatment of depressive symptoms of children with ADHD. Future studies should involve significantly larger sample size to ensure sufficient model power. Nevertheless, the current study was able to offer sufficient quantitative results to justify the position that there is a clear value of culturally sensitive arts therapies for improving emotional wellbeing and relational/social skills of children suffering from emotional and behavioural disorders. Additionally, the interviews with parents and teachers offered an unparalleled insight into the symptoms, problematic behaviours and, ultimately, positive changes in children assigned to the treatment group. The benefits of arts therapies are likely to exceed immediate improvements in emotional and behavioural issues and reduce the risk of developing depression in adult life. Most importantly, this study demonstrated that, despite cultural differences, UK-inspired arts therapies can be successfully adapted for the KSA context and can be enthusiastically welcomed by parents and teachers in the country.

Developing culturally sensitive interventions is crucial for adopting arts therapies worldwide and has real implications for both clinical and academic practice. The current study suggests a pathway for consideration for many countries in the Arab world to evaluate arts therapies as a viable alternative practice that is compatible with their culture and society. Although arts therapies are internationally recognised, a broader, more scientifically-based body of research would raise the reputation and interest in arts therapies in educational and healthcare settings in developing countries.

Note

1 The age range has been selected on the grounds that this is the age where ADHD prevalence is most noticeable with the diagnostic methods currently used.

References

Abu Taleb, R. A., & Farheen, A. (2013). A descriptive study of attention deficit hyperactivity disorder in Sabia City, Saudi Arabia. *International Journal of Current Research and Review*, 5(11), 36–41.

Alavinezhad, R., Mousavi, M., & Sohrabi, N. (2014). Effects of art therapy on anger and self-esteem in aggressive children. *Procedia – Social and Behavioral Sciences*, 113(0), 111–117.

Al-Habeeb, A. A., Qureshi, N. A., & Al-Maliki, T. A. (2012). Pattern of child and adolescent psychiatric disorders among patients consulting publicly-funded child psychiatric clinics in Saudi Arabia. *Eastern Mediterranean Health Journal*, 18(2), 112–119.

Al-Haidar, F. A. (2003). Co-morbidity and treatment of attention deficit hyperactivity disorder in Saudi Arabia. *The Eastern Mediterranean Health Journal*, 9(0), 988–995.

Al-Hamed, J. H., Taha, A. Z., Sabra, A. A., & Bella, H. (2008). Attention deficit hyperactivity disorder (ADHD) among male primary school children in Dammam, Saudi Arabia:

Prevalence and associated factors. *Journal of the Egyptian Public Health Association*, 83(3–4), 165–182.

Al-Khashrami, S., & Ali, A. (2009). ADHD scale: A standardized study. *Arabian Journal of Special Education*, 2(14), 83–133.

Alkhenaini, N. (2013). Fostering creativity in elementary school art education in Saudi Arabia through the use of selected art therapy techniques. Master ed. The University of the Arts.

Al Mulla, S. (2008). Psychodrama program for reducing attention deficit hyperactivity disorder in kindergarten in the United Arab Emirates (MEd thesis ed). Cairo University.

Alotaibi, A. (2014). A study of the impact of a movement therapy programme on perceptual-motor abilities and emotional well-being for children with mild learning difficulties in primary schools in Saudi Arabia (PhD ed). Queen Margaret University.

Alrazain, B. (2016). Developing and evaluating an arts therapies programme for children with attention deficit hyperactivity disorder (ADHD) in primary schools in the Kingdom of Saudi Arabia (KSA) (Doctoral thesis). Queen Margaret University.

Alyami, A. (2005). A proposed higher educational training program for art therapists in Saudi Arabia. *Saudi Journal of Higher Education*, 3(3), 108–143.

Alyami, A. (2009). The integration of art therapy into physical rehabilitation in a Saudi hospital. *The Arts in Psychotherapy*, 36(5), 282–288.

Amighi, J. K., Loman, S., Lewis, P., & Sossin, M. (1999). *The meaning of movement: Developmental and clinical perspectives of the Kestenberg Movement Profile*. New York: Taylor & Francis.

Biederman, J., Ball, S. W., Monuteaux, M. C., Mick, E., Spencer, T. J., McCreary, M., Cote, M., & Faraone, S. V. (2008). New insights into the comorbidity between ADHD and major depression in adolescent and young adult females. *Journal of the American Academy of Child & Adolescent Psychiatry*, 30(4), 426–434.

Bojner-Horwitz, E., Anderberg, U. M., & Theorell, T. (2003). Dance/movement therapy and changes in stress-related hormones: A study of fibromyalgia patients with video-interpretation. *Arts in Psychotherapy*, 30(5), 255–264.

Bower, P., Garralda, E., Kramer, T., Harrington, R., & Sibbald, B. (2001). The treatment of child and adolescent mental health problems in primary care: A systematic review. *Family Practice*, 18(4), 373–382.

Bowlby, J. (1997). *Attachment and loss* (vol. 1, 2nd ed). London: Pimlico.

Chang, W., & Liu, W. (2006). A study of the application of the drama therapy on ADHD students' social abilities at the resource class of the elementary school. *The International Journal of Arts Education*, 36–64.

Chen, S., Lin, S., Lin, C., Chen, H., Lai, C., & Tseng, S. (2012). Effect of music therapy on children with attention deficit hyperactivity disorder. *Journal of Rehabilitation Medicine*, 44, Supplement 52, 53–53.

Chong, H. J., & Kim, S. J. (2010). Education-oriented music therapy as an after-school program for students with emotional and behavioral problems. *The Arts in Psychotherapy*, 37(3), 190–196.

Classi, P., Milton, D., Ward, S., Sarsour, K., & Johnston, J. (2012). Social and emotional difficulties in children with ADHD and the impact on school attendance and healthcare utilization. *Child Adolesc Psychiatry Ment Health*, 6(1), 1–8.

Coholic, D., Fraser, M., Robinson, B., & Lougheed, S. (2012). Promoting resilience within child protection: The suitability of arts-based and experiential group programs for children in care. *Social Work with Groups*, 35(4), 345–361.

Cope, M. (2009). Circus in the creative arts therapies: The 'CITCAT' approach. In S. Scoble, M. Ross & C. Lapoujade (Eds.), *Arts in arts therapies: A European perspective* (19–29).

Craig, P., Dieppe, P., MacIntyre, S., Michie, S., Nazareth, I., & Petticrew, M. (2013). Developing and evaluating complex interventions: The new Medical Research Council guidance. *International Journal of Nursing Studies*, 50(5), 587–592.

Creswell, J. W. (2009). *Research design: Qualitative, quantitative, and mixed methods approaches* (3rd ed). California: Sage Publications.

Czamara, D., Tiesler, C. M., Kohlböck, G., Berdel, D., Hoffmann, B., Bauer, C., Koletzko, S., Schaaf, B., Lehmann, I., & Herbarth, O. (2013). Children with ADHD symptoms have a higher risk for reading, spelling and math difficulties in the GINIplus and LISAplus cohort studies. *PloS One*, 8(5), 1–7. Doi: 10.1371/journal.pone.0063859.

Dokter, D., & Hills de Zarate, M. (2016). *Intercultural arts therapies research: Issues and methodologies*. Oxon: Routledge.

Eisa, Y., & Abdulrashed, N. (2010). The effectiveness of a counseling program based on art therapy to reduce locomotor hyperactivity and improve attention by a sample of learning disabilities children in primary school. *Journal of Research in Education and Psychology*, 23(2), 1–68.

Erfer, T., & Ziv, A. (2006). Moving toward cohesion: Group dance/movement therapy with children in psychiatry. *Arts in Psychotherapy*, 33(3), 238–246.

Freilich, R., & Shechtman, Z. (2010). The contribution of art therapy to the social, emotional, and academic adjustment of children with learning disabilities. *The Arts in Psychotherapy*, 37(2), 97–105.

Goodill, S. W. (2005). *An introduction to medical dance/movement therapy: Health care in motion*. London: Jessica Kingsley.

Goodman, R. (1997). The Strengths and Difficulties Questionnaire: A research note. *Journal of Child Psychology and Psychiatry*, 38(5), 581–586.

Goodman, R., Ford, T., Simmons, H., Gatward, R., & Meltzer, H. (2000). Using the Strengths and Difficulties Questionnaire (SDQ) to screen for child psychiatric disorders in a community sample. *The British Journal of Psychiatry: The Journal of Mental Science*, 177(6), 534–539.

Goodman, A., & Goodman, R. (2009). Strengths and difficulties questionnaire as a dimensional measure of child mental health. *Journal of the American Academy of Child & Adolescent Psychiatry*, 48(4), 400–403.

Grönlund, E., Renck, B., & Weibull, J. (2005). Dance/movement therapy as an alternative treatment for young boys diagnosed as ADHD: A pilot study. *American Journal of Dance Therapy*, 27(2), 63–85.

Hamre, H. J., Witt, C. M., Kienle, G. S., Meinecke, C., Glockmann, A., Ziegler, R., Willich, S. N., & Kiene, H. (2010). Anthroposophic therapy for attention deficit hyperactivity: A two-year prospective study in outpatients. *International Journal of General Medicine*, 3, 239–253.

Henley, D. R. (1998). Art therapy in a socialization program for children with attention deficit hyperactivity disorder. *American Journal of Art Therapy*, 37(1), 2–12.

Homidi, M., Obaidat, Y., & Hamaidi, D. (2013). Prevalence of attention deficit and hyperactivity disorder among primary school students in Jeddah city, KSA. *Life Science Journal*, 10(3), 280–285.

Karkou, V. (2010). Introduction. In V. Karkou (Ed.), *Arts therapies in schools: Research and practice* (pp. 9–24). London: Jessica Kingsley.

Karkou, V., Fullarton, A., & Scarth, S. (2010). Finding the way out of the labyrinth through dance movement psychotherapy: Collaborative work in a mental health promotion programme for secondary schools. In V. Karkou (Ed.), *Arts therapies in schools: Research and practice* (pp. 59–84). London: Jessica Kingsley.

Karkou, V., & Sanderson, P. (2006). *Arts therapies: A research-based map of the field.* Edinburgh: Elsevier Health Sciences.

Kearns, D. (2004). Art therapy with a child experiencing sensory integration difficulty. *Art Therapy*, 21(2), 95–101.

Kennedy, H., Reed, K., & Wamboldt, M. Z. (2014). Staff perceptions of complementary and alternative therapy integration into a child and adolescent psychiatry program. *Arts in Psychotherapy*, 41(1), 21–26.

Koepfer, S. R. (2000). Drawing on the spirit: Embracing spirituality in pediatrics and pediatric art therapy. *Art Therapy*, 17(3), 188–194.

Koshland, L. (2010). PEACE through dance movement therapy: The development and evaluation of a violence prevention programme in an elementary school. In V. Karkou (Ed.), *Arts therapies in schools: Research and practice* (pp. 43–58). London: Jessica Kingsley.

Lanzillo, A. A. (2009). The effect of dance/movement therapy on incidences of aggression and levels of empathy in a private school for children with emotional and behavioral problems. Master ed. Drexel University.

Levy, F. J. (2005). *Dance movement therapy: A healing art* (2nd ed). Reston: AAHPERD.

Lundy, H., & McGuffin, P. (2005). Using dance/movement therapy to augment the effectiveness of therapeutic holding with children. *Journal of Child and Adolescent Psychiatric Nursing*, 18(3), 135–145.

Majorek, M., Tuchelmann, T., & Heusser, P. (2004). Therapeutic eurythmy – Movement therapy for children with attention deficit hyperactivity disorder (ADHD): A pilot study. *Complementary Therapies in Nursing and Midwifery*, 10(1), 46–53.

Murphy, J., Paisley, D., & Pardoe, L. (2004). An art therapy group for impulsive children. *International Journal of Art Therapy*, 9(2), 59–68.

NHS Choices (2016). Attention deficit hyperactivity disorder (ADHD) – Symptoms. Available from: www.nhs.uk/Conditions/Attention-deficit-hyperactivity-disorder/Pages/Symptoms.aspx.

Novy, C. (2003). Drama therapy with pre-adolescents: A narrative perspective. *The Arts in Psychotherapy*, 30(4), 201–207.

Orth, U., Robins, R. W., & Roberts, B. W. (2008). Low self-esteem prospectively predicts depression in adolescence and young adulthood. *Journal of Personality and Social Psychology*, 95(3), 695–708. Doi: 10.1037/0022–3514.95.3.695.

Papageorgiou, V., Kalyva, E., Dafoulis, V., & Vostanis, P. (2008). Differences in parents' and teachers' ratings of ADHD symptoms and other mental health problems. *The European Journal of Psychiatry*, 22(4), 200–210.

Petruta-Maria, C. (2015). The role of art and music therapy techniques in the educational system of children with special problems. *Procedia – Social and Behavioral Sciences*, 187(0), 277–282.

Pratt, R. R. (2004). Art, dance, and music therapy. *Physical Medicine and Rehabilitation Clinics of North America*, 15(4), 827–841.

Redman, D. (2007). The effectiveness of dance/movement therapy as a treatment for students in a public alternative school diagnosed with attention deficit hyperactivity disorder: A pilot study. Master ed. Drexel University.

Remschmidt, H. (2005). Global consensus on ADHD/HKD. *European Child & Adolescent Psychiatry*, 14(3), 127–137.

Reynolds, M. W., Nabors, L., & Quinlan, A. (2000). The effectiveness of art therapy: Does it work? *Art Therapy*, 17(3), 207–213.

Rickson, D. J. (2006). Instructional and improvisational models of music therapy with adolescents who have Attention Deficit Hyperactivity Disorder (ADHD): A comparison of the effects on motor impulsivity. *Journal of Music Therapy*, 43(1), 39–62.

Rickson, D. J., & Watkins, W. G. (2003). Music therapy to promote prosocial behaviors in aggressive adolescent boys – A pilot study. *Journal of Music Therapy*, 40(4), 283–301.

Riley, S. (2003). Using art therapy to address adolescent depression. In Malchiodi (Ed.), *Handbook of art therapy*. New York: The Guilford Press.

Rogers, C. (2003). *Client-centered therapy: Its current practice, implications and theory*. London: Constable.

Safran, D. (2002). *Art therapy and AD/HD: Diagnostic and therapeutic approaches*. London: Jessica Kingsley.

Saudi Ministry of Health (2014). About the ministry. Retrieved from: http://www.moh.gov.sa/en/Ministry/About/Pages/default.aspx.

Sherborne, V. (2001). *Developmental movement for children: Mainstream, special needs and pre-school* (2nd ed). London: Worth.

Skounti, M., Philalithis, A., & Galanakis, E. (2007). Variations in prevalence of attention deficit hyperactivity disorder worldwide. *European Journal of Pediatrics*, 166(2), 117–123.

Sowislo, J. F., & Orth, U. (2013). Does low self-esteem predict depression and anxiety? A meta-analysis of longitudinal studies. *Psychological Bulletin*, 139(1), 213–240. Doi: 10.1037/a0028931.

Tsal, Y., Salev, L., & Mevorach, C. (2005). The diversity of attention deficits in ADHD: The prevalence of four cognitive factors in ADHD versus controls. *Journal of Learning Disabilities*, 38(2), 142–157.

Van der Merwe, S. (2010). The effect of a dance and movement intervention program on the perceived emotional well-being and self-esteem of a clinical sample of adolescents. Master ed. University of Pretoria.

Van Nieuwkerk, K. (2008). Creating an Islamic cultural sphere: Contested notions of art, leisure and entertainment: An Introduction. *Contemporary Islam*, 2(3), 169–176.

Waite, R., & Ivey, N. (2009). Promoting culturally sensitive ADHD services for women: An individual example and a call to action. *Journal of Psychosocial Nursing and Mental Health Services*, 47(4), 26–33.

Part II

Arts therapies with adults experiencing depression

Chapter 5

Collaborative discourse analysis on the use of drama therapy to treat depression in adults

Nisha Sajnani, Aileen Cho, Heidi Landis, Gary Raucher and Nadya Trytan

Introduction

According to the World Health Organization, "depression is the leading cause of ill health and disability worldwide" (WHO, 2017). Clinical depression causes long-lasting symptoms and often disrupts a person's ability to perform routine tasks. A person's vulnerability to developing depression is often related to many factors, including life stresses and circumstances, changes in brain function, and genetics. Yet, little is known about how drama therapy, the "intentional use of drama and theatre processes to achieve therapeutic goals" (nadta.org), may be used to improve the quality of life for persons suffering from depression across the lifespan. As Zubala et al (2013) observed, "There is growing evidence that arts therapies may be under-used treatments for the 'global burden' of depression. However, the experiences of arts therapists, their methods, tools and ways of working with this client group remain unclear" (p. 458). In this chapter, four drama therapists in different settings reflect on their *ways of working* with adults suffering from depression. Our hope is that by hearing the voices of fellow practitioners, we will be better able to identify the specific therapeutic mechanisms associated with drama therapy in the treatment of depression and that readers will come away with a richer understanding of the guiding assumptions and practices used when working with this population.

Methodology: narrative inquiry and collaborative discourse analysis

A narrative approach to inquiry assumes that knowledge is held in stories that can be shared, stored, and retrieved (Barter & Renold, 1999; Bevir, 2006; Bruner, 1990; Polkinghorne, 1988). Discourse analysis "is the study of social life, understood through analysis of language in its widest sense including face-to-face talk, non-verbal interaction, images, symbols and documents" (Shaw & Bailey, 2009: 413). Narrative inquiry and discourse analysis are linked in that both involve an investigation of the ways that language informs meaning and both serve to illuminate "systems in practice" in that textual and otherwise narrated accounts make visible the conditions and resources that shape or restrict possibilities and practices (Hardin, 2003). What these approaches also have in common is an appreciation of the cultural and communicative patterns and contexts which inform behaviour and perception, an assumption that "social reality is socially constructed," and that language is not always literal in that the words we choose reveal investments and tensions (Shaw & Bailey, 2009: 414). The use of discourse analysis through narrative vignette research has been used in drama therapy to investigate practitioner notions of change as well as destructiveness and creativity (Jones, 2009, 2011, 2013). Drama therapist Jones (2011) notes that, as a methodological approach, discourse analysis offers insight into how "dramatherapists describe, respond, and think about how dramatherapy is used by clients" as well as what "dramatherapists see and value within their accounts of what is effective about their practice" (Jones, 2011: 23–24).

In this study, Nisha Sajnani (primary researcher) asked the leaders of major drama therapy training programs in the US and Canada to recommend practitioners who used drama therapy to treat depression. This snowball sampling technique, in which participants were recruited from acquaintances, resulted in the identification of four colleagues who confirmed that they used drama therapy to treat depression: Aileen Cho, Heidi Landis, Gary Raucher, and Nadya Trytan. Drawing on Jones' (2011, 2013) vignette research in which accounts of practice were shared and analyzed using online technologies, Sajnani asked her colleagues to join her as co-researchers, to respond to a list of relevant questions about their practice by email, and to engage in a collaborative analysis of the resulting data through the use of an online document sharing platform (Google Docs). Collaborative discourse analysis, as an approach to coding data, shares values with participatory action research (PAR) (Reason & Bradbury, 2008). It permits reflection and analysis of how power in relationships informs practice while also creating the conditions to share authority within the research process itself. While preliminary in nature, qualitative accounts from providers offer a useful point of departure at this early stage in our body of knowledge concerning drama therapy in the treatment of depression.

Data representation

The data was originally presented as a script inspired by ethnodramatic methods pioneered by Mienczakowski (2001) and Saldana (2003, 2005), as this aesthetic reflects the conversational approach underlying this enquiry and, in the words of Mundel (2003), allows for a transparent *performance of process* by which we arrived at our findings. This approach also encourages readers to participate in the process of meaning-making. However, for the purposes of this chapter, each narrative account has been edited in order to privilege the results of the analysis. A full transcript of this conversation may be accessed online.[1]

Trustworthiness

Trustworthiness in this study is reliant on the combination of documented conversation, reflection on the conversation through an accessible online exchange, and collaborative analysis. Readers may refer to the full transcript for elaboration on the questions and responses offered by the co-authors.

Four drama therapists engaged in the treatment of depression

The four drama therapists interviewed by Nisha Sajnani were:

> Aileen Cho, a recent graduate of the California Institute of Integral Studies (CIIS, 2013), is a bi-cultural drama therapist who provides treatment in both Korean and English. She works as a program director treating children and adolescents suffering from eating disorders and co-occurring disorders such as depression in a residential treatment program in Menlo Park, California. She also works in private practice on a wide variety of treatment issues and in her words, she "sees many Korean/Korean-American clients, especially those struggling with parent-child relationship issues and family conflict, victims of sexual abuse/incest, transracial Korean adoptees and Korean-American LGBTQ children with their immigrant parents."
>
> Heidi Landis is the past clinical and training director at Creative Alternatives of New York where she provided trauma-informed drama therapy groups for children who had experienced complex trauma, PTSD, and complex PTSD in a variety of settings including hospitals and schools. Heidi maintains a private practice with adults, teenagers, and couples in New York City. In her words, "Most of the clients who I am working with are dealing with depression, anxiety or a combination of the two."
>
> Gary Raucher is a drama therapy educator at CIIS and in part-time private practice as a Marriage Family Therapist and Registered Drama Therapist in San Francisco. In his words, "common presenting issues among [my] clients are depression, anxiety, life transitions, relational stress, traumatic stress, addictions coupled with other compulsive behaviors, sexual identity, and existential disorientation."
>
> Nadya Trytan primarily provides group therapy for adolescents, adults, and geriatric patients in an inpatient setting at a hospital in St. Paul, Minnesota, as well as in an intensive outpatient and partial hospitalization program (PHP). In her words, "Patients with depression typically stay only for a couple of days and then they are discharged to PHP or outpatient treatment. Most of the clients that we treat for depression are middle-class and appear to be White. Many have a co-occurring chemical dependency, eating disorder, or personality disorders. It is not uncommon for our clients to have some form of permanent physical or mental health disability. Their education levels vary but tends to be higher than average in this city."

Themes, trends and tensions in accounts of practice

In this section, we present our observations about the themes, trends, and tensions arising from our analysis of each other's accounts of practice. We begin with an analysis of how depression is understood by this group of drama therapists in their specific contexts followed by an analysis of ways of working and, finally, approaches to assessing and evaluating change. Where possible, these observations are grounded in literature about the use of drama therapy in the treatment of depression.

"An absence of play": situated understandings of depression

As drama therapist Langley (2006) observed, "dramatherapy may be an appropriate intervention at most stages of depression" and that attention to the duration and severity of symptoms will enable specific interventions" (p. 108). It is apparent from the descriptions of practice that this group of practitioners is cognizant of standard diagnostic criteria concerning depression and its manifestation along a continuum of varying degrees of severity from mild, to moderate, to severe (WHO, 2015). They conceptualize depression as having a dual impact on physiology and psychology, and one practitioner, Gary, stressed the relationship between depression and spiritual health.

However, what is perhaps more interesting about these accounts is that they reveal how drama therapists tend to understand existential and clinical phenomena through their own particular orientation, dramatic worldview, in relation to the people they serve, the contexts in which they work, and their prior training. For example, Aileen, who works primarily with children, adolescents, and adults struggling with eating disorders in a treatment program and in private practice, describes working from an integrative, relational, and strength-based approach. She describes depression in those she works with as "an absence of play" and writes of the need to explore "underlying emotional, social and environmental factors" such as "unresolved experiences" and "intergenerational trauma" that might be contributing to presenting symptoms. Like many of her clients who may rigidly deprive themselves of food, she writes of the *deprivation* of imagination:

> Clients with depression are deprived of the imagination they need to change and create something new to better their health and lives. What is unique about drama therapy from other creative arts modalities is the simultaneously active and reflective elements that help to integrate the cognitive, emotional and physical levels of experience.

As previous research has shown, the metaphors that we use to describe existential phenomena influence reasoning (Thibodeau & Boroditsky, 2011). Aileen responds to states of rigidity and deprivation by offering opportunities "to enhance interpersonal relationship skills by moving out of rigid roles and discover more satisfying ways of relating with themselves and others."

Heidi, who describes working from a "trauma-informed" perspective (see Sajnani & Johnson, 2014), works primarily with young adult groups in a variety of settings and with adults in her private practice. She shares Aileen's notion of absence stating that "depression takes away the ability to imagine and that the innate creativity that we all have feels like it is nowhere to be found." She uses the analogy of "a tightly tangled ball of black yarn" to describe depression and, consequently, describes the use of drama therapy, and psychodrama in particular, to "begin to pull apart the yarn and actually work on the individual knots." She describes embodiment as being central to discovering where these knots, the depression and trauma, reside in the body.

On the other hand, Gary, who approaches his clinical practice from a "transpersonal-humanistic orientation with somatic leanings" understands depression "through an energy lens, as a congestive block to free circulation in a person's psychological process." He writes of the need to attend to the relational wounds that reinforce negative cognitive schema. His observations about attachment are resonant with a trauma-informed perspective and create a bridge to currently accepted research on cognitive therapy (CT) which has considerable evidence for its efficacy in the treatment of depression (Hollon et al., 2005; Gibbons et al., 2010; Strunk & DeRubeis, 2001). He writes,

> I view many forms of depression as conflicted states within the psyche around self-love and self-acceptance. In these cases, a person's sense of value and self-worth is challenged by conditioned belief structures born of adverse life experiences. Thoughts backed by the power of emotional conviction take on an aura of reality, even when such thoughts do not align with what is considered to be objective or consensual reality. When we no longer believe that we are worthy or deserving of love, we unknowingly block the natural circulation of its healing and resiliency factors throughout the whole mind-body dynamic. I see working towards restoration of the circulation of the energies of love and acceptance (for these are energies) as the primary antidote to depression.

Gary also offered insight into the difference between a textbook understanding of depression and the experience of treating depression. His words underscore the value of practicing with a balance of evidence, intuition, imagination, and experience:

> The DSM-V (APA, 2013) taxonomy of depressive disorders may be somewhat practical for diagnostic purposes, but it is not that helpful for understanding or formulating treatment for people who present with depressive symptoms. . . . My thinking owes a lot to Aaron Beck's (1967) concept of

> the cognitive triangle – the mutual feedback loop between thinking, feeling, and behavior. Cognitive treatments for depression place emphasis on entering this loop by challenging negative thoughts and self-talk. However, my experience with the energetics of healing has convinced me that negative thoughts only gain debilitating power when they are reified emotionally through deep-seated belief. A fleeting negative thought is relatively harmless, but the emotional conviction that accompanies severely negative thoughts (such as 'I am worthless') resulting from developmental wounds turns them into destructive schemas that fuel depressive self-negation and psychological stagnation. Circulation of health and resiliency factors such as hope, love, connection, and joy are then largely calcified.

Finally, Nadya, who works primarily with older adults, speaks of play in drama therapy as "breaking up the darkness" of depression to let a sense of lightness in. She highlights the unique presentation of depression among geriatric adults and advocates for a developmental perspective. She writes,

> At the facility where I work, depression manifests in a manner consistent with the DSM-V (APA, 2013) symptoms associated with this diagnosis. . . . Often it is a concurrent diagnosis with physical disability, chemical dependency, eating disorders, anxiety and/or personality disorders. I've seen cases of existential depression that don't carry the mood symptoms typically associated with a typical geriatric presentation in that they report feeling, for example, that they have completed their time. Often many friends and family members have died and the person wants to commit suicide. There is also a form of depression that we see, primarily in men, about a year or so after retirement. These are people who were very committed to their work, and who didn't really have any interests, hobbies or activities outside of work. After retirement they lack a focus for their time and energy and sink into depression. A classic presentation of geriatric depression . . . comes with anxiety or panic in the morning. . . . However, it is important to note the nuances that make existential depression different from what we label as geriatric depression. It's also important to distinguish between dementia and depression as this can often be confused when treating the elderly. Apathy is a common symptom of dementia, so when someone has dementia, they will sometimes be brought in to the hospital by caregivers who want them treated for depression. On the other hand, depression can have cognitive symptoms, and sometimes people assume that the cognitive symptoms are dementia, when they are actually caused by depression. A good geriatric psychiatrist is very good at teasing out what is going on.

Nadya's words highlight another tension that is often present for drama therapists working within multidisciplinary treatment teams in that she refers to the psychiatrist as the person with the expert knowledge (see Foucault, 1973). This reflects her respect for how diverse roles share in the responsibility for effective care but also calls attention to how hierarchies, while not necessarily harmful, exist within the healthcare system and reveal themselves in the experience of drama therapists.

Ways of working: play, role, metaphor, story, and enactment in relationship

Drama therapy, as a field, is comprised of a variety of approaches (Johnson & Emunah, 2009). What they share in common is a commitment to facilitating treatment through an engagement with dramatic reality, a general orientation to working in the "here and now," and being actively involved while working alongside their clients to establish safety, trust, and a sense of control (Cassidy et al., 2014, see Jones, 2007). Where they diverge is in, "(1) the degree of engagement by the therapist in the dramatic action; (2) the use of physical touch and proximity; (3) the balance of cognitive versus emotive forms of expression; and (4) the emphasis on the past versus the present" (Johnson & Emunah, 2009: 26).

These four practitioners vary in similar ways as well as in terms of their emphasis on free play versus structured enactment. For example, Aileen uses Developmental Transformations (DvT) (see Johnson, 2009), an improvisational, relational approach, to cultivate a sense of playfulness amongst those in her care. She writes that DvT, through its emphasis on "non-verbal movements, expression, gesture and stillness," expands her capacity to communicate with her clients and, in turn, offers them a broader palette with which to express their inner experience. She writes,

> DvT is an embodied psychotherapy where clients are not just bringing their thoughts and feelings, but also their physical bodies where there is value placed on the non-verbal movements, expression, gesture and stillness – expanding the access of communication for both the clients and myself. This is valuable for clients with depression who often express an inability to verbalize their experience of depression in a way they feel seen, heard and understood.

She sees DvT, with its stated intention to expand capacities to cope with instability, as an approach to "examine, explore, and liberate" the "stuck patterns" and "restrictive behaviors" such as "hibernation, isolation, procrastination and disengagement from tasks and activities" that arise in response to depression. By changing movement patterns, roles, and imagery in the play, clients are able to experience "new insights and change in mood and energy." She offered an example of a mid-20's female who had a history of alcohol abuse in remission but who was diagnosed with Anorexia Nervosa (Binge-Purge Type), Major

Depressive Disorder (Recurrent), Generalized Anxiety Disorder, Obsessive-Compulsive Disorder, and Non-Suicidal Self-Injury (in the form of cutting):

> In our first individual session, this client presented with severely depressed mood and reported with intrusive suicidal ideation and urges to self-harm. She was restless and fidgety throughout the session with minimal to restricted affect. In the non-drama therapy groups, she was quiet, withdrawn, would often dissociate or sometimes even become catatonic. In her first week of treatment, she threw a tantrum refusing to attend the Equine-Assisted Therapy group due to her fear of horses and germs. Later that same day, in her very first DvT drama therapy group, the image of animals surfaced and eventually the whole group took on the role of a team of imaginary horses circling around her for her to pet. The client's face lit up with a mixture of disgust and curiosity, but mostly awe at the contradicting experience of being able to play with something that she dreaded while also enjoying it.

From her example, it is clear that Aileen's clients experience a possibly rare opportunity to express their very *real* disturbing thoughts and destructive feelings in a safe and harmless manner without the *real* consequences. They practice accessing and expressing their feelings and desires, while also demonstrating healthy impulse control within this pretend play.

Gary also discusses the use of DvT in his example of working with a client who presented with rigid "perseverative thinking," but also relies on more structured and directive approaches such as role-play (see Landy, 2009) and psychodrama (see Moreno, 1946) to achieve "insight, the corrective realignment of self-identification (with healthy self-objects), and [the] adaptive integration of the parts." He offered this example:

> One factor that most of the cases of depression I've treated have had in common is significant inner conflict between different points of self-identification within the psyche. It is almost as if different sub-personalities or clusters of them are at war with one another, though for the most part, not consciously. As an example, one adult female client had internalized the voice of a mother who had routinely dismissed her childhood craving for affection as 'attention-seeking.' This client experienced unrecognized inner conflict between residues of this dismissive maternal voice and the inchoate cries of her inner child, whose emotional needs had not been adequately recognized or met. When multiple conditioned patterns within the psyche are in an unacknowledged war like this, and especially when attachment has been compromised, the healing, integrative, and resiliency enhancing circulation of healthy self-love is impeded. Submerged conflicts such as these seem to cry out for drama therapy, which I think has a unique capacity to externalize and concretize the voices of inner conflict, lending

> them a chance to declare themselves consciously. Once surfaced, these disparate voices can be explored, interrogated, linked to their sources, and facilitated in mutual conversation.

The use of embodied action to externalize internal conflicts is also valued by Heidi and Nadya. Like Gary, Heidi draws on psychodramatic techniques to encourage those in her care to "concretize what is going on and physically move around and within . . . projected pieces of the self." She also wrote about the value of metaphor within role work and storytelling to recover a sense of spontaneity, challenge negative thinking, and foster supportive relationships in group work. Consistent with storymaking approaches in drama therapy (Gersie & King, 1989) and with Landy's (1997) insights about the therapeutic value of aesthetic distance in drama therapy, Heidi connects the use of metaphor in drama therapy as the means through which safety is established and creativity and playfulness encouraged. She offered this example from an inpatient psychiatric unit in New York City:

> The energy was extremely low as the clients entered the room for drama therapy group. As we checked in group members described their current states as sad, agitated, bored, and hopeless. Clients in this group had struggled with entering into the creative process in the previous weeks, so we decided that using a projective technique might be helpful and a bit more containing. We brought in a deck of cards with mythical and fantastical pictures on them and we asked each group member to choose a card and begin narrating a story inspired by the picture that had been randomly picked. The second client was asked to do the same, adding onto the story in some way with the card that was chosen. . . . There was an anticipation that began to emerge as each person added their piece. Spontaneously, some group members invited quieter participants to add on, helping to guide those who seemed to feel lost or confused. After the story was created, the group members were invited to choose a character or piece of the story to take on and we told the story again, this time as new characters in relationship to others. New dialogue and insights emerged as characters connected in scene work. The story they created told the tale of a garden, a communal garden where each of the characters had planted one thing that could be used by themselves but also by others.

In this example, the group transitioned from a room full of individuals consumed with their own pain to a group that could help and support each other. Through the metaphor of the garden, group members were able to reflect on what they would like to grow and what they would like to have "weeded" from their lives suggesting a sense of hope that wasn't there before.

Nadya described her use of projective devices, psychodramatic, and sociodramatic techniques with geriatric adults in her care. She highlighted the value of psychodramatic techniques like the empty-chair, doubling, and role-reversal in particular. She writes,

> The techniques that I use are often tailored to the individual or group that I am working with but because it is a short-term setting where people may have been admitted involuntarily, I often aim to help people get in touch with their strengths. As a warm up, I often use a concrete object like a card or a stone with strengths written on them to open up conversations about individual strengths. Drawing from the Therapeutic Spiral Method (Hudgins, 2002) which has its roots in psychodrama, I build on these strengths by asking the protagonist to identify a strength that would help them in a particular situation or with an issue they have identified. Once they have a name for the strength (e.g. courage), then I ask them to choose a scarf to represent that strength and a person from the group to play the strength. I set up 2 chairs – one for the protagonist and one for the strength. The person playing the strength sits in one of the chairs and wears the scarf. The protagonist sits in the other chair and engages in a dialog with their desired strength. We usually do a role reversal pretty quickly so that the protagonist gets to play the strength, and it helps the other group member get a sense of how to play the strength. Once there is some depth and the conversation is finished, the person playing the strength stands behind the protagonist and, with consent, places a hand on protagonist's shoulder. From there we may create a scene with the person playing the strength supporting the protagonist in a challenging situation. We might create more strengths or create a dialog with a part of the person that feels stuck. In the de-roling, we shake out the scarf and the group member does a gesture to give the strength back to the protagonist. . . . I also use sociodrama (Garcia & Sternberg, 2000) to work on boundaries and assertiveness. It allows clients to gain insight through observing interactions and experimenting with different interpersonal choices [and] practice new skills. This is a way of building confidence, and build success in interpersonal interactions, since difficulty with boundaries and a sense of failure in relationships can be a factor for some people with depression. Since many of our clients with depression have issues with anxiety, anger or chemical abuse, I also use the doubling techniques from the Therapeutic Spiral model which uses limbic resonance to teach emotional regulation on a body level.

"Beyond the role of the depressed one": evaluating progress and assessing change

A discussion around how drama therapists assess progress and evaluate change in drama therapy, and specifically in the treatment of depression, emerged through our online exchange. What came through in reading these accounts of practice was the careful and ongoing way in which these practitioners assess change through a combination of observation, collaboration, and drama-based assessments. Each practitioner wrote about the use of "check-ins" at the start of most sessions and elaborating on specific ways of assessing progress and change.

For example, Aileen, wrote about a team approach in which the client is involved in tracking a reduction in relevant symptoms. She also highlighted the need to look beyond a linear trajectory of progress and symptom reduction toward increases in the internal capacity of her clients to tolerate conflict and change. Referring to the example provided earlier she writes,

> Her depression often got the best of her. It would get in the way of accessing any motivation for her to recover from her eating disorder. Halfway through her stay, she was hospitalized due to her self-harm and suicidal behaviors that briefly worsened. . . . She always brought in her imaginary trademark weapon to destroy and destruct things as much as she desired [in drama therapy]. There was almost a direct correlation of reduction in actual self-harm behaviors and urges outside of the playspace the more she was able to dramatize and release her urges in the drama therapy groups. Through increased positive engagement and connection with others, she reported less and less suicidal ideation and increased motivation for recovery and life in general. . . . At the time of her discharge and stepping down a lower level of care, she was still struggling with eating disordered thoughts and preoccupation with urges to lose weight. However, she was able to stay accountable for following her meal plan 90–100% without 24-hour supervision. Power struggles were no longer an issue with the staff as she willingly followed her treatment recommendations. Her depression was in full remission with no suicidal ideation and reported little to no urges to self-harm. She was excited about re-enrolling in community college and also had a part-time job lined up. She had a much brighter and hopeful outlook on her life and future.

Of course, this example also calls up the degree to which compliance with treatment plans may be conflated with progress. Gary also emphasized the need to avoid superficial indications of progress and to involve those receiving treatment in the evaluation of change. He describes doing this by "asking clients at least every several weeks about their sense of progress in relationship to their goals" even if self-reports may dismiss positive changes observed by the therapist. He wrote,

> In the early to mid phases of treatment for depression, I have found that clients may at various times either dismiss some progress that I have seen signs of (such as presenting with a subtle but discernible brightening of affect for several weeks), or alternatively, fantasizing a 'flight-to-wellness' that I don't yet think is realistically grounded, based on my past experience.

> The most telling and, I think, reliable measures of improvement concerning depression with drama therapy clients are positive changes that sustain and build upon themselves over time, for example: discernible improvements in mood, affect, energy level, attitudes, self-image, and behavior that both the client and I have observed, discussed, and agree on.

Each practitioner endorsed the use of informal measures in the form of a mini mental status exams or self-reporting scales coupled with observation. For example, Nadya wrote, "I may also assess progress by asking them to rate their anxiety or distress on a 1–10 scale at the beginning of the session and again at the end." She describes her use of observation:

> Some clients have reported that drama therapy helps them learn how to self-regulate. When I'm using doubling to teach self-regulations, I will assess if the attunement is effective as the session progresses. I do this by observing their body tension, breathing and any movement. Are they able to follow me in slowing and relaxing breathing? If they have psychomotor agitation, does it decrease?

Heidi also emphasized the use of formal quantitative instruments and assessments to track symptom reduction. She writes,

> Quantitative measures at Creative Alternatives of New York included the use of an in-house scale that measures creativity and validated trauma scales, focusing on the four central domains of impairment in complex trauma that Creative Alternatives of New York groups address: Attachment, Affect Regulation, Behavioral Control and Sense of Self. The data collected revealed that over time clients develop empathy and social bonding skills, increase emotional intelligence and awareness, regulate destructive and impulsive behaviors, and build a positive sense of self through expanded roles.

In addition to this, most endorsed the use of drama based assessments [see Snow et al., 2014) on an ongoing basis. For example, Gary wrote that he "observed that a client's capacity to participate in play or to enter into and sustain dramatic reality (Pendzik, 2006) with increasing flexibility, spontaneity, and pleasure is a reliable marker of therapeutic progress." Heidi wrote that she constantly looks for evidence of "new roles, stories and or enactments that might allow the client to look outside the role of the 'depressed one' and imagine and create new roles for themselves."

In the final instance, each practitioner was concerned with how the skills and experiences shared in drama therapy might transfer to everyday life. As Nadya writes,

> The goal is for them to be able to develop skills to practice self-soothing on their own without a therapist-guide present. I assess that based on what

> they report to me when they come back for the next session. So, for example, are they able to self-soothe and decrease episodes of anger at home?

Heidi writes that she often wonders,

> Is the therapy allowing the client to understand the situations, emotions, and ideas that make up the depression? Are they able to step out and gain a different understanding even if it is for just a moment? How does the client adapt this new role and take it out in the world? And, once the new roles are internalized does it allow for restructuring of old thought patterns?

Conclusions

Because of its prevalence in our society, drama therapists will continue to encounter clients with depression, regardless of the setting in which they choose to work. Examinations of practice such as the one offered in this chapter push us forward in that they illuminate how drama therapists who work with depression conceive of their work and carry it out in different contexts. This collaborative discourse analysis revealed a relationship between therapists' orientations and the ways in which they conceive of depression. Sometimes, this correlation was apparent in that the metaphors chosen to describe depression (e.g. as an absence of play, as a tightly tangled ball of black yarn, or as a darkness in need of light) also shed light on how each drama therapist conceived treatment (e.g. as making play a visible, integral part of the process or as undoing knots). Examining practice in this way seemed to give us a window into each drama therapist's very unique way of working while also offering examples of how general theories and approaches might be expressed in actual choices made in the therapeutic encounter.

We also remarked on how collaborative discourse analysis is an approach to research that bears similarity to peer group supervision in that reading through and commenting on accounts of practice facilitated greater understanding. Indeed, this is consistent with writing on supervision in the arts therapies and in drama therapy in particular (Jones & Dokter, 2008). However, there are also several limitations to this approach to research. First of all, sampling within one's own network of peers can lead to bias as there is no guarantee about the representativeness of the sample. There are also limitations to conducting a discourse analysis of narrative accounts of practice (Jenkins, 2010). Participants may convey their accounts through a "normative screen" that "minimizes the potential" for concerns and feelings that the participant may not wish to communicate to the researcher (Hookway, 2008). Hookway (2008) adds that narrative accounts rely on memory and is "therefore susceptible to memory impairment and retrospective reconstruction" (p. 95).

Going forward, it will be necessary to design studies that account for the qualitative experience of those participating in drama therapy to treat depression, retrospective and prospective cohort studies to assess the impact of drama therapy on a particular group over time, and randomized control trials involving reliable, culturally appropriate, and valid measures to compare the use of drama therapy with treatment as usual and to compare outcomes between drama therapeutic approaches such as Psychodrama, Role Method, or Developmental Transformations amongst other approaches referenced in this chapter.

Note

1 The transcript of the full conversation between the authors of this chapter may be found here: https://goo.gl/F7gmKW

References

APA (2013). *DSM V.* Washington DC: American Psychiatric Publishing.

Barter, C., & Renold, E. (1999). The use of vignettes in qualitative research. *Social Research Update*, 25.

Beck, A. (1967). *Depression: Clinical, experimental, and theoretical aspects.* Philadelphia: University of Pennsylvania Press.

Bevir, M. (2006). How narratives explain. In Dvora Yanow and Peregrine Schwartz-Shea (Eds.), *Interpretation and method: Empirical research method and the interpretive turn* (pp. 281–290), New York: M.E. Sharpe.

Bruner, J. (1990). *Acts of meaning.* Cambridge, MA: Harvard University Press.

Cassidy, S., Turnbull, S., & Gumley, A. (2014). Exploring core processes facilitating therapeutic change in Dramatherapy: A grounded theory analysis of published case studies. *The Arts in Psychotherapy*, 41, 353–365.

Foucault, M. (1973). *The birth of the clinic.* London: Tavistock.

Garcia, A., & Sternberg, P. (2000). *Sociodrama: Who's in your shoes?* (2nd ed.). Westport, CT: Praeger Publishers.

Gersie, A., & King, N. (1989). *Storymaking in education and therapy.* London, UK: Jessica Kingsley.

Gibbons, C. J., Fournier, J. C., Stirman, S. W., DeRubeis, R. J., Crits-Christoph, P., & Beck, A. T. (2010). The clinical effectiveness of cognitive therapy for depression in an outpatient clinic. *Journal of Affective Disorders*, 125, 169–176. Doi: 10.1016/j.jad.2009.12.030.

Hardin, K. (2003). Constructing experience in individual interviews, autobiographies and online accounts: A poststructuralist approach. *Journal of Advanced Nursing*, 41(6), 536–544.

Hollon, S. D., DeRubeis, R. J., Shelton, R. C., Amsterdam, J. D., Salomon, R. M., O'Reardon, J. P., Lovett, M. L., Young, P. R., Haman, K. L., Freeman, B. B., & Gallop, R. (2005). Prevention of relapse following cognitive therapy vs medications in moderate to severe depression. *Archives of General Psychiatry*, 62, 417–422.

Hookway, N. (2008). 'Entering the blogosphere': Some strategies for using blogs in social research. *Qualitative Research*, 8(1), 91–113.

Hudgins, K. (2002). *Experiential treatment for PTSD: The therapeutic spiral model.* New York, NY: Springer Publishing Company.

Jenkins, N., Bloor, M., Fischer, J., Berney, L., & Neale, J. (2010). Putting it in context: the use of vignettes in qualitative interviewing. *Qualitative Research*, 10(2), 175–198.

Johnson, D. R. (2009). Developmental transformations: Towards the body as presence. In D. R. Johnson & R. Emunah (Eds.), *Current approaches in drama therapy* (pp. 89–106). Springfield, IL: Charles C. Thomas.

Johnson, D. R., & Emunah, R. (2009). *Current approaches in drama therapy*. Springfield, IL: Charles C. Thomas.

Jones, P. (2007). *Drama as therapy*. London: Routledge.

Jones, P. (2009). Research into therapists' perceptions of therapeutic change using vignettes and aMSN messenger. *European Journal of Psychotherapy and Counselling*, 11(3), 251–266.

Jones, P. (2011). Creativity and destructiveness: A discourse analysis of dramatherapists' accounts of the work. In D. Dokter, P. Holloway & H. Seebohm (Eds.), *Dramatherapy and destructiveness: Creating the evidence base, playing with Thanatos*. London, UK: Routledge.

Jones, P. (2013). Narrative vignettes and online enquiry in researching therapist accounts of practice with children in schools: An analysis of the methodology. *Counselling and Psychotherapy Research*, 14 (3), 227–234.

Jones, P., & Dokter, D. (2008). *Supervision of drama therapy*. London, UK: Routledge.

Landy, R. (1997). Drama Therapy and distancing: Reflections on theory and clinical application. *The Arts in Psychotherapy*, 23 (5), 367–373.

Landy, R. (2009). Role theory and the role method of drama therapy. In D. R. Johnson& R. Emunah (Eds.), *Current approaches in drama therapy* (pp. 65–88). Springfield, IL: Charles C. Thomas.

Langley, D. (2006). *An introduction to drama therapy*. London, UK: Sage.

Mienczakowski, J. (2001). Ethnodrama: Performed research – limitations and potential. In Paul Atkinson, Sara Delamont, Amanda Coffey, John Lofland & Lyn Lofland (Eds.), *Handbook of ethnography* (pp. 468–476). London: Sage.

Moreno, J. L. (1946). *Psychodrama first volume*. Beacon, New York: Beacon House.

North American Drama Therapy Association (n.d.). 'What is drama therapy?' Retrieved from www.nadta.org. Accessed July 1, 2017.

Pendzik, S. (2006). On dramatic reality and its therapeutic function in drama therapy. *The Arts in Psychotherapy*, 33(2006), 271–280.

Polkinghorne, D. (1988). *Narrative knowing and the human sciences*. Albany: SUNY Press.

Reason, P., & Bradbury, H. (Eds.) (2008). *The Sage handbook of action research: Participative inquiry and practice*. Thousand Oaks, CA: Sage.

Sajnani, N., & Johnson, D. R. (2014). *Trauma-informed drama therapy: Transforming clinics, classrooms, and communities*. Springfield, IL: Charles C. Thomas.

Saldaña, J. (2003). Dramatizing data: A primer. *Qualitative Inquiry*, 9(2), 218–236.

Saldaña, J. (2005). *Ethnodrama*. London: AltaMira Press.

Shaw, S., & Bailey, J. (2009). Discourse analysis: what is it and why is it relevant to family practice? *Family Practice*, 26(5), 413–419. Retrieved from http://doi.org/10.1093/fampra/cmp038.

Snow, S., Pendzik, S., & Johnson, D. R. (2014). *Assessment in drama therapy*. Springfield, IL: Charles C. Thomas.

Strunk, D. R., & DeRubeis, R. J. (2001). Cognitive therapy for depression: A review of its efficacy. *Journal of Cognitive Psychotherapy*, 15, 289–297.

Thibodeau, P., & Boroditsky, L. (2011). The metaphors we think with: The role of metaphor in reasoning. *PLOS One*. Retrieved March 1, 2017 from http://journals.plos.org/plosone/article?id=10.1371/journal.pone.0016782.

World Health Organization (2017). Depression: Fact sheet no 369. www.who.int/mediacentre/factsheets/fs369/en/. Retrieved February 11, 2017.

Zubala, A., MacIntyre, D. J., Gleeson, N., & Karkou, V. (2013). Description of arts therapies practice with adults suffering from depression in the UK: Quantitative results from the nationwide survey. *The Arts in Psychotherapy*, 40, 458–464. Doi: 10.1016/j.aip.2013.09.003.

Chapter 6

An essence of the therapeutic process in an art therapy group for adults experiencing depression

Therapy process mapping

Ania Zubala

A few years ago, I embarked on, I expect, a lifelong journey of discovery. It followed naturally from my clinical practice and experiences of the transformative power of the arts and particularly the engagement in the creative process. It might be that I had been on this journey long before then but my doctoral work, if nothing else, helped me understand its meaning – which, being the subject of my research since, is evolving and shifting constantly. I have dedicated a big part of my academic work so far to examining the arts therapies' role in empowering those who experience depression; the challenge is how to break the vicious circle of a tendency to withdraw and a desire to connect within this most prevalent form of mental ill-health (Zubala, 2013).

In this chapter, based on an unpublished part of my doctoral work, I guide you through the therapy process in a small art therapy group for adults with depression. Firstly, I briefly describe the rationale behind this project and the context in which the group was facilitated and the study undertaken. I then explain the research methodology of this particular section of work and within the wider context of the larger research study. Following that, I present the findings, discuss them in relation to psychotherapy (and particularly arts psychotherapy) research and highlight areas for potential further scientific exploration. Finally, I propose how the "therapy process map" method I developed may be applied more widely to psychotherapy and community arts-based research projects.

Art therapy group evaluation: context and methods

As part of my doctoral project I evaluated an art therapy group for adults with depression, using multiple methods originating in quantitative, qualitative and arts-based paradigms – a mixed-method approach, often considered most suited to arts therapies research (Kaiser & Deaver, 2013; Robb, 2015; Meldrum, 1999). The art therapy group included five adults of ages between 33 and 65, who attended nine therapy sessions delivered over five weeks. Participants' levels of depression, anxiety and subjectively perceived wellbeing were measured at three points in time and similarly spaced interviews enabled understanding of their expectations and experience of therapy. A unique opportunity for participant observation allowed me to witness the therapy process and to devise a method of identifying and sequentially recording significant moments in therapy, which I later called "therapy process mapping". Elements of arts-based research provided an additional creative exploration of the therapeutic process and its meaning and allowed for a deeper understanding of how certain outcomes were achieved.

In this project, the quantitative data offered a more general guide and an indication of tendencies, while qualitative data enriched the overall findings by giving them a more comprehensive and simultaneously a much deeper perspective with additional layers of meanings unfolding through the process of analysis. The use of arts-based reflection completed the creatively designed quasi-experimental study and, I believe, brought its understanding to a level not necessarily commonly available to clinical trials and purely quantitative research.

Here, I focus on the observation and arts-based exploration of the therapeutic process. Hence, although psychometric testing was an important part of this research as a whole, it will not feature in the forthcoming sections. I invite those readers interested in a more complete picture of this project and the interconnectedness of the methods, data sources and their place in the research timeline, to refer to my doctoral thesis (Zubala, 2013) and previous publications (Zubala et al., 2013, 2014a, 2014b).

Observation-as-participant

I was present in each of the nine art therapy sessions and took notes in a research journal, usually two to three pages of writing and graphs, immediately after the session finished. During the time of intervention, I became an "observer-as-participant" (Johnson & Christensen, 2010) and my primary role in group sessions was to observe actively while being useful to the group, offering additional support for the participants or technical help for the main art therapist facilitator, as and if needed. I aimed to simultaneously immerse myself in the therapy process and at the same time to retain a degree of research distance by employing reflexivity throughout the process.

I feel that my physical position in therapy space was important: while the group was gathering in a circle (at the beginning and towards the end of each session), I was taking one of the free places alongside participants and the therapist. As the group members were gathering by a large table for art-making, I was usually the last to take one of the available seats. By physically positioning myself within the group, I was able to observe the therapy process closely from an "insider's" perspective. This way I avoided taking an unwanted role of a distant outsider-observant, which, I felt, might have caused additional anxiety in the group and either prevented or instilled emotions not necessarily helpful in a brief therapy process.

The participants appeared to accept my presence as a "silent part of the group" and seemed aware of the very different roles the therapist and I had. In order to minimise the impact of my presence on the group, I withstood from verbal comments during the discussion part of the sessions and limited my communication with participants to the minimum during the course of therapy. This included contacts during and outside therapy times. Participants similarly made no attempts to verbally dialogue with me during the sessions, although occasional non-verbal contacts were made to similar degree to which participants made connections with each other and the therapist.

A set of ideas emerged from every session, uncovering the meaning of unique and potentially significant moments in therapy. Some of those themes appeared in more than one session, while others found their place in single sessions never to be repeated. The ideas could range from totally abstract to tangibly concrete and originated from three sources: 1) the process of art-making and artwork itself; 2) the group discussion towards the end of each session; 3) my reflections after each session. The order of the sources is important, as most time was spent in art-making and this is when and where the first and most unconscious ideas emerged in every session. Group discussion, by bringing in a verbal perspective, often named those concepts, verified them and sometimes offered new ideas, inspired by what happened in the session. Eventually, my recording of notes after every session and simultaneous reflection on their meaning occasionally provoked additional ideas. These were added to the notes only when I felt that the set was otherwise incomplete and when the new concepts seemed to be hidden behind the ideas emerging from artwork and/or those verbalised.

Notes from observation were organised in a table and later coded systematically. This revealed repeating themes, which were named, listed and eventually placed on a matrix of sessions (see Figure 6.1) – a process I further call "therapy process mapping". This visual technique was adopted when it started to be clear to me that the themes seemed to be forming patterns, only visible on the therapy timeline, and that this emergence and interaction of themes throughout the course of therapy revealed the nature of the therapy process.

Arts-based reflection

In addition to recording notes in the research journal, within a couple of hours after each therapy session I took time (usually half an hour up to one hour) to reflect on the therapy process and to create, while immersing myself in thoughts about the themes which seemed significant in the particular session. I avoided focussing on individual members of the group or particular problems they experienced. Instead, I was trying to contemplate on the group as a whole, and on the phenomena I observed within the therapy process. Such an approach

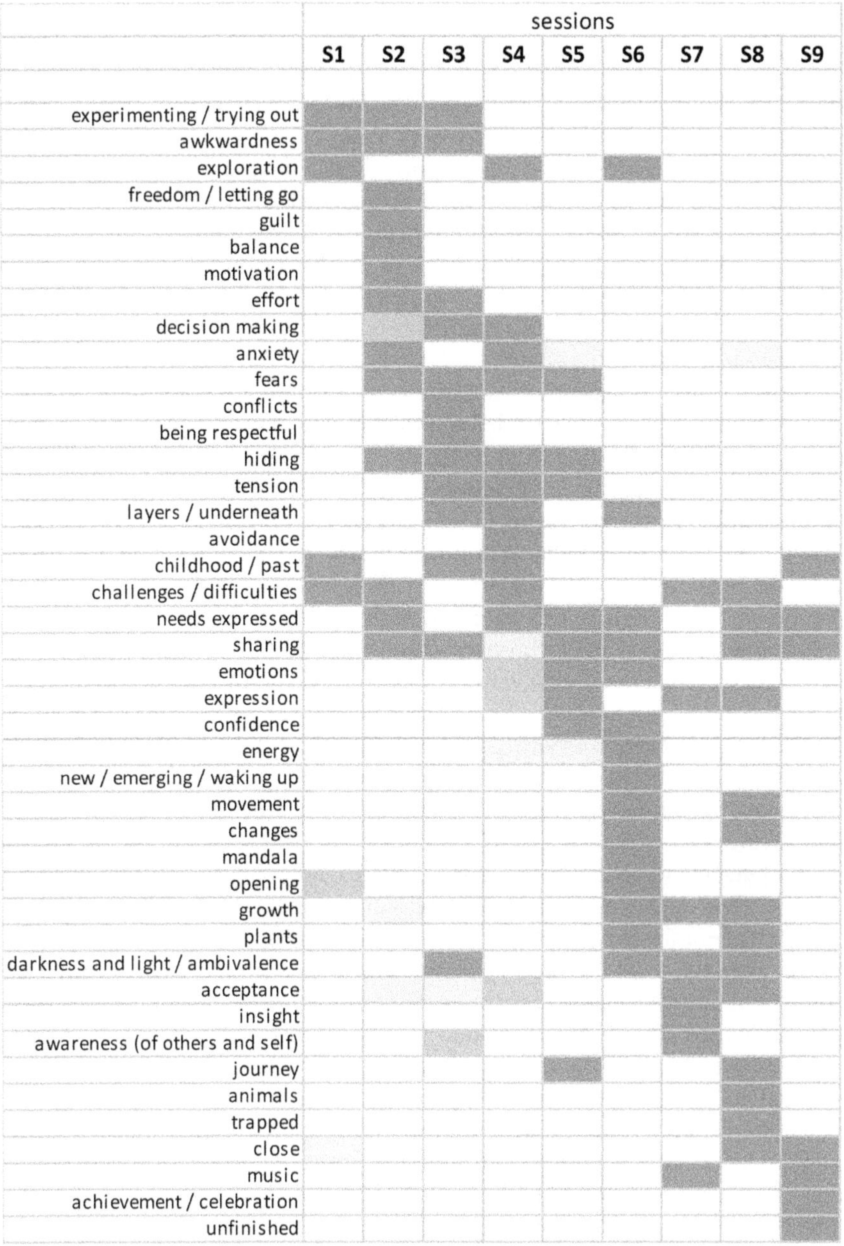

Figure 6.1 Therapy process map: Themes emerging from analysis of observation in nine art therapy sessions. (Lighter shades indicate emergence of a theme but a lack of the idea it represented.)

helped me to deconstruct the meanings of the most intense themes rather than individual concerns brought in by group members.

In effect of this practice, on an evening following each session I created an image in a designated visual journal. In my work, I used a set of art materials similar to the one available to the group members. Not being a trained artist, I believe that my art-making reflected to some extent the process, which the participants experienced. I was faced with similar resentment and anxieties in the beginning and experienced more confidence and growth with increasing familiarity with art materials and the process of art-making itself.

Nine different images were the result of the described process – the "data" (see Figure 6.2). Once the images were produced, I kept them safe and have not looked at them for several months to allow for incubation to take place (Moustakas, 1990).

Apparent lack of guidance on how to analyse data derived through arts-based inquiries (Colucci, 2010) led me to adopting elements of artistic inquiry (Hervey, 2000), originating from dance movement psychotherapy research and active imagination (Jung & Chodorow, 1997), with its roots in analytical psychology and the work of Carl Gustav Jung. The process I engaged in both making and exploring the created images could be described as an arts-based (McNiff, 2007; Simons & McCormack, 2007) systematic "immersion in creative process and scholarly reflection" (Kossak, 2012: 22).

Following a period of "incubation" (Moustakas, 1990) of several months after they were created, I connected with the nine artworks again and immersed myself in the process of deep reflection by silently studying their qualities for half an hour. Feelings and thoughts that emerged during this time, through the technique of active imagination (Jung & Chodorow, 1997), were immediately sketched or written down. I anticipated that by interacting with the nine artworks "while maintaining waking level of consciousness" (Tomlinson, 2011), I, as researcher, may more clearly perceive ideas that could have easily remained hidden if approached by other methods alone. In effect of these reflections, a final "essence" (Hervey, 2000) was created – a single image and a single, however complex, finding. Contrary to what I expected, I did not experience any hesitation while choosing art materials at this point. I was changing them numerous times, often coming back to the tools previously used. The process of creation was also unexpectedly quick.

In order to improve the trustworthiness of generating and processing observational and image-based data, I engaged in de-briefing sessions with the art therapist after each group session, this way allowing for a valuable perspective of a key professional and a central person in this project to be included in the findings (however inevitably filtered by my personal understanding). Though not directly taking part in the research procedures, the art therapist had indirectly contributed and shaped the research process and is just as present in the findings of this inquiry as are the group members and all of us who were present in this therapy space.

Findings: therapy process map and visual essence of the therapy process

As described earlier, findings in the form of themes are based on analysis of notes, which incorporated observations of the actual art-making and of discussions at the end of sessions, as well as my own reflections. Themes visually represented on a matrix (Figure 6.2) give an almost instant idea of how and when they were appearing in the therapy process, indicating therapeutic progress and varying meanings of individual sessions.

I describe the themes that emerged in hope to offer the reader an experience of travelling through an intimate process of therapy, which I was privileged to explore. I introduce the themes as they appeared throughout the nine therapy sessions to capture their changing character. As noted above, however, most themes were not bound to single sessions and will be placed in text

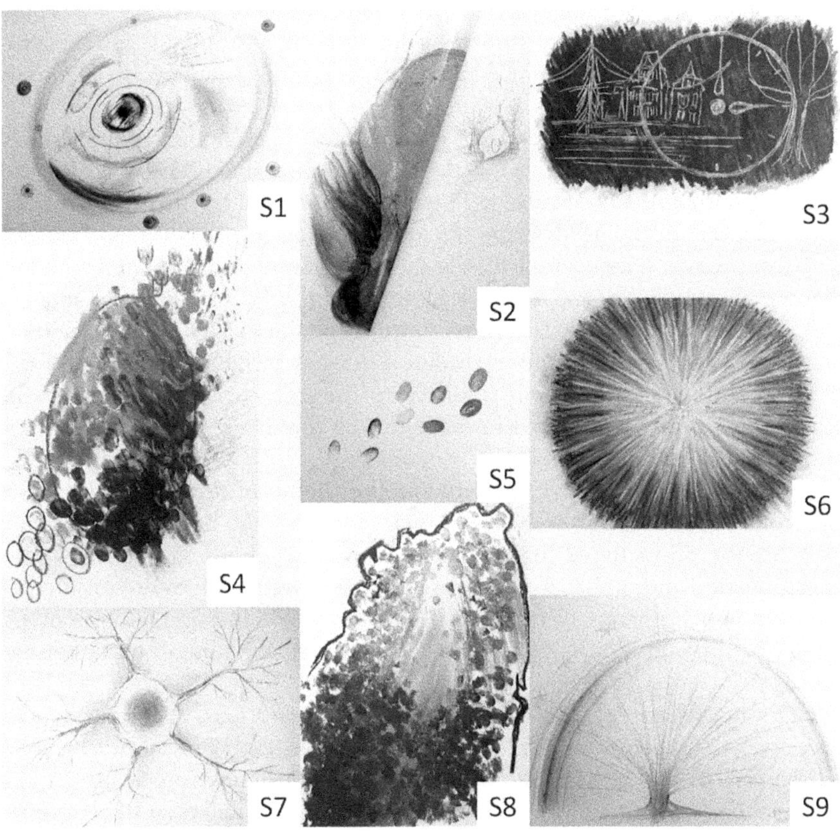

Figure 6.2 Nine images emerging from arts-based reflection (with session numbers).

where they feel particularly prominent (in italics and followed by appropriate number(s) of sessions in which they emerged). If not stated otherwise, all citations come directly from my reflective journal. Participants are quoted using fictional names.

Journey through the therapy process

Not surprisingly, at the very beginning of therapy *experimenting/trying out* (S1, S2) was the main emerging theme. It included *experimenting with colours* (S3) and also meant *getting out of comfort zone* (S3). *Awkwardness* of art-making in front of others (S1, S2) and speaking about one's artwork (S3) seemed also a natural theme in the first few sessions.

The first session started the process of *exploration* (S1), which did not finish there but was present in several following sessions (S4, S6). Exploration concerned new art media in general (S1, S6), but also explored spontaneity, letting the paint lead and learning (and accepting) to follow it (S4). *Freedom/letting go* understood as an attempt to act without too much thinking and analysis, although not the most pronounced theme, was noticeable at the very beginning of therapy (S2).

Session S2 brought the feeling of *guilt* for not using enough colour, which seemed to have been perceived as desirable in art-making. This was also the time when the theme of *balance* (S2) appeared. Initially, I felt that *balance* could have been one of the needs expressed in this session (see further), but striving for balance might have been a ballast at the same time, especially paired with the themes of *experimenting* and *letting go*. A theme of *motivation* (S2) seemed important at that point and while lack of motivation could initially be expected, there was a lot of courage in the group, readiness to work seemed apparent and I felt that motivation was huge. This is related to the next theme of *effort* (S2, S3), which the group was prepared to make during the therapy, including putting effort into art-making itself.

First sessions of therapy also brought the theme of *decision making* with decisions about what to draw and which colour to use being very difficult (S2). Session S3 included further decisions beyond choosing colours, while engaging in a more challenging work and making effort were considered. The theme of *acceptance*, or rather lack of it, emerged in session S2 with mentions of a difficulty with acceptance of artwork making being witnessed by others.

Beginning of therapy also saw a rise in *anxiety* and *fears*, which seemed to have appeared first in session S2 and remained consistently present until session S5. Anxiety in session S2 arose in the context of little structure while session S4 saw increase in difficulties and challenge, which was understandably accompanied by increasing anxiety and fear "of something to emerge". It seemed to me that anxiety was slightly relieved in session S5, when I noted that "some problems may be touched". Later, in session S8, one participant noticed that anxiety she/he was expecting in the beginning of therapy was relieved once she/he learned what would happen in the sessions.

Rise in anxiety and fears was followed by an attempt to express *conflicts* is session S3. As conflicts were expressed for the first time (S3), there didn't seem to have been an *acceptance* (S3) of them as yet and the group reaction seemed to have been an attempt to keep status quo. Fear of the exposure of conflicts could have its origins in the group *being respectful* (S3), caring for each other, considering feelings of other group members and in the generally present tendency to "rescue" each other from challenges. A theme of *hiding* appeared for the first time in session S2, when some of the group members decided, contrary to the agreed group structure, not to turn their artwork facing others in the discussion time. In session S3 *tension* appeared which could not be released and meant that something could be felt hiding beneath the surface, touching it, but still remaining hidden. This is when the themes of *layers/underneath* and *darkness and light/ambivalence* emerged (S3), and I noted in my journal:

> Colour underneath black and coming out. Layers. What is on the surface? What is underneath? How much am I ready to share? Do I want to expose fears/conflicts? Is darkness disguised as colour?

Tension "under the surface" could again be felt in session S4, when the need for "something to emerge" and a simultaneous fear of it and hiding behind the masks ("everything is well, all is pretty, all will be fine") seemed to have been present. *Avoidance* (S4) of emotions and of sharing them verbally seemed apparent and the theme of *energy* (S4), or rather the lack of it, emerged.

Session S4 brought the themes of *emotions* and *expression*, as the group seemed to have been wondering: "What are we here for? How art therapy may help us express emotions?" and also "I wonder how it is to be able to do that", meaning how it is to paint spontaneously, with no plan. Some of the group members appreciated recognition of emotions in artwork and shared feelings of jealousy of others being able to "let go" and express emotions through art. Could those emotions have been this previously mentioned "something", hiding under the surface and causing tension? Practising of *making decisions* (S4) with slightly more confidence and *acceptance* (S4) of a challenge seemed to be present and it is possible that the group's readiness to make effort led to further developments in therapy process.

Session S5 saw "energy and humour lost from the group", while there seemed to have been a "willingness to engage in a more in-depth work, to share and express emotions", accompanied by "a strong fear and still hiding away". Session S5 introduced artwork making in response to a theme chosen by the group, and I made a note: "towards relaxation". Possibly a theme was needed to relieve tension before more meaningful work could be done?

A thought is shared in the group: "If not given a theme, I would only attempt to paint nice pictures, I will not want to touch the emotions or problems" (Helen, S5).

The themes of *confidence* and *journey* appeared as members of the group were taking "small steps on the journey towards confidence" (S5), which were "slowly becoming bolder and more defined", as I noted. It seemed important that "confidence was changeable, present on one day, absent on another, it's not given, it comes and goes, changes from rain to sun" and that "it's good to have tools to help through the rain" (Mary, S5).

Themes of *layers/underneath* and *confidence* were still very much present in session S6. Different layers were recognised in the artwork. Emotions were finally very present, the group started noticing different shades and textures and making associations to mood and emotions, while some members were facing them for the first time. Confidence and readiness to share (further introduced) was growing in the group.

The theme of *energy* (S6) reappeared in participants' images and verbalisations, this time literally, as the group noticed how energy was present "in every image, they all have it". The theme of *new/emerging/waking up* (S6) seemed to be dominating throughout. There was an exploration of new art media, new life pictured in artwork and new qualities emerging in individual members of the group, who seemed to have gathered enough confidence to start exploring aspects of themselves, which were previously unavailable to them. *Waking up* was represented in an image of a sun which allowed to sleep better and wake up fresher and which was bringing hope. *Opening*, although sensed already in session S1, became another theme in session S6 while the group decided to use previously unopened boxes with art materials and "openness and dialogue" seemed to be present along with the new theme of *changes* (S6). Something *emerging* and *changes* were recognised in the group with an attempt to depict *movement* (S6) in several artworks.

While the theme of *growth* appeared first is session S2, when I felt the "need for growth, starting point (for something beautiful to grow)" within the group, it only fully developed in session S6, accompanied by the theme of *plants* (S6). Confidence was growing, new life and plants were growing in artwork, "despite the turmoil and darkness": "they come out whether you like it or not" (Mary, S6). Alongside changes and energy, a theme of *darkness and light/ambivalence* was very present in all artwork. New life was surrounded by dark skies, lighter centre of an image had darkness around it ("light and colours layered with winter, darkness – intertwined") and there was also a "calmness and turmoil amongst it". *Mandala*, which appeared in several artworks (S6), became another theme, possibly corresponding to (or representing?) growth.

Following the rich themes in session S6, session S7 seemed to have explored new ideas and given new meanings to previous themes. *Expression* and *darkness and light /ambivalence* were still present while dark colours dominated artwork ("predominantly black, but rather expressive and strong"). The theme of *acceptance* was revisited, while difficulties seemed to have been accepted and I noted that this might have brought a feeling of "satisfaction from overcoming them". *Insight* was identified as a theme as the group acknowledged its importance, and I felt that session S7 offered new understandings. *Awareness* (S7) seemed to have been a predominant theme in the session, although it previously appeared briefly in session S3, when the group started to "be curious of others and their intentions". Session S7, however, brought a new depth to this theme, with growing awareness and appreciation of others and the surroundings ("images, landscapes, family history, the past"). Two types of awareness seemed apparent: one pertaining to the inner and the other to the outside world.

Self-awareness seemed to have grown in the group. Mary shares: "I know that I build walls around me, so that people cannot touch me" (S8). Theme of *music* appeared while it was recognised as facilitating growth of awareness, "of what is happening around". Session S8 revisited the themes of *expression, changes* and *growth* once again. A theme of *journey* (S8) and *darkness and light/ambivalence* emerged again. This time they were depicted as a dark tunnel and then another with a light at the end of it – "the therapy was a journey", noted Dave (S8). Crossroads signified another journey, as there was no certainty of what would happen next. Vivid, expressive images suddenly appeared in the session. A surreal tropical scene included *plants* (S8) and *animals* (S8), which became a theme, as they significantly materialised in yet another artwork of "the wildest animals" (Helen, S8).

A theme of being *trapped* (S8) seemed very strongly present, in varying contexts. It related to inability to engage spontaneously in art-making, but also to the wild animals being trapped, going through the tunnel, possibly the group being "trapped, together in a small, suffocating space". Another theme of *close* (S8) seemed very much related, when the feeling of being trapped originated in "being so close to others and having to share". The tropical jungle was also an "enclosed space, humid and crowded" for Dave (S8). The theme of *close* seemed to have appeared for the first time in session S1, when "difficulty being in a group, so close at one table" was mentioned. There was an acceptance as well, again, while the "animals needed to accept each other in this confined space and needed to coexist in peace" (Helen, S8).

Session S9 gave the theme of *close* another meaning, when the desire to be close to others seemed to have been explored. Obviously, *close* would also relate to the closing of therapy. Music and movement appeared again in artwork. Additionally, the theme of *achievement/celebration* emerged when it was recognised that the fact that "everyone went through therapy and completed it" (Maya, S9) deserved celebration ("there is something today to celebrate", Dave, S9) and was an achievement which the group shared ("we are all there", Mary, S9). A feeling that some processes were not complete led to the last theme – *unfinished* (S9). Artwork seemed unfinished and there was a sense that the group did not want the therapy to end.

More frequent stops along the way

Some more generic but not less important themes were present throughout the therapy process and therefore did not seem to suit the chronological order of the journey described above.

Childhood/past: In session S1 exploration of art materials resembled a "childlike experience" (Dave, S1). Session S3 brought memories, by "revisiting technique known from school" and artwork seemed to have been used to connect to events and feelings from the past in sessions S4 and S9.

Challenges/difficulties: Challenges emerged in session S1 as difficulty being in a group and continued in session S2 as "difficulty with acceptance of artwork making being witnessed by others" and difficulty with making decisions. In sessions S7 and S8 difficult observations about self were made and the group themes were considered particularly challenging.

Needs expressed: Expression of needs started early, in session S2, and continued in different forms until the very end of therapy. Session S2 brought the need for calm and peace as well as "simplicity, honesty, ideal place to be and balance". Session S4 saw the need for expression of emotions through art and for "something to emerge" counterbalanced by the need to relieve tension and relaxation in session S5. Calmness was mentioned again in session S6, while session S8 brought in animals which "needed to accept each other" and to "coexist in peace" (Dave, S8). In the last session, S9, a need for "something relaxing" resurfaced and thus, celebration followed.

Sharing: "Sharing" appeared for the first time in session S2 and became progressively more difficult in further sessions. Session S3 saw increase of sharing ("of pastels, of the theme, of colour") and recognition of looking at "the same image and colours differently, sharing different perceptions", but it also brought doubts about willingness to share ("How much am I ready to share?") and whether the "environment is safe enough for sharing of self". Avoidance of sharing emotions seemed to have been present in session S4, while session S5 saw the group better prepared to share and express again, despite associated challenges. Sharing of art materials, "recognition of common themes in artwork, dialoguing" seemed to have reached a peak level in session S6, while it was accompanied by the feeling of being too close and trapped. The culminating session S9 included sharing of personal memories – "powerful" (Jane, S9) experience.

Reflecting using arts: visual essence of the therapy process

A series of nine images are the "data", both the effect and the subject of arts-based reflection, while the "essence" image is the actual core finding (Figure 6.3). As words accompanied this artwork from the very beginning, it seemed appropriate to describe it verbally, which I later attempted to do. I decided to layer the words over the image – both visually (literally layering words over the image – see Zubala, 2013, Appendix 31) and verbally (in the form of a narrative – Box 6.1).

The image and the text were inspired purely by the data collected (nine images). The "essence" image emerged in response to artwork through the method of active imagination and no consciously intellectual activity was involved.

Figure 6.3 An "essence" of arts-based inquiry.

Box 6.1 Narrative to findings from arts-based inquiry

There is a centre here, a core. And a mixture of parts – separate in form but connected. Grey is the beginning, then colours unfold. Black joins, adds definition. Eventually all colours, all shades are there. They are approaching, with energy, take turns, don't waste time. Some are stepping out with caution and subtlety. Layers emerge, one after another, covering. Then revealing. Some are hidden, some are growing under, there's life underneath, deep inside. It is reaching out. In the pre-growth shadows and light appear. Darker or lighter shades may not dominate the story, they all have place, they need to be in balance, controlled. Balancing colours, balancing forms. In and out. Towards the boundary, outside the walls, outwith. Growing.

I would like to avoid unnecessary interpretations, but reflecting on the image reluctantly leads me to thinking that it was perhaps responding to the complexity of depression, its various representations, layers, paradoxes within it, anxiety and longing for connections, striving for balance and meaning. The circle, the core, may also be seen as a therapy space, through which growth and breaking of the walls become possible. In this light, the narrative may not only be considered a description of the art-making process, but possibly a symbolic representation of the therapy process itself. Including a narrative added another layer of meaning to the created essence and was for me an important way of retaining the process and not only the outcome of this arts-based inquiry. This interest in a research process reflected the importance of the therapy process itself – the very core of this project.

Discussion: creative tension and moments of change

As I mentioned earlier, in the complete research study, the findings presented above complemented qualitative finding from interviews and quantitative results from psychometric scales. Synthesis of all these complex data from such diverse sources proved to be a challenge, however a very satisfactory one. For a detailed description of how I identified concepts core to this study and to approaching depression within arts therapies realm, please refer to my doctoral thesis (Zubala, 2013). For the purpose of this chapter, it is important to mention that a common theme across the findings was the tension between the tendency to withdraw and the desire to connect experienced by the group members. There seems to be a unique potential in the nature of arts therapies to address this phenomenon – to work with the tension and not against it, to utilise its creative qualities and guide the client on their journey to re-establishing balance and re-connecting – with self and others (Van Lith et al., 2009). Balancing between just enough tension (needed for creative energy to emerge) and flow (allowing for release of this energy and making connections) in the therapy process is a challenging task for both the therapist and the client. However, the arts seem to have a potential to assist us in this process, as explained by De Botton and Armstrong (2013, 32): "Art can put us in touch with concentrated doses of our missing dispositions, and thereby restore a measure of equilibrium to our listing inner selves".

The described journey through the therapy process is an effect of a systematic (however inevitably subjective) analysis of my observations and creative reflections from an art therapy group. As such, it allows for a deepened understanding of how therapeutic change happened in this particular group and how the unique qualities of art-making, and working with both the process and outcomes in the form of images helped facilitate the progress and new insights.

Observation of therapy sessions offered me a unique opportunity to reflect on the therapy process (Greenberg, 1999), an experience usually unavailable to non-participants. Ball (2002) argues, for example, that some of the art therapy processes, like nonverbal communication and the power of images within the session, may only be accessible to a direct observer of therapy sessions and that "the intensive analysis of significant episodes may lead to a deeper and more specific understanding of change processes and treatment effectiveness" (Ball, 2002: 80). Important issues around ethics and how the presence of an observer in therapy sessions impacts the therapeutic process should not be disregarded, of course. However, as shown in this project, the big advantage of observation lies in the opportunity to not only identify but also map significant themes and moments in therapy across sessions and on therapy timeline – it this sense, observation offers us a unique chance to follow the individual's or the group's "developmental" journey through the therapy, not dissimilar to our growth as humans according to Winnicott's developmental theory (Winnicott, 1964). In addition, using art as a mode of investigation and not only an object of inquiry (McNiff, 2007) brings the scientific understanding a little bit closer to the actual experience of therapy.

It is now commonly recognised in psychotherapy research that therapy processes as well as outcomes need to be examined and not only whether but, most importantly, how and why the therapy presents value for patients and clients (Roth & Fonagy, 1996; Laurenceau et al., 2007; Timulak & Creaner, 2010), appreciating the challenges of such research (Kazdin, 2009). Similar approach is advocated by arts therapies researchers (Kapitan, 2012; Gilroy, 2006; Meldrum, 1999) and research on the processes and mechanisms in art therapy was identified as most needed by a panel of practice and research experts, after outcome/evidence-based and neuroscience-related research (Kaiser & Deaver, 2013). Indeed, therapeutic factors or mechanisms of change in arts therapies are increasingly more often studied (Blomdahl et al., 2013, 2016; Gabel & Robb, 2017; Sporild & Bonsaksen, 2014; Czamanski-Cohen & Weihs, 2016; Cassidy et al., 2014; Zubala, 2014b).

Since the process of therapy happens over time, in addition to enabling factors that lead to change, it seems just as important to locate the significant moments of change on the therapy timeline or even within individual sessions – those brief points in time, indicating either individual or group shifts towards meeting the aims of treatment (Greenberg, 1994; Timulak & McElvaney, 2013; Laurenceau, 2007). Researchers in psychotherapy also discuss the course of change (whether change occurs smoothly over the course of therapy or whether the trajectory of change decreases and increases at different stages of therapy) and argue that the therapy process is almost always dynamic, characterized by a nonlinear and irregular trajectory (Hayes et al., 2007; Gelo & Salvatore, 2016; Salvatore, 2015; Laurenceau et al., 2007).

The therapy process mapping method described in this chapter identified moments in therapy when anxiety in the group seemed apparent and helped understand how expression of emotions through art-making eventually enabled growth and acceptance but simultaneously triggered feelings of being trapped and the process being difficult. This nonlinear trajectory of change is consistent with ideas that change in therapy may require getting worse before getting better (Mahoney, 1991) and not dissimilar to the concept of "depression spike" described by Hayes et al. (2007). Such phenomena would not be apparent in the more usual pre-post analyses of data, regardless of their form.

The therapy process map is essentially a method of analysis and visualising observational material, and, while being inspired by a more conventional method of thematic analysis, seems to have a clear advantage over it – not only does it allow to instantly "see" the themes in place of reading lengthy paragraphs of text, but it also enables tracking of these themes across time. While in the therapy described in this chapter, the "visual" themes seemed to often provide a symbolic representation of the therapy process (e.g. "light/darkness" or concrete objects or settings – "jungle", "animals"), the use of the tool in other arts therapies could instead focus on the qualities of their corresponding arts. For example, in music therapy themes related to tempo, rhythm, noise, perhaps whisper, perhaps waterfall, would hold similar symbolic value and could be similarly mapped across the course of therapy. Therapy process mapping could equally be a useful method to observe and visualise any therapy process or in community-based interventions (particularly those involving arts) where change across time is important and the outcomes themselves would be enriched by insights into how the process evolved and enabled change to happen.

Conclusions: towards understanding

The single study presented here does not of course reflect the entire complexity of art therapy practice with depression. Expanding our understanding of how change happens, including identifying mechanisms of change and pivotal moments in therapy, requires many more studies of creative design, in a variety of settings and contexts and with diverse groups of clients and patients.

Nevertheless, the findings from this research project bring us a little closer to realising how group art therapy might empower those who experience depression to rebuild balance and lost connection with self and others. This work aligns with the growing body of research indicating that arts therapies have the power to transform tension creatively, to reverse withdrawal common in depression and to build relationships – it is now essential that we continue our creative research and practice to understand how this happens.

Acknowledgements

With special thanks to the group Members and to Kim Chapman, who facilitated the art therapy – thank you for allowing me to witness the therapy process and to share it on these pages.

References

Ball, B. (2002). Moments of change in the art therapy process. *The Arts in Psychotherapy*, 29 (2002), 79–92.

Blomdahl, C., Gunnarsson, A. B., Guregård, S., & Björklund, A. (2013). A realist review of art therapy for clients with depression. *Arts in Psychotherapy*, 40(3), 322–330. Doi: 10.1016/j.aip.2013.05.009.

Blomdahl, C., Gunnarsson, B. A., Guregård, S., Rusner, M., Wijk, H., & Björklund, A. (2016). Art therapy for patients with depression: Expert opinions on its main aspects for clinical practice. *Journal of Mental Health*, 25, 6, 527–535, Doi: 10.1080/09638237.2016.1207226.

Cassidy, S., Turnbull, S. & Gumley, A. (2014). Exploring core processes facilitating therapeutic change in Dramatherapy: A grounded theory analysis of published case studies. *The Arts in Psychotherapy*, 41(4), 353–365. Doi: 10.1016/j.aip.2014.07.003.

Colucci, E. (2010). Arts-based research in cultural mental health. In Y. Kashima, E. Kashima, & R. Beatson (Eds.), *Steering the cultural dynamics: Selected papers from the 2010 Congress of the International Association for Cross-Cultural Psychology*. Melbourne, Australia: International Association for Cross-Cultural Psychology. Available at: www.iaccp.org.

Czamanski-Cohen, J., & Weihs, K. L. (2016). The bodymind model: A platform for studying the mechanisms of change induced by art therapy. *The Arts in Psychotherapy*, 51, 63–73. Doi: 10.1016/j.aip.2016.08.006.

De Botton, A. & Armstrong, J. (2013). *Art as therapy*. London: Phaidon Press Limited.

Gabel, A., & Robb, M. (2017). (Re)considering psychological constructs: A thematic synthesis defining five therapeutic factors in group art therapy. *The Arts in Psychotherapy*, 55, 126–135. Doi: 10.1016/j.aip.2017.05.005.

Gelo, O. C. G., & Salvatore, S. (2016). A dynamic systems approach to psychotherapy: A metatheoretical framework for explaining psychotherapy change processes. *Journal of Counseling Psychology*, 63(4), 379–395, Doi: 10.1037/cou0000150.

Gilroy, A. (2006). *Art therapy, research and evidence-based practice*. London: Sage Publications.

Greenberg, L. S. (1994). The investigation of change: Its measurement and explanation. In R. L. Russell (Ed.), *Reassessing psychotherapy research* (pp. 114–143). New York: The Guilford Press.

Greenberg, L. S. (1999). Ideal psychotherapy research: A study of significant change processes. *Journal of Clinical Psychology*, 55(12), 1467–1480.

Hayes, A. M., Laurenceau, J.-P., Feldman, G., Strauss, J. L., & Cardaciotto, L. (2007). Change is not always linear: The study of nonlinear and discontinuous patterns of change in psychotherapy. *Clinical Psychology Review*, 27, 715–723. Doi: 10.1016/j.cpr.2007.01.008.

Hervey, L. W. (2000). *Artistic inquiry in dance/movement therapy: Creative research alternatives*. Springfield: Charles C Thomas Publisher.

Johnson, B., & Christensen, L. (2010). *Educational research: Quantitative, qualitative, and mixed approaches*. London: SAGE.

Jung, C. G., & Chodorow, J. (1997). *Jung on active imagination*. Princeton, NJ: Princeton University Press.

Kaiser, D., & Deaver, S. (2013). Establishing a research agenda for art therapy: A Delphi study. *Art Therapy: Journal of the American Art Therapy Association*, 30(3), 114–121. Doi: 10.1080/07421656.2013.819281.

Kapitan, L. (2012). Does art therapy work? Identifying the active ingredients of art therapy efficacy. *Art Therapy*, 29(2), 48–49, Doi: 10.1080/07421656.2012.684292.

Kazdin, A. E. (2009). Understanding how and why psychotherapy leads to change. *Psychotherapy Research*, 19(4–5), 418–428, Doi: 10.1080/10503300802448899.

Kossak, M. (2012). Art-based enquiry: It is what we do!, *Journal of Applied Arts & Health*, 3(1), 21–29. Doi: 10.1386/jaah.3.1.21_1.

Laurenceau, J.-P., Hayes, A. M., & Feldman, G. C. (2007). Some methodological and statistical issues in the study of change processes in psychotherapy. *Clinical Psychology Review*, 27, 682–695, Doi: 10.1016/j.cpr.2007.01.007.

Mahoney, M. J. (1991). *Human change processes: The scientific foundations of psychotherapy*. New York, NY: Basic Books.

McNiff, S. (2007). Art-based research. In J. G. Knowles, & A.L Cole (Eds.), *Handbook of the arts in qualitative research: Perspectives, methodologies, examples, and issues*. London: Sage Publications.

Meldrum, B. (1999). Research in the arts therapies, In A. Cattanach (Ed.), *Process in the arts therapies*. London: Jessica Kingsley.

Moustakas, C. (1990). *Heuristic research: Design, methodology, and applications*. London: Sage.

Robb, M. A. (2015). Overview of historical and contemporary perspectives on art therapy research. In D. Gussak & M. Rosal (Eds.), *The Wiley handbook of art therapy*. Chichester, UK: Wiley and Sons, Ltd.

Roth, A., & Fonagy, P. (1996). *What works for whom?: A critical review of psychotherapy research*. New York: Guilford Press.

Salvatore, S., Tschacher, W., Gelo, O. C. G., & Koch, S. C. (2015). Editorial: Dynamic systems theory and embodiment in psychotherapy research: A new look at process and outcome. *Frontiers in Psychology*, 6(914), Doi: 10.3389/fpsyg.2015.00914.

Simons, H., & McCormack, B. (2007). Integrating arts-based inquiry in evaluation methodology. *Opportunities and Challenges, Qualitative Inquiry*, 13(2), 292–311.

Sporild, I. A., & Bonsaksen, T. (2014). Therapeutic factors in expressive art therapy for persons with eating disorders. *Groupwork*, 24(3), 46–60. Doi: 10.1921/10201240104.

Timulak, L., & Creaner, M. (2010). Qualitative meta-analysis of outcomes of person-centred/experiential therapies. In M. Cooper, J. C. Watson & D. Holldampf (Eds.), *Person-centred and experiential psychotherapies work*, 65–90. Ross-on-Wye: PCCS Books.

Timulak, L., & McElvaney, R. (2013). Qualitative meta-analysis of insight events in psychotherapy. *Counselling Psychology Quarterly*, 26(2), 131–150, Doi: 10.1080/09515070.2013.792997.

Tomlinson, K. L. (2011). Working with the imaginal: Art-making and dialogue with figures of soul. [Dissertation] ProQuest, UMI Dissertation Publishing.

Van Lith, T., Fenner, P., & Schofield, M. J. (2009). Toward an understanding of how art making can facilitate mental health recovery. *Australian e-Journal for the Advancement of Mental Health (AeJAMH)*, 8(2), 183–193, Doi: 10.5172/jamh.8.2.183.

Winnicott, D. W. (1964). *The child, the family and the outside world*. England: Pelican Books.

Zubala, A. (2013). Description and evaluation of arts therapies practice with depression in the UK (Doctoral thesis). Queen Margaret University. Retrieved from http://etheses.qmu.ac.uk/1775/.

Zubala, A., MacIntyre, D. J., Gleeson, N., & Karkou, V. (2013). Description of arts therapies practice with adults suffering from depression in the UK: Quantitative results from the nationwide survey. *The Arts in Psychotherapy*, 40(5), 458–464. Doi: 10.1016/j.aip.2013.09.003.

Zubala, A., MacIntyre, D. J., Gleeson, N., & Karkou, V. (2014a). Description of arts therapies practice with adults suffering from depression in the UK: Qualitative findings from the nationwide survey. *The Arts in Psychotherapy*, 41(5), 535–544. Doi: 10.1016/j.aip.2014.10.005.

Zubala, A., MacIntyre, D. J., & Karkou, V. (2014b). Art psychotherapy practice with adults suffering from depression in the UK: Qualitative findings from depression-specific questionnaire. *The Arts in Psychotherapy*, 41(5), 563–569.

Chapter 7

Embodied treatment of depression

The development of a dance movement therapy model

Päivi Pylvänäinen

Introduction

Depression visits many people's lives, briefly or more chronically, in milder or more severe form. It is considered an epidemic. The global burden of disease studies shows depressive disorders as the leading cause of years lived with disability (YLD) in the adult population in the world (WHO, 2016). The situation was the same in the previous report, year 2013.

In this chapter, I assume that as complex adaptive dynamic systems (Claxton, 2015), all living humans constantly respond to their environment, to others and to themselves. Following Claxton's phrasing, "a System is a constellation of processes that are themselves Systems" (p. 52), the central feature is that these processes resonate in reciprocal and reverberatory ways with each other. Furthermore, in this chapter I will argue that at its core, the human responding happens in and through the body. As a result, when someone becomes depressed, the body can be seen as holding information about the person's experience and at the same time as becoming the realm for potential solutions. Dance Movement Therapy (DMT) is a body-based practice, which may be able to offer some treatment options to people with depression.

To understand how the information about lived experiences and the potential solutions are shaped in the body, the concept of body image is useful. Body image, while differentiated into body-self, image properties, and body memory (Pylvänäinen, 2003), is seen as a concept that functions as information organizer and assists in perceiving the patterns of embodied interaction. Body image can act as the container of lived experiences and relationships to others, environment and the self. Body image is a shaping process from the beginning of life, continuing throughout the lifespan.

This chapter will present a view on depression from embodiment-perspective. The concept of body image will be described theoretically and research findings on the body image of patients with depression will be presented. Stemming from the concept of body image, this chapter then proposes and discusses a DMT model for the treatment of depression. The central aspects of this model are encountered as embodied phenomena: the modulation of stress levels, safety, interaction, and dialogue.

Depression is embodied

How persons' subjective, felt experiences of their bodies in action provide the fundamental grounding for human behavior, cognition, and also language, is at the core of an embodied view on humans (Gibbs, 2005; Hommel, 2015). Depression is resonated in the felt experiences, behaviors, and cognition. Concrete, felt experiences are also relevant in constructing the attachment style the person learns and develops through the interaction with others. Simply put, attachment style shapes our social and emotional action patterns. Research indicates that insecure, i.e. avoidant or anxious-ambivalent attachment style characteristically can be observed in patients with depression (Siegel, 1999; Bifulco et al., 2002; Slade, 2014). Insecurity in the attachment style produces difficulties in behavioral self-regulation and also in interpersonal regulation (Mikulincer & Shaver, 2007; Schore, 2012; Messina et al., 2016). It has been argued that attachment styles are stored to a large extent into implicit memory and are essentially embodied (Schachner et al., 2005; Bentzen, 2015). In interaction, attachment can be reshaped during the whole life-time (Levy et al., 2011), but through the interactional expectations and learnt, automated response patterns that constitute the attachment style, an individual spontaneously has a tendency to maintain what he/she has acquired already.

It is not only the other humans, but also the physical and non-personal environment, that we respond to with our body. Building on an interactionist view of perception and action, the concept of "affordances" (Gibson, 1966) proposes that people perceive the environment in terms of their ability to act in it. Affordances are the organism's possibilities for action in certain situations (Rietveld, 2008), which inevitably shape the behaviour and felt experiences. Factors that affect physical ability and thus influence perception include body size, body control and coordination, energetic potential, and the challenges of the task (Witt, 2011). This physicality creates a basis for cognitive and social interactional abilities (Jaswal, 2016). Triberti & Riva (2016) perceive presence as the relevant link between intentions and affordances.

In depression the person perceives meager affordances, and when this is joined with the insecure attachment, the situation becomes even more stressful, because coping and completing actions in the situation becomes perturbed (see also Micali, 2013; Ratcliffe, 2013). Consequently, a self-enhancing, stressful, negative spiral develops, and the person may begin ruminating on it and distancing oneself from sensing the body. Stress causes the individual to reduce attention given to internal information and focus on the external information instead (Fogel, 2013; Cloninger, 2004). According to Fogel (ibid.), the interoceptive information, i.e. information about internal sensations in the body and arousal, are transmitted in the nervous system through the non-myelinated axons and thus the transmission of information is slower. The information from the external environment and from the proprioceptive system (stretching of muscles and ligaments, balance, movement coordination) travels through a fast lane in the spinal cord and is thus dominating. As depression is provoked by stress experiences, and produces stress experiences, this creates a particular relationship to interoceptive and proprioceptive systems. Due to stress, the connectedness to interoceptive system tends to become weakened, thus fragmenting the experience of presence. On the other hand, stress and physical action evoke signals, for example muscle movement, coordination, and balance sensations, in the proprioceptive system.

The symptoms of depression, i.e. low energy, anhedonia, pain, sleeping problems, anxiety, and suicidality in severe depression, can be seen as features and outcomes, which are fueled by opted and infused predispositions to respond to others, environment, and self. The patterns of responding in patients with depression are often tuned by insecurity and avoidance, and by action expectations that are not perceived enabling. These result in increased stress levels in the individual. It is possible that developing skills to be attentive to embodied proprioceptive system signals brings a way to maintain and cultivate connectedness and presence in one's embodiment even in stress situations that are linked to depression. This is an antidote to the tendency to detach from embodiment in stressed states. Connectedness and presence in one's embodiment can be strengthened through movement and mindfulness practices, which are included in DMT. Connectedness and presence in one's embodiment means also that one is more connected with and more aware of one's body image.

Body image – containment and shaping of lived experience in the body

Phenomenologically-oriented approaches to body image perceive the concept to refer to the multilayered experiential totality we perceive within our body, about our body, and by our body (Koch et al., 2012; Sheets-Johnstone, 2009; Gallagher, 2005; Bermudez et al., 1995; Pylvänäinen & Lappalainen, 2017). Body image can therefore be seen as referring to the lived experience contained in the body and the psychological significance of the body. Within the context of DMT, a tri-partite model of body image has been proposed (Pylvänäinen, 2003, 2010, 2012). In this model, body image consists of three elements: body-self, body memory, and image-properties.

The body-self (see also Dosamantes-Alpersson, 1981; Pallaro, 1996; Campbell, 1995; Pylvänäinen, 2003) refers to the body responses and action, often carrying emotional qualities, in the present moment. The body-self is interactive and emotional, the core sense of self. We relate to ourselves and to environment through the body-self. A sense of continuity in this relating in the present moment is an essential feature of mental health. The body self-actualizes the individual's relatedness to the internal and external environment in the present moment in body shapes, tensions, arousal levels, gestures, and motion. The body-self shapes the responses in close connection to body memory.

Body memory (Casey, 1987; Koch et al., 2012, 2013) refers to the implicit memory, an embodied storage of body sensations and tension patterns, which relate to habits, suffering and trauma, and pleasure and sexuality. The living body and its nervous system learn from the sensations received from the environment and from the body itself (see Kandel, 2006). The organism needs the integration of sensory, tactile, and proprioceptive information and motor efferent information. This integration is the essence of the organism's ability for intelligent action. Body memory stores the integrated patterns, the capacities and dispositions (Koch et al., 2012, 2013) that are shaped in the body and nervous system through life experiences.

The image-properties (Pylvänäinen, 2003, 2010) refer to the beliefs, judgments, and attitudes the person has about his/her body and its looks in particular. The person obtains these in the context of social and cultural environment. The image-properties are what stereotypically have been addressed by the concept of body image. The image-properties the person perceives in his/her body evoke emotional responses in the body-self. This impact is reciprocal: the person may also have beliefs and judgements about his/her embodied responses arising in the body-self.

Body image, in the elements described above, contains the individual's relatedness to the physical/spatial and social environment, and to oneself. It contains the body as a subject, the body as an object and as a body for others, i.e. an interactional and relating body, a body in togetherness. The attachment style, i.e. the secure or insecure response patterns and expectations, are ingrained in body image. Affordances, which refer to an individual's perception of possibilities for action provided by environment (Rietveld, 2008, 2013) are also essentially resonating in the body image.

Body image is created in the interactional relating experiences with others and the environment (Pylvänäinen, 2003; Sandel et al., 1993). Body image holds embodied motor, behavioral, and emotional patterns. The complex adaptive dynamic system manifests here: the responses created in the present moment influence how the patterns develop and how the individual perceives himself/herself in the present moment, and how the patterns develop. Resilient body image is sufficiently integrated, enabling flexible and realistically responsive behavioral patterns. It supports the experience of wellbeing, ability, and security. Experiences of secure attachment promote these qualities in body image as secure attachment cultivates the experiences of presence, attunement, responsiveness, modulation of emotions, communication, and reflection (Siegel, 1999, 2007). The level of awareness of the body image contents varies in individuals.

Body image concept can be utilized in clinical practice. For a clinician, it is of interest, what are the expressive characteristics of body posture and movement that are typical for patients with depression. Enquiring about the experiential contents linked to the body image can bring into communication essential features of the patient's living and condition. Furthermore, observing changes in the condition becomes possible when systematically reviewing the person's body image.

Body image characteristics in depression modulated by DMT

Based on clinical observation by the author and studies by Papadopoulos and Röhricht (2014), Michalak et al. (2012), and Punkanen et al. (2017), the characteristics of the expressive shapes and patterns arising in the body of a person with depression are as follows:

- a sunken chest
- hunched shoulders
- narrow body stance
- downcast eye-line gaze with an internal and withdrawn focus
- breathing typically shallow and mainly involving upper chest region
- core characteristic in movement and bodily presence is bound flow
- walk: slower tempo, smaller arm swings, pronounced swaying and lateral movements of the upper body, reduced vertical movement
- in emotionally expressive motion, patients with depression move more slowly, use less acceleration, use less open postures; move generally less than healthy controls

Pylvänäinen and Lappalainen (2017) explored the body image of the adult psychiatric outpatients (N = 18) suffering from depression. The Body Image Assessment (BIA) was completed as part of an interview before a DMT group treatment (12 sessions of 90 min each) and as a questionnaire after the intervention, to find out the patients' experience of their body image. BIA was developed in the clinical practice by the author on the basis of the tri-partite model of body image. It consists of the following questions:

1 How do you perceive your body and its appearances? (*image-properties*)
2 What is it like for you to take physical action? (*body-self*)
3 In your body, how do you typically sense or feel your everyday interactions with others? (*body-self*)
4 What is the basic mood like in your body when you are by yourself? (*body-self*)
5 Do you have bodily memories of moments, when you have suffered or felt ill at ease? Please give an example of such a memory. (*body memory*)
6 Do you have bodily memories of moments when you have felt good and enjoyed? Please give an example of such a memory. (*body memory*)
7 What is important for you in your body? (integrative personal evaluation; relationship to the body image)

BIA-responses were analyzed qualitatively by organizing them around central themes arising from the material. A scoring system based on the negativity-neutrality-positivity of the responses to the questions A-D was developed so that the change patterns in the pre- and post-intervention BIA-responses could be assessed numerically as well.

In this study sample, before the DMT treatment, the problems with body image in depression were lack of energy and direction in action, lacking sense of agency (in social situations), pain, fragmentation of body experience, shallow consciousness of one's body, difficulty to have peaceful rest, worry about weight, and embodied body-memories of traumatizing events or circumstances in childhood (abuse, losses of family members, bullying). In other published studies (Papadopoulos & Röhricht, 2014; Stötter et al., 2013; Segal et al., 2002), it has been reported that the characteristics of body image in patients with depression were poor mindful body awareness, feelings of being detached and distant from own body, difficulties in finding grounding, and experiences of fatigue and pains. Also, patients with depression frequently had an experience that their body boundaries were easily penetrated in social interactions. The findings portray a very similar image as was discovered in the present study. This accumulation offers validation of the findings.

DMT interventions have been found to produce change in the body image of patients with depression. Papadopoulos and Röhricht's (2014) report, that the essential outcome from the 20 bi-weekly sessions of body psychotherapy group, facilitated by an experienced dance movement therapist, was that the patients became more aware of their embodiment, their bodily sensations, and their movement patterns, and they were able to see how these related to their depression.

After the DMT treatment in the Pylvänäinen and Lappalainen (2017) study, the participants expressed positive change in body image: feeling comfortable with the motility of the body, its strength, sensing one's body as balanced and healthy. The positive experiences of physical activity were described as a pleasure of moving, ease, enjoying physical work, and finding liveliness in physical activity. Perceptions of the impact of social interaction in one's body varied from tension to non-recognition to comfort and relaxedness. In several responses, the varying quality of one's basic, embodied mood was noted. Positive perceptions of one's embodied state when alone were described as pleasant, free, relaxed, and happy. The question "what is important to you in your body" yielded a selection of topics: health, harmony, and a kind and interested attitude towards one's body.

Quantitative analysis of BIA responses revealed, that the body image of these patients was statistically significantly more positive after a 12-session DMT group intervention (Pylvänäinen & Lappalainen, 2017). The body image change explained approximately 30% of the positive change in these same patients' scores in their self-evaluations on depressive symptoms and level of functioning (Pylvänäinen & Lappalainen, 2017; Pylvänäinen et al., 2015). The BIA scores were higher, i.e. more positive, after the DMT treatment for 66% of the respondents. Among these patients, the positive change in depression levels (Pylvänäinen et al., 2015), measured by pre-, post- and follow-up self-evaluation questionnaires (BDI, HADS, SCL-90, CORE-OM) and positive change in body image scores appeared to go parallel. In their written feedback of the DMT-group treatment, 63% of the patients reported that they had noticed alleviation in their depression after the intervention. These patients reported that they had experienced positive changes during the intervention:

- Improvement in wellbeing: less sleeping problems, more positive perception of one's body, decrease or cessation of anxiety, improved activity level
- Reduction of tension
- Strengthening of feeling safe
- Increased consciousness of self: attending to oneself, recognizing physical experience and its influence, strengthening of trust in one's body, adjustment of actions on the basis of observations from the body
- Improved social interaction: better tolerance for other people, courage to approach others and to be more active in social situations, positive experience of peer support

These findings provide a new research evidence, that DMT group treatment can promote positive change in body image, mood, and social functioning (Pylvänäinen & Lappalainen, 2017; Pylvänäinen et al., 2015; Punkanen et al., 2014, 2017; Röhricht et al., 2013).

DMT treatment model for depression

Recognizing depression as a stressed systemic state, which is fed by troubled, insecure attachment styles, meager affordances, and a continuously high stress level in the individual, the therapy for depression should be able to address these themes in an experiential way. For the treatment of depression, a DMT model consisting of the following four factors, is proposed here:

1 modulation of stress level
2 safety
3 interaction
4 dialogue

The use of movement and dance enable creative ways for structuring action and presence, which allow these four factors to be explored and learnt about during the therapy process. It is argued that these four processes are directly related to changes in the body image and its three constituents. For example, the body-self resonates in the process experiences, body memories can be activated, and new memories can be shaped, while image-properties may be recognized and re-worked.

Looking at the model more closely, the first factor, *modulation of the stress response* involves, in essence, managing the activation of the autonomous nervous system. This, essentially requires behaviors that support the body and produce balancing change in the body arousal state. Movement activities provide a wide range of options for modulating the arousal level in the body. Increasing individual's knowledge and awareness of the characteristics of the information processing in stress response can support coping with stress response. The stress response in not the only option in responding, but instead, there is also the option of creative playful exploration and social connecting (see Panksepp, 1998), which is concretely practiced in DMT. Experientially, recognizing this can bring more behavioral choices for the individual in everyday life. This, in turn, creates change in the body-self.

The playful creative exploration is possible only in sufficiently safe interaction (Winnicott, 1971). Thus in DMT, the second factor named in this model, *safety*, is essentially and deeply important. There needs to be a sufficient sense of physical, emotional, and psychological safety. The therapist's task is to communicate safety on all levels:

- to guard the safety of the therapy room (privacy, comfortableness, commitment to accurate therapy time),
- to verbally express the ground rules that create safety, namely confidentiality, respect of the body experience, non-harming, and each participant's right to move the way that is suitable to him/her,
- to express and model a non-judgmental attitude, acceptance, and respect of the participant and, in particular, his/her embodied experiences and movement; this is reflected in both non-verbal behavior and in verbal communication,
- to offer the patient space to be and to support grounding, i.e. connectedness to the supporting ground surface and presence, settling in the bodily felt sensations,
- to adequately support the patient in the mutual affect regulation; attunement to the expressions and movement qualities of the patient, resonating with them and reflecting them back in interaction in an adequate and compassionate way.

Safety and *interaction* are interconnected; they mutually enhance each other. In safety, there is a possibility for freedom and creative exploration, which allows a richer, more flexible information processing and action possibilities with the other and the environment. Thus, the individual's experience of affordances gains a more positive tone. In DMT this is learnt through experience – bodily activities, interactional responses, settling into the body and self – and thus the process creates new embodied learning for the participant. The process allows the participant to discover his/her relationship to the sensitivity of the body. Also, the behavioral responses and patterns can become explicit in creative action, and safety allows them to be explored with increasing awareness and to be understood in integrating and more compassionate ways.

Interaction is action in the present, and in the therapy setting it provides an *in vivo* lab for exploring behavioral patterns and ways of responding. Karkou and

Sanderson (2006) identify three types of interactions in arts therapies: an internal level of interaction, dyadic level of interaction, and group level of interaction. Internal level refers to body sensations and imagery. Dyadic level attends to the communicative exchange between two persons, whether it is between peers or between the therapist and the patient. Group level interaction is significant as it provides experiences about joining in or staying out, or finding a position somewhere in between, regarding the distance to the emotions, communication, and activities in the group.

Dialogue is a specific form of interaction as it also can involve reflection of what may have happened a moment ago. Sufficient safety makes dialogue possible (Seikkula, 2011). In DMT group, there is interpersonal dialogue, which particularly gives attention to sensory experiences and bodily responses: movements and their qualities, body shapes, distances, and the feelings, images, and memories relating to those. The participant learns to use this kind of dialogue also in intrapersonal dialogue, which increases his/her awareness of what his/her embodied responses and state are. This awareness decouples automaticity (Siegel, 2007) and allows space for choice making, for example making subtle changes in movement pattern, gaze direction, body position, tempo or other movement quality, which will then modulate the individual's experience in the interaction. Dialogue in DMT context has an integrative nature; it integrates experience and information, emotion and cognition, sensory events and verbal expressions, unconscious and conscious contents, and inner and external worlds. Dialogue enables sharing, validation, and recognition of phenomena. When the dialogue is grounded in the embodied experiences, it functions as a practice to strengthen the consciousness of and connectedness to the self, to develop mindfulness skills. All this is very much rooted in implicit information processing, i.e. body responses in perception, being and action. In DMT the body responses – movement qualities, changes in arousal and breath, tensions in the body, reaching in the personal kinesphere and to surrounding space – are central in the interaction, and skills to observe them, to relate to them, and to communicate about them verbally are developed.

In interaction and dialogue, validation is an important aspect. Validation shapes interactional patterns. Embodiment continues whether one is conscious about it or not, but in order to validate an experience, response, or sensation, one has to be aware of it. The sphere of consciousness enlarges as one becomes better able to stay present to embodied responses. Accessing the present embodied responses i.e., connecting with the body image strengthens the presence, clarifies boundaries, and supports communication about them, which in consequence can enhance the body image.

Creativity is inherent in DMT. In the context of arts therapies and building on the work of Winnicott, Rogers, Fromm, and May, Karkou and Sanderson (2006) define creativity as "the capacity to find new and unexpected connections, new relationships and therefore new meanings" (p. 53). Creativity is a feature of interaction, play, exploration, and choice making. Creativity means the ability to see through the tacit assumptions gained via implicit learning (Nachmanovitch, 1990). Creativity means learning to translate your sensations. Creativity arises from working with what you have at hand, responding to it in new ways. Creativity is part of improvisation, and improvisation is acceptance; what arises in the moment is accepted and responded to. The moments of relaxation and quietude, that may take place in a DMT session, allow space for creative insights to emerge, as creative insights and surprises often arise at moments of surrender and repose. Nachmanovitch (ibid.) identifies the prerequisites of creation: playfulness, compassion, concentration, practice, skill, using the power of limits, using the power of mistakes, risk, surrender, patience, courage, and trust. These are also the features that need to be present in therapy. In the proposed model, the dance movement therapist aims to maintain openness to these features and prerequisites of creativity, while allowing the patient to choose how s/he wants to create his/her explorations in the therapy session.

In the proposed DMT model, the therapist's task is to create possibilities for attending to the tactile, interoceptive, and proprioceptive information that can emerge in the individual participating in the interaction of the group. The structuring and facilitation of a DMT group process for patients suffering from depression is always a unique process. Much of it happens in the flow of the moment, as a response to what is perceived in the group interaction. Based on a literature review on DMT practice with patients suffering from depression, (Meekums e al., 2015; Bräuninger, 2014a, Bräuninger, 2014b; Lin & Payne, 2014; Papadopoulos & Röhricht, 2014; Punkanen et al., 2014; Zubala, 2013), Table 7.1 summarizes the themes arising from previous research and offers

Table 7.1 The levels of rationale behind the chosen DMT method: Themes arising from a literature review on the DMT practice aiming at treating depression. The most essential aspect of each level is printed in bold.

METALEVEL
Mindfulness skills
Interconnectedness of the internal and external world
Verbal reflection of experiences
Integration
INTERACTIONAL LEVEL
Safety
Engagement
Responsiveness
Attunement – to oneself and between persons
BODY LEVEL
Grounding
Body boundaries
Movement improvisation
Expressive movement; movement narrative
Sensing the body and sensory perceptions in it; sensing breath

rationale for the choice of movement practices and themes in DMT aiming to help patients suffering from depression. The DMT treatment evolves in the context of embodiment. Embodiment can be encountered on three levels: 1) metalevel refers to the skills of *attending to information* that constitutes the embodiment in the present moment; 2) interactional level refers to the qualities that can *support secure attachment and pro-social behavior*; and 3) body level addresses the concrete movement activities which allow *stress modulation, build safety in the body*, and allow creative exploration, i.e. *dialogue in movement*.

The movement practices provide stimuli and experiences, explorations of variability. The action and interest toward how action is experienced develop the skill of attending to one's own embodied experience, which then, in a group setting, enables peer sharing and support. The essentials are safety, presence, and modulation in embodiment. These open up a potential space for learning new ways of relating to oneself, others, and action. The movement explorations and interaction in the group can be utilized to promote creatively problem-focused coping, social support seeking, and cognitive restructuring, which have been identified as the central behaviors that would support recovery from depression (McInnis et al., 2015).

Built on the experiences with the four DMT groups, which produced the material for the study of the impact of DMT on depression and body image (Pylvänäinen et al., 2015; Pylvänäinen & Lappalainen, 2017), a model of 12 x 90 mins weekly sessions was structured as an example of a possible flow of therapy process. These themes can be explored through various activities and communications, created in reciprocal resonance with the people in the group. This is where the creativity is needed and also, this is where the creativity sparks the process and offers insights. It makes the process unique to the group.

Table 7.2 An example model of a 12 × 90 min DMT group process flow for patients suffering from depression.

	Theme	*Process movement practices*
1	Introduction, start	Circular motion in joints. Improvisation with name gestures. With picture cards, expressing one's expectations of the DMT group.
2	Familiarizing with the space, moving, and collaboration	Exploring the space/room by moving in it in various ways and acknowledging the others. In a dyad, mirroring of each other's movement.
3	Safety and agency, playfulness	Recognizing how one directs attention: outwards, inwards. Sensing body boundaries. Moving with eyes open or closed. Exploring the spatial options in movement.
4	Playfulness, agency, finding different options	Exploring spine motility. Imagery & improvisation: If you were an animal, how would the animal move? In a circle, moving by holding hands.

	Theme	Process movement practices
5	Grounding, intuition, sensitivity	Activation of the body, starting from the feet. Playing with different movement qualities. Mindfulness skills and breathing: sensing one's walking.
6	Relieving achievement pressure	Sensing hands through different movements. Breathing exercises. Basic movement exercises allowing grounding and sensing the kinesthetic connections in the body structure. Mindfulness skills: breathing and seeing the other. Polarity: familiar and unfamiliar in movement.
7	Boundaries, distances, directions	Activating hands and breathing, sensing body boundaries, sensing center/core also with strength. Movement improvisation with a focus on near space, middle space, far space. Walking in a dyad and sensing the connection. Drawing a picture of one's experience.
8	Space for motion, boundaries, surfaces – balancing being and action	Self-nurturing movement and moving on the floor level. Basic movement exercises allowing grounding and sensing the kinesthetic connections in the body structure. Getting into vertical slowly and through different postures.
9	Emotion – acceptance and agency in one's life and in relation with environment/others	Movement improvisation from the words selected to express one's present state. Exploring earth, water, air and fire through movement improvisation – expressing and describing associated feelings.
10	What do I need – attention and focusing in action	In a dyad, hand massage. On a tape line, improvising movement in relation to the line; working with a partner who accompanies the movement in the way one asks for.
11	Accepting needs – nurturing, simplicity, freedom	Moving with breath, gradually engaging the whole body. Simple movement exercise (breath, clear movement pattern, a sense of opening/stretching, focusing). Requesting from a pair something one needs in movement and/or presence. Homework: to write a poem of one's experiences in this group.
12	Closure – what have I learnt?	Activating the body, grounding, being aware of the body. Simple movement exercise (same as in the session 11) Poems: sharing them, improvising movement on them. Feedback of the process.

Conclusions

DMT and creative arts therapies are seen here are interaction-based interventions: exploring the embodied experience in the here and now, in the encounter between patient(s), therapist, and the dance/movement. In this chapter, it is argued that the body image reflects depression in essential ways, and therapeutic work on body image helps to alleviate depression. A DMT model that is embodied and explores the concept of body image was proposed. The four essential factors to actively work on in DMT groups that aim to alleviate depression are the modulation of stress level, safety, interaction, and dialogue. It is argued that addressing these factors enables the therapy process and carries it on. As DMT techniques engage the sensory system, movement capacities, and attention, and they evoke creative responding in the interactional moment; it is possible to access and modulate the implicit and explicit patterns of responding that constitute the individual's ways of relating with the environment and the self. This can allow the individual to learn more flexible, reflective, and gratifying ways of relating, thus alleviating depression.

In the future, it will be interesting to study the application of this model with a larger sample of patients with depression participating in the DMT groups. The goal in this kind of study is to refine the understanding of the reverberatory links between body image and depression, and to develop more accessible and natural DMT- based practices to help people to cope with depression and to support their agency and their connectedness to themselves and others.

References

Bentzen, M. (2015). Dances of connection: Neuroaffective development in clinical work with attachment. *Body, Movement and Dance in Psychotherapy*, 10(4), 211–226. Retrieved from http://dx.doi.org/10.1080/17432979.2015.1064479.

Bermúdez, J. L., Marcel, A., & Eilan, N. (Eds.) (1995). *The body and the self.* Cambridge, MA: A Bradford Book.

Bifulco, A., Moran, P. M., Ball, C., & Bernazzani, O. (2002). Adult attachment style. I: Its relationship to clinical depression. *Social Psychiatry and Psychiatric Epidemiology*, 37, 50–59.

Bräuninger, I. (2014a). Specific dance movement therapy interventions – Which are successful? An intervention and correlation study. *Arts in Psychotherapy*, 41, 445–457. Doi: 10.1016/j.aip.2014.08.002.

Bräuninger, I.B (2014b). Dance movement therapy with the elderly: An international internet-based survey undertaken with practitioners. *Body, Movement and Dance in Psychotherapy*, 9(3), 138–153. Doi: 10.1080/17432979.2014.914977.

Campbell, J. (1995). The body image and self consciousness. In J. L. Bermúdez, A. M. & N. Eilan (Eds.), *The body and the self* (pp. 27–42). Cambridge, MA: The MIT (Massachusetts Institute of Technology) Press.

Casey, E. S. (1987). *Remembering: A phenomenological study*. Bloomington, IN: Indiana University Press.

Claxton, G. (2015). *Intelligence in the flesh: Why your mind needs your body much more than it thinks*. London: Yale University Press.

Cloninger, R. E. (2004). *Feeling good: The science of well-being*. New York: Oxford University Press.

Dosamantes, I. (1981). Experiencing movement in psychotherapy. *American Journal of Dance Therapy*, 4(2), 33–44.

Fogel, A. (2013). *Body sense: The science and practice of embodied self-awareness*. New York: W.W. Norton & Company, Inc.

Gallagher, S. (2005). *How the body shapes the mind*. New York: Oxford University Press.

Gibbs, R. W. (2005). *Embodiment and cognitive science*. New York: Cambridge University Press.

Gibson, J. J. (1966). *The senses considered as perceptual systems*. Boston MA: Houghton.

Hommel, B. (2015). The theory of event coding (TEC) as embodied-cognition framework. *Frontiers in Psychology*, 6, 1318. Doi: 10.3389/fpsyg.2015.01318.

Jaswal, S. (2016). Editorial: The balanced triad of perception, action, and cognition. *Frontiers in Psychology*, 7, 991. Doi: 10.3389/fpsyg.2016.00991.

Kandel, E. R. (2006). *In search of memory: The emergence of a new science of mind*. New York: W.W. Norton & Co.

Karkou, V., & Sanderson, P. (2006). *Arts therapies: A research based map of the field*. London: Elsevier Science Limited.

Koch, S. C., Caldwell, C., & Fuchs, T. (2013). On body memory and embodied therapy. *Body, Movement and Dance in Psychotherapy*, 8(2), 82–94. Doi: 10.1080/17432979.2013.775968.

Koch, S. C., Fuchs, T., Summa, M., & Müller, C. (Eds.) (2012). Body, metaphor and movement. *Advances in Consciousness Research* 84. Amsterdam: John Benjamins Publishing Company.

Levy, K. N., Ellison, W. D., Scott, L. N., & Bernecker, S. L. (2011). Attachment style. In J. C. Norcross (Ed.), *Psychotherapy relationships that work: Evidence based responsiveness* (2nd ed, pp. 377–401). New York: Oxford University Press.

Lin, Y., & Payne, H. (2014). The BodyMind Approach, medically unexplained symptoms and personal construct psychology. *Body, Movement and Dance in Psychotherapy*, 9(3), 154–166. Doi: 10.1080/17432979.2014.918563.

McInnis et al. (2015). The moderating role of an oxytocin receptor gene polymorphism in the relation between unsupportive social interactions and coping profiles: Implications for depression. *Frontiers in Psychology*, 6, 1133. Doi: 10.3389/fpsyg.2015.01133.

Meekums, B., Karkou, V., & Nelson, E. A. (2015). Dance movement therapy for depression. *Cochrane Database of Systematic Reviews*, (2), CD009895. Doi: 10.1002/14651858.CD009895.pub2.

Messina, I., et al. (2016). Abnormal default system functioning in depression: Implications for emotion regulation. *Frontiers in Psychology*, 7, 858. Doi: 10.3389/fpsyg.2016.00858.

Micali, S. (2013). The alteration of embodiment in melancholia. In R. T. Jensen & D. Moran (Eds.), *The phenomenology of embodied subjectivity* (vol. 71, pp. 203–219). Switzerland: Springer International Publishing.

Michalak, J., Burg, J. M. & Heidenreich, T. (2012). Mindfulness, embodiment, and depression. In S. C. Koch, T. Fuchs, M. Summa, & C. Müller (Eds.), *Body, metaphor and movement. Advances in Consciousness Research* 84 (pp. 393–413). Amsterdam: John Benjamins Publishing Company.

Mikulincer, M., & Shaver, P. R. (2007). *Attachment in adulthood: Structure, dynamics, and change*. New York: Guilford Press.

Nachmanovitch, S. (1990). *Free play: Improvisation in life and art*. New York: Tarcher/Putnam.

Pallaro, P. (1996). Self and body-self: Dance/movement therapy and the development of object relations. *The Arts in Psychotherapy*, 23(2), 113–119.

Panksepp, J. (1998). *Affective neuroscience: The foundations of human and animal emotions*. New York: Oxford University Press.

Papadopoulos, N. L. R., & Röhricht, F. (2014). An investigation into the application and processes of manualized group body psychotherapy for depressive disorder in a clinical trial. *Body, Movement and Dance in Psychotherapy*, 9(3), 167–180. Doi: 10.1080/17432979.2013.847499.

Punkanen, M., Saarikallio, S., & Luck, G. (2014). Emotions in motion: Short-term group form dance/movement therapy in the treatment of depression: A pilot study. *The Arts in Psychotherapy*, 41, 493–497. Doi: 10.1016/j.aip.2014.07.001.

Punkanen, M., Saarikallio, S., Leinonen, S. O., Forsblom, A., Kulju, K., & Luck, G. (2017). Emotions in motion: Depression in dance-movement and dance- movement in treatment of depression. In V. Karkou, S. Oliver & S. Lycouris (Eds.), *The Oxford handbook of dance and wellbeing*. Oxford: Oxford University Press.

Pylvänäinen, P. (2003). Body image: A tri-partite model for use in dance/movement therapy. *American Journal of Dance Therapy*, 25, 39–56.

Pylvänäinen, P. (2010). The dance/movement therapy group in a psychiatric outpatient clinic: explorations in body image and interaction. *Body, Movement and Dance in Psychotherapy*, 5(3), 219–230.

Pylvänäinen, P. (2012). Body memory as a part of the body image. In S. C. Koch, T. Fuchs, M. Summa, & C. Müller (Eds.), *Body, metaphor and movement: Advances in Consciousness Research* 84 (pp. 289–306). Amsterdam: John Benjamins Publishing Company.

Pylvänäinen, P., Muotka, J., & Lappalainen, R. (2015). A dance movement therapy group for depressed adult patients in a psychiatric outpatient clinic: effects of the treatment. *Frontiers in Psychology*, 6, 980. Doi: 10.3389/fpsyg.2015.00980.

Pylvänäinen, P., & Lappalainen, R. (2017). Change in body image among depressed adult outpatients after a dance movement therapy group treatment. The Arts in Psychotherapy, Doi: 10.1016/j.aip.2017.10.006.

Ratcliffe, M. (2013). The structure of interpersonal experience. In R. T. Jensen & D. Moran (Eds.), *The phenomenology of embodied subjectivity* (vol. 71, pp. 221–238). Switzerland: Springer International Publishing.

Rietveld, E. (2008). Situated normativity: The normative aspect of embodied cognition in unreflective action. *Mind*, 117(468); 973–1000.

Rietveld, E. (2013). Affordances and unreflective freedom. In R. T. Jensen & D. Moran (Eds.), *The phenomenology of embodied subjectivity: Contributions to phenomenology* (vol. 71, pp. 21–42). Switzerland: Springer International Publishing.

Röhricht, F., Papadopoulos, N. L. R., & Priebe, S. (2013). An exploratory randomized controlled trial of body psychotherapy for patients with chronic depression. *Journal of Affective Disorders*, 151, 85–91. Doi: 10.1016/j.jad.2013.05.056.

Sandel, S. L., Chaiklin, S., & Lohn, A. (Eds.) (1993). *Foundations of dance/movement therapy: The life and work of Marian Chase*. Columbia, MD: The Marian Chase Memorial Fund of American Dance Therapy Association.

Schachner, D., Shaver, P. R., & Mikulincer, M. (2005). Patterns of nonverbal behavior and sensitivity in the context of attachment relationships. *Journal of Nonverbal Behavior*, 29(3), 141–169. Doi: 10.1007/s10919–10005–14847-x.

Schore, A. N. (2012). *The science of the art of psychotherapy*. New York: W.W. Norton & Company.

Seikkula, J. (2011). Becoming dialogical: Psychotherapy of a way of life? *The Australian and New Zealand Journal of Family Therapy*, 32(3), 179–193.

Segal, Z. V., Williams, J. M. G., & Teasdale, J. D. (2002). *Mindfulness-based cognitive therapy for depression: A new approach to preventing relapse*. New York, NY: Guilford Press.

Sheets-Johnstone, M. (2009). *The corporeal turn: An interdiciplinary reader*. Exeter, UK: Imprint-Academic.

Siegel, D. J. (1999). *The developing mind: How relationships and the brain interact to shape who we are*. New York: The Guilford Press.

Siegel, D. J. (2007). *The mindful brain: Reflection and attunement in the cultivation of well-being*. New York: W.W. Norton & Company, Inc.

Slade, A. (2014). Imagining fear: Attachment, threat, and psychic experience, psychoanalytic dialogues. *The International Journal of Relational Perspectives*, 24, 3, 253–266. Doi: 10.1080/10481885.2014.911608.

Stötter, A., Mitche, M., Endler, P. C., Oleksy, P., Kamenscheck, D., Mosgoeller, W., & Haring, C. (2013). Mindfulness-based touch therapy and mindfulness practice in persons with moderate depression. *Body, Movement and Dance in Psychotherapy*, 8(3), 183–198. Doi: 10.1080/17432979.2013.803154.

Triberti, S., & Riva, G. (2016). Being present in action: A theoretical model about the "interlocking" between intentions and environmental affordances. *Frontiers in Psychology*, 6, 2052. Doi: 10.3389/fpsyg.2015.02052.

WHO (2016). *Global Health Estimates 2015: Burden of disease by cause, age, sex, by country and by region, 2000–2015*. Geneva: World Health Organization. www.who.int/healthinfo/global_burden_disease/estimates/en/index2.html.

Winnicott, D. W. (1971). *Playing and reality*. London: Routledge.

Witt, J. K. (2011). Action's effect on perception. *Current Directions in Psychological Science*, 20(3), 201–206.

Zubala, A. (2013). Description and evaluation of arts therapies practice with adults suffering from depression in the UK (PhD thesis). Queen Margaret University, Edinburgh.

Chapter 8

Reversing a sub-cultural norm

Art therapy in treating depression in prison inmates

David Gussak and Ashley Beck

Working as an art therapist in a prison many years ago, I found that depression always appeared to be a natural byproduct of a restrictive and degrading system. Often, as an inmate was questioned in his treatment team meetings, ultimately, among other complaints, he would admit that he was feeling depressed. While the team identified his other conditions and ailments as problematic-i.e., his delusional tendencies, irrational thoughts, organicity-like symptoms, paranoid developments, and heightened anxiety; the depression was viewed almost as a rational response. Quite frankly, the team reasoned, if he *wasn't* depressed, there might be more of a concern. Locked up in a tiny cell or crowded dorm, away from loved ones, stripped of identity and potential purpose in life, it would seem that depression was a sign of good mental health and awareness. He would then be prescribed antidepressants by the psychiatrist, signed up for various activities, and sent on his way.

However, after spending many years in various correctional settings, I have come to recognize just how cynical and misinformed my previous perspective was, and really how systemic and compounding the issue of depression is for the entire US prison system. As a result, I have come to focus on how art therapy can alleviate symptoms of depression for those in prison, and I have conducted a number of studies and theoretical explorations to see how and why such services impact those who suffer depression within the prison walls.

This chapter, co-authored with a current art therapy graduate student who has been focusing on art therapy within the correctional arena and has been interning in various forensic units, will provide an overview of the most prevalent issues confronting mental healthcare in the prison system, of which depression is quite pervasive. This chapter will provide a general summation of the benefits of art therapy in prison, the empirical studies that demonstrate the effectiveness of art therapy in reducing depression in male and female inmates, and a theoretical examination of why this might happen. This chapter will conclude with a call to arms on providing more comprehensive art therapy services to the prison population to reduce and mitigate this illness.

The criminalization of the mentally ill

To understand the difficulties in addressing depression, it is helpful to first understand the overall mental health challenges inside prisons. Prisons are becoming a bastion of mental health attention simply because, as a culture, we tend to criminalize the mentally ill (Gibbs, 1978).

> As a consequence, many of the mentally ill, particularly those who are poor and homeless, are unable to obtain the treatment they need . . . large numbers commit crimes and find themselves swept up into the burgeoning criminal justice system. Jails and prisons have become, in effect the country's front line mental health providers.
>
> (Human Rights Watch, 2003)

To compound the problem, understandably, the prison milieu continues to exacerbate the preexisting mental illnesses (Morgan, 1981). This includes, as previously indicated, major depression.

In 1994, Eyestone and Howell evaluated 102 inmates at different security levels, finding that 25% maintained symptoms of severe depression. Another 30% maintained depressive-like symptoms, but did not meet all of the standards of the then DSM-III-R (American Psychiatric Association, 1987) classification system used. More recent surveys reveal that about 23% of state prisoners and 30%of jail inmates reported symptoms of major depression (James & Glaze, 2006).[1] As a primary illness, depression may naturally emerge from the environmental surroundings, particularly from the limitations and restrictions placed upon the inmates, or it may secondarily emerge as a derivative of other mental and physical health challenges.

The compounding issues of depression in prison

Yet, while cynical members of society maintain that depression is a normal reaction to incarceration, long-term depressed inmates "can affect the prison community as a whole" (Boothby & Durham, 1999: 110). Depressed inmates may commit suicide, or self-abuse (Toch, 1992), and more depressed inmates inside may increase the proliferation of drugs and alcohol as a means to escape (Winfree et al., 1994). Such mental illnesses may be instead misidentified as behavioral problems; in particular, inmates may be perceived as resistant to reprogramming as they appear disinterested and uncommitted, resulting in further deterioration; possibly producing a vicious cycle (Torrey et al., 2014). Even still, there is a disproportionate amount of those with mental illness, including depression, placed in solitary confinement, once again compounding the very disease. Additionally, those who suffer accordingly are seen as weak and vulnerable and may be victimized by others within the system (Gussak, 1997a).

Aside from the human costs, the financial impact of taking care of mentally ill inmate populations includes requiring additional staff to monitor those who are depressed and possibly suicidal and providing the psychotropic medication administered to alleviate these mental illnesses (Baillargeon et al., 2002). Overall, there is a disproportionate rate of recidivism for those suffering from depression (Torrey et al., 2014).

Some would argue that mental health is being addressed within the prison system. In 2000, it was reported that 89% of public and private adult correctional facilities reported providing mental health services to their inmates. In fact, "fewer than 1.8% of all State inmates were held in facilities in which mental health services were not available" (Beck & Maruschak, 2001: 2). Despite the overwhelming empirical support that underscores the availability of mental health services in the correctional system, I have long argued that the types of therapy offered may not be the most advantageous (Gussak, 1997b, 2016).

Challenges for treatment in prison

Prison inmates cope with mental health issues differently than those outside the prison gates. Unfortunately, many times inmates most in need of services find it difficult to ask for help. They often do not know how or hold the belief that, for their own safety, they should not seek it. Oftentimes, staff view inmates who ask for help as manipulative, and fellow inmates view them as susceptible. Asking for help can be risky in an environment where survival of the fittest is the axiom and the weak are preyed upon (Gussak, 1997b). "Inmates with mental illness are the most vulnerable in our state prisons. They can be victimized by predatory inmates or untrained staff" (Warner, on-line article obtained 3/9/2005). As a result, inmates are constantly vigilant of their surroundings, knowing that how they are seen and what they say is always being evaluated by others. What seems harmless outside the prison system may have negative repercussions inside.

Consequently, there are major obstacles faced by therapists working with inmates (Gussak, 1997a, 2016). "There is an inherent mistrust for such verbal disclosure, and a well-grounded fear of prisoners taking advantage of others' voiced vulnerabilities; rigid defenses are built to achieve basic survival." (Fenner & Gussak, 2006: 414). Moreover, increased illiteracy, developmental or intellectual disability, and inability to verbally communicate make it difficult for prison inmates to give voice to the mental, emotional, and/or physical problems they experience (Fox, 1997; Gussak, 2016). Thus, admitting to a mental illness, the sadness of one's circumstances or an inability to adjust to the setting may be seen as an unfavorable or even impossible option.

Clearly, providing therapy is crucial. However, it is not nearly enough to provide treatment to inmates that suffer from psychiatric disorders. Equally important is protecting the inmate and not leaving him susceptible to being targeted.

He must adapt to his new subculture and learn that he may not be able to trust anyone, including, therapists.

> If a therapist tries to break through necessary barriers, the inmate/patient may become dangerous even if initially charming and cooperative. The inmate's defenses take over, making him anxious and angry, perhaps even violent, to a much greater extent . . . than clinicians are accustomed to with the general population.
>
> (Gussak, 1997a: 1)

In order to succeed, therapists need to be armed with tools that address these vulnerabilities without doing so verbally, considering the substantial difficulties and risks associated with verbal expression of emotional difficulties or mental illnesses. Art therapy has been effective in addressing the needs of the clients ultimately bypassing these survival-based defenses.

Art in prison

Creative expression is a natural byproduct of the prison subculture, emerging from the instinctual impulses, specifically aggression, sexuality, and the need for escape, already prevalent in the institutionally restrained and vapid environment (Fox, 1997). Dissanayake (1992) linked the need to express art through the libidinal impulses of sexuality and aggression through shared primal needs of expression, bonding, and release. For one to survive, even thrive, such impulses require attention. But, releasing those impulses in this subculture can have dire consequences, as they are seen as antithetical to the correctional mission of security. Contrarily, creative expression is more socially acceptable as a means to sublimate these primitive, instinctual, and, sometimes destructive reactions (Kramer, 1993; Rank, 1932; Rubin, 1984). The act of creating also allows the inmate to "escape" for a few moments or hours into his or her own created world; it provides a necessary diversion (Gussak, 1997b; Gussak & Cohen-Liebman, 2001; Hall, 1997). It is not a coincidence that early empirical studies examining the effectiveness of art therapy in prison populations demonstrated that art-making decreased the number of disciplinary reports written on inmates who participated in an Arts – in-Corrections program (Brewster, 1983) and recidivism (California Arts In Corrections, 1987). Thus, creating art may provide a safer, less visible outlet for inmates.

The benefits of art therapy in prison

Previous publications have emphasized the benefits of art therapy in prison (Gussak, 1997a, 2004, 2016; Gussak & Cohen-Liebman, 2001). As already discussed, making art allows the inmate to express their instinctual libidinal impulses, while those around him or her are none the wiser. In this sense, the hidden process becomes the core of the art therapy. It allows disclosure without vulnerability, helping the inmate express himself with little fear of retaliation in a manner that is valued by both the inside and outside culture. It provides a much-needed diversion and emotional escape. The process of creating can diminish pathological symptoms without verbal interpretation and provide an opportunity for the inmate to express himself, even if there are other restraints like illiteracy or diminished capacity. It can bypass certain conscious and unconscious defenses, including evasion and dishonesty; art cannot lie.

Just as significantly, it provides an opportunity for the inmate to create a new identity, above that of simply being an "inmate." In order for the institution to control their wards, they objectify them, making it easier to take away their basic human rights (Fox, 1997). By its very nature, creating art is humanizing. When an inmate creates art, it constructs a bridge between the inside and the outside, between those that control and those that are controlled. In a sense, it de-objectifies the inmate. This, in turn, provides the person the opportunity to rise above the label placed upon them by the culture at large; they are no longer merely an "inmate." Such changes create a safer environment for all those that comprise an institution and can facilitate the transition into society following release.

Art therapists have documented such advantages in various other correctional environments, not solely prison. These include juvenile justice settings (Bennink et al., 2003; Gussak & Ploumis-Devick, 2004) and jails (Day & Onorato, 1989, 1997). Much of the literature supports these benefits through case vignettes (Day & Onorato, 1989; Liebmann, 1994). However, while anecdotal information has long been available, empirical support on the benefits of art therapy in correctional settings has only recently surfaced.

Studying the effectiveness of art therapy in prison[2]

Pilot study

Beginning in 2003, a series of studies were conducted in various correctional institutions throughout the Northeast region of Florida. The summer of 2003 yielded a pilot study that was the first to quantify the effects of art therapy in prison (Gussak, 2004). This 4-week, 8-session study used a standardized art therapy assessment, the Formal Elements Art Therapy Scale (FEATS) (Gantt & Tabone, 1998), to evaluate a drawing (*The Person Picking an Apple from a Tree – [PPAT])* completed using standardized materials prior to and following the sessions. The FEATS is designed to evaluate the formal elements of a drawing; in other words, how a drawing is completed, not on its content. These elements include: prominence of color; color fit; implied energy; space; integration; logic; realism; problem-solving; developmental level; details; line quality; person; rotation; and perseveration. Each scale is measured along a Likert Scale with a manual that standardizes the measurement and score criteria. Various combinations of any of these 15 scales have been correlated with various diagnostic criteria: Schizophrenia, Depression, Mood disorder, Mania; and Organicity. As well, the assessment can be used to determine problem-solving. For example, if a drawing reflects unusual scores in space, implied energy, prominence of color and fit, realism, details, and person, then the person may be deemed depressed, such as seen in Figure 8.1.

In addition, surveys evaluating institutional resilience, behavior, problem-solving, and improved socialization, were developed and implemented by the primary researcher and facility's mental health counselor pre- and post-sessions to determine the changes in those receiving art therapy services (Gussak, 2004). Simple paired *t*-tests were implemented to compare the mean scores of the surveys and the FEATS scales to determine if indeed these results demonstrated significant differences of all those who participated.

The trajectory of the group sessions, made up of six–eight participants per group, followed a standard series of art-based directives; from simple to complex tasks, from individually focused directives to those that would be more group-oriented. For example, early directives might be a name embellishment (Figure 8.2) or white paper sculptures (Figure 8.3).

These were considered simple and individually-focused. As sessions advanced, the tasks would become gradually more complicated and require cooperation and negotiation, culminating in a group project such as a three-dimensional paper sculpture reflecting their "dream environment" [as seen in Figure 8.4] or mural.

These tasks were designed particularly to address the strengthening of identity, self-reliance, socialization, and problem-solving. These activities, in turn, were believed to assist in improving mood, focus, and cooperation.

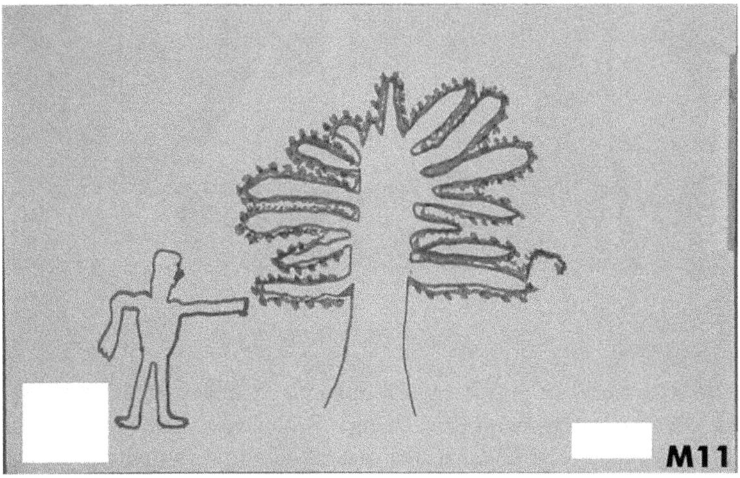

Figure 8.1

Figure 8.2

Figure 8.3

The post evaluations and drawings did indeed reflect change. Along with marked and statistically significant change in behavior, resilience, compliance, and socialization, the study revealed a marked improvement in mood. For example, Figure 8.5 is a PPAT drawing done by the same artist who did Figure 8.1 after the sessions were completed.

Figure 8.4

Figure 8.5

Follow up study

Due to the success of this pilot, a follow-up study was developed and conducted the following summer. Distinct changes in the methodology and delivery of services were implemented; while the therapeutic trajectory remained the same [simple to complex and individually-focused to group-oriented] new psychological assessment was used: the Beck Depression Inventory-Short Form [BDI-II] (Beck et al., 1974; Beck & Steer, 1993). This assessment, a 21-item self-report, has been found to be instrumental in measuring the change in mood of prison inmates (Boothby & Durham, 1999). As well, a control group was added; thus, the experimental group received eight weeks of sessions whereas the control group received none. Participants were randomly assigned to either the control or experimental group. After the study was over, those in control group also received future art therapy services.

Along with the FEATS, the BDI-II was administered to both the experimental and control groups before and after the eight-week period. If there were significant changes in the FEATS drawing categories that specifically revealed depression and problem-solving between the two drawings, and in the scores between the pre- and post-administered BDI-II, then it could be concluded that change in the participants' mood and problem-solving abilities occurred (Gussak, 2006). Simple paired *t*-tests were conducted to statistically demonstrate these changes in the quantitative scores. Despite a few inconsistencies outlined in the Gussak 2006 publication, the results yielded significant improvement in mood in the experimental group particularly as compared to those in the control.

Expanded studies

These successful findings led to two expanded studies conducted from 2006–2008. A number of changes occurred to augment the previous study. The studies were conducted in yet another men's prison; a woman's prison was also added (Gussak, 2009a). The number of sessions was increased from 8 to 15 over a 15-week period. Along with the FEATS and the BDI-II, another assessment tool was introduced: the Adult Nowicki-Strickland Locus of Control Scale (ANS) (Nowicki & Duke, 1974). Often used by the Department of Corrections, the ANS had, in the past, specifically been used to ascertain whether or not the participants had primarily an internal or an external locus of control (LOC) (Watt et al., 2000). Two hypotheses were created to expand upon the results obtained in the previous study: 1) if male inmates receive art therapy services, then they will exhibit marked improvement in mood, socialization, problem-solving abilities and locus of control within the correctional environment; and 2) if female inmates receive art therapy services, then they will exhibit marked improvement in mood, socialization, problem-solving abilities, and locus of control within the correctional environment. To be clear, improvement in locus of control indicates a shift from external to internal LOC.

Group art activities with both the men and women followed the same therapeutic trajectory as the previous studies – tasks gradually increased in complexity, from individually focused to group focused. Once again, participants in both settings were randomly assigned to an experimental group and a control group. As before, they received the same assessments over the same designated period as the experimental group members. The assessments (i.e. the FEATS, BDI-II and the ANS) were administered before and after the 15-week period in which the art therapy sessions were provided, to both the control and experimental groups.

The results yielded significant yet curious outcomes. Indeed, there were greater amounts of significant change when comparing the mean score of the pre-tests to the post-tests in depression and LOC in the experimental group as compared to the control group, with both the men and the women. Yet, an unintended outcome emerged. Both the men and women demonstrated change, however, it appeared, based on the difference of means, that the women changed more drastically than the men. In other words, it seemed that they developed a significantly better mood and more internal LOC. Thus, an additional hypothesis was added to examine this apparent anomaly:

> Although both male and female inmates will exhibit marked improvement, the male inmates will exhibit different responses to the art therapy services in mood and locus of control than female inmates within their respective correctional environments.

As first revealed, statistically, this final hypothesis was supported: the female inmate population demonstrated more marked change in LOC and mood than the male inmate population. While both the men's and women's respective groups ended the sessions with similar scores on the measurement tools, the women exhibited scores that reflected greater depression and external locus of control than their male counterparts *prior* to receiving treatment (Gussak, 2009a, 2009b). Upon deeper examination, the results were even more revealing.

The comparison between male and female inmates

While the statistical analysis of the BDI-II and the ANS demonstrated that the women improved more than the men in both mood and LOC, the final average scores on the various assessments administered were fairly similar. The study revealed that the *pre-test* assessments were dramatically different – the women's scores in both mood and LOC were considerably lower [and external, in the case of the LOC] prior to receiving the services than those of the men. In other words, the assessments revealed that the women were significantly more depressed and demonstrated more of an external LOC than their male counterparts.

This analysis supported the literature stating that female inmates may be more susceptible to depression than their male counterparts (Harris, 1993). It is understood that men do indeed experience depression; however, as Butterfield (2003) indicated, women, particularly female inmates, are more likely to experience – and be adversely effected – by this mood disorder. In addition, women were seen as potentially more influenced by external factors such as familial and societal interactions and expectations, revealed through a more external LOC (DeWolfe et al., 1988; Zingraf, 1980). This seems to coincide with the types of crimes women commit.

It is likely that women are more provoked toward crime as a reaction to domestic and sexual abuse; this, in turn, may result in retaliatory and defensive assaults against their partners or abusers. It is possible they may also be more pressured or compelled by a loved one to commit a crime or feel that they must do so to protect their family. Male inmates may have committed more crimes that were more personally and independently driven and focused; in other words, while both genders' crimes are a result of poor impulse control, the men may be less influenced by others to commit their crime than the women. Even when a man is coerced or pressured to commit a crime by another, or *because* of another, he would be less likely to admit that the decision was beyond his control [unless, of course, claiming such a reason would reduce his sentence]. Thus, while a man's crimes are prone to be a consequence of particular social interactions (Gussak, 2009a), they are liable to be less so than a woman's.

Once imprisoned, female inmates may be considered by others to be more dependent. Eventually, such labels and considerations may be internalized, paradoxically revealing itself as an external LOC. However, male inmates are less likely, given the cultural expectations inside, to exhibit such a dependent and perceived weakness.

Also, notably significant for this chapter, the female inmates are likely to show greater rates of depression than the male inmates as a result of the social and maternal difficulties female inmates experience by being sent to prison. Women may also be more willing to admit struggling with depression, as they are more likely than the men to receive empathy and emotional support from the others inside.

This naturally translated to changes in the pre- and post-test scores on the BDI-II and ANS (Gussak, 2009a) with the female inmates demonstrating a greater range of change. This may support the notion that the women may prefer alternative therapies, and thus they may be more responsive to creative approaches such as art therapy.

Indeed, both the men and women responded positively to the approach; yet they differed in response. The male inmates seemed to focus on the final product whereas the women seemed content with creating the art piece with less consideration for what it was they created. This could be due to the men's natural competitive tendencies compelling them to produce what they saw as good art. While the women did care about the final piece, even going so far as to compliment each other on their work, the women did not compare the quality of their products with each other. In addition, the women used the art-making process as an impetus for empathic discussion.

> In other words, while the men may have realized that they needed to interact with one another in order to succeed in creating a final product, the women seemed content simply with the interactions, drawing energy from the group cohesiveness and socialization, with the final piece of secondary importance.
>
> (Gussak, 2009b: 205)

In addition, while the women's pre-test scores revealed greater depression and a more external LOC, the post-test scores between the men and women were actually quite similar. "By the end of the sessions, the men and women may have been exhibiting, on average, near-similar levels of mood and internal LOC; the women just had further to rise" (p. 205), empirically demonstrating greater improvement.

Overall, as these previous studies revealed, despite the apparent differences, the men and women in prison did indeed benefit from art therapy in improving mood. The following section will reevaluate some of the guiding theoretical constructs of how art therapy benefits an inmate population outlined earlier in the chapter and provide a brief argument on what is it about the art and art therapy that makes it so effective.

The why

The previous sections argued that art therapy is beneficial in changing prison inmates' mood. While such studies answer the "what" and the "how,", it does not necessarily explain the why. The following rationales on why art and art therapy may change mood within the prison setting draws from previous understandings used by clinicians to approach and develop particular goals in addressing depression as a treatable mental illness.

Throughout a therapeutic experience, clinicians identify negative or distorted thinking patterns that may contribute to feelings of hopelessness and helplessness, which frequently worsen depressive symptoms. In turn, therapists often help clients restructure these learned thoughts and behaviors. Clinicians may focus on helping those suffering from depression recover a sense of control, in turn regaining a pleasure in life (Pardini et al., 2014). Tailoring these steps to overcome depressive symptoms for those stuck within the confines of the prison settings may seem antithetical – changing such hopeless thoughts, regaining a sense of control, and recognizing positive aspects of life within the limitations imposed by the correctional institution seems nigh impossible. Yet, drawing upon years of theoretical and epistemological considerations on the benefits of art therapy in prison, such aims are indeed within reach. As a result, four specific points emerge on why art therapy may help prison inmates address and cope with depression.

While prison strips away the inmates' identity and sense of self, art and art therapy allows them to re-establish an identity above that of inmate

As underscored above, prisons dehumanize the inmate population in order to control them. One of the ways prisons control their populations is by objectifying the inmates – it is easier to control those who are seen as inferior or subhuman (Fox, 1997). Essentially, they are stripped of their identity, labeled with numbers, all required to wear the same clothes. They are seen as nothing; and while valuable for instituting security, such dynamics are detrimental to change and mental health, and can stand in the way of true rehabilitation. What eventually emerges is a person who either rebels against such treatment, becoming violent, aggressive and/or manipulative, or one who develops a sense of apathy, distance, and depression. Eventually an inmate may continue to feel beaten down, resulting in a tendency to become withdrawn and downtrodden: depressed.

Art provides an opportunity to reinforce individual identity and sense of self (Gussak, 2006); it may even provide an opportunity to re-define themselves. As one inmate stated, "I still have something to contribute." To ultimately cause a positive transformation or change, the inmates, through art-making, may be able to "remain human in an inhuman environment" (Brown, 2002: 28). One of the most challenging roles of a therapist within the institution is to assist the inmate in rising above the detrimental labels imposed on him, and to eventually buck the system by developing a distinct and unique identity capable of thriving independently. In so doing, the very factors that can contribute to depression can be alleviated, even removed. A sense of identity and worth, even pleasure, can help alleviate the depressive symptoms pervasive in the institution. What emerges, then, is a connection with those outside this primitive subculture. This leads to the next benefit.

Art provides a connectedness, a bridge between the outside and inside culture, underscoring for those outside that those inside are indeed real people

Those inside are oftentimes dehumanized and forgotten by the outside culture. As well, their societal and familial relationships are put on hold, and at times, denied, making them even further removed. Such barriers from their loved ones diminish their sense of belonging. When these roles are diminished, the inmate is likely to have overpowering feelings of helplessness and hopelessness, a sense of disengagement and loss. However, what can emerge through art therapy is that the inmates learn to re-engage with others, develop new societal roles that can continue to be reinforced and reflected through their art, and in a sense, develop a new self-[re]creation. During this process the inmate can reconcile lost meaning and correspondence with the outside world in the therapeutic environment.

In a much more pragmatic sense, whereas the inmate is locked inside, their art may "exit" the walls. Such art, when viewed by others, reflects the very humanity of the creator. In turn, this allows societal members to recognize those who create inside as real people, those with a purpose, those with an opportunity to contribute to the greater culture. As a result, some of the factors that cause loss of self-worth and depression may be reversed. For example, in 2008, the Florida Department of Cultural Affairs hosted a gallery show of inmate art. Those inmates whose artwork was to be exhibited expressed feelings of engagement and value; family members of the inmates whose work was on display reflected how proud they were. Community members, who would otherwise not acknowledge the marginalized members of their own society, marveled at the creations on the walls. The art became a mediator and mirror for those inside, thus allowing a connection between the two cultures.

I had an opportunity to co-present with Piper Kerman, author of the book *Orange is the New Black*, on the value of art and creativity in prison. She indicated that her fellow inmates would often make arts and crafts inside. This was more than a mere distraction; she reflected that this would often provide a sense of value and worth, and contemplated how the women's mood would brighten when their work was accepted by others, inside and out. It reminded the women that they were not forgotten; they were reminded that they were human.

Art-making process provides a means to sublimate and channel the very impulses and emotions that can cause depression

Previous publications have underscored that art can be used to sublimate the aggressive and violent tendencies that emerge as a natural byproduct of the prison subculture (Gussak, 1997b, 2006, 2016). As well, art-making may provide a means to sublimate and channel the very impulses and emotions that can also cause depression. Sublimation, much more advanced and complex than catharsis, is a psychic phenomenon that allows for the socially productive manifestation of harmful acts and ideas by displacing and neutralizing the negative drive. It does so by symbolizing and identifying the undesirable energy, in turn integrating it through a creative process or activity (Kramer, 1993). While the aftermath of cathartic expression may result in a loss of self-worth or anxiety, sublimating negative emotions and impulses assists an inmate in regulating the sentiments that contribute to depression. In other words, an inmate that demonstrates his anxiety, fear, or aggression through harming someone or himself may feel a sense of loss, emptiness, and shame after. However, if such emotions are expressed and contained through the art, a sense of resolution and accomplishment emerges. There is a sense of mastery, of control, over the negative impulses contributing to the detrimental feelings.

In addition, when this artistic expression is accepted by others, the inmate comes to feel more accepted and validated. As a result, his own concept of true self is strengthened as he sees himself as an individual within a productive societal context rather than dependent on an illicit one (Gussak, 2016). Art reinstates a sense of control and provides an avenue to feel valued and in charge.

Art-making facilitates socialization

Providing art therapy groups directly seeks to reverse one of the behaviors resultant of depression: self-isolation. Fostering a new context for socialization and positive regard from others may reverse depressive symptoms as inmates relearn positive communication techniques. For example, in 2008, a mural program was established through the Florida Department of Corrections, and the inaugural project was conducted in a prison in North Florida. Through the process, the inmates who completed the 22 x 47 foot painting on the side of one of the prison buildings facing the public parking lot, learned to negotiate and developed positive self-regard and social skills. The group was in charge of conceptualizing and planning the mural as well as executing its creation on a wall (Argue et al., 2009).

This was the first of several such projects. Many of those selected to participate in the projects were identified as having depression. In such large-scale ventures, participants learned how to demonstrate mutual respect for the contributions of each member and effectively give and receive constructive criticism from their group members. Ultimately, what materialized was a greater sense of pride in their work and accomplishment, positive social relationships and ultimately a positive self-regard. This, in turn, alleviated and mitigated depressive symptoms by providing a sense of community, an opportunity for expression, and an engagement in a project deemed worthwhile by the institution and the outside culture.

Caveat – a call to arms

While depression is a detrimental and debilitating illness in greater society, it is pervasive and overwhelming inside constrictive prison walls. In such an environment, the admittance of an illness, a perceived weakness, may be taken advantage of and mark someone as an easy target. Thus, mitigating these symptoms, improving one's mood and removing the impediments that cause diminished functioning, must occur beyond traditional verbal counseling practices.

Art therapy has been demonstratively instrumental in working behind an imposed mask to alleviate depression in male and female inmates successfully.

However, while this chapter provides empirical support for the benefits of art therapy with depressed inmates, and it ruminates on why this likely occurs, more work needs to be done. Over the years, there seems to have been a marked increase in the number of artists and art therapists who provide such services in the prison system, several of whom have made their work known. It is not enough. It is important that we continue to reach out to the prison and correctional communities to invoke the power of art in reversing the negative symptoms that the environment compounds and continue to conduct research and publish findings on how art with prison inmates can be beneficial to both the inside and outside cultures.

While depression may indeed be a natural by-product in the prison, it does not have to be a passively accepted response to the experience. Art therapy can provide an opportunity to reverse the debilitating effects of depression and provide a hopeful option for the inmate to rise above the weight of this illness.

Notes

1 To differentiate, in the US a jail is often run by a county or local law enforcement agency. Inmates are placed in jail for a short duration, to either await trial or sentencing. Prisons are run by the state or federal systems, and inmates are placed in these facilities to complete the sentence received, usually for a much longer duration.

2 Further details of the empirical statistics and methodology can be found in [First Author's] works listed in the References section.

References

American Psychiatric Association (1987). *Diagnostic and statistical manual of mental disorders* (3rd ed., revised). Washington, DC: Author.

Argue, J., Bennett, J., & Gussak, D. (2009). Transformation through negotiation: Initiating the inmate mural arts program. *The Arts in Psychotherapy*, 36(5), 313–319. Doi: 10.1016/j.aip.2009.07.005.

Baillargeon, J., Black, S. A., Contreras, S., Grady, J., & Pulvino, J. (2002). Anti-depressant prescribing patterns among prison inmates with depressive disorders. In *National Criminal Justice Reference Service*. Washington, DC: U.S. Department of Justice.

Beck, A. T., & Maruschak, L. M. (2001, July). Mental health treatment in state prisons, 2000. *Bureau of Justice Statistics-Special Report*, (1–8).

Beck, A. T., Rial, W. Y., & Rickets, K. (1974). Short form of depression inventory: Cross-validation. *Psychological-Reports*, 34(3), 1184–1186.

Beck, A. T., & Steer, R. A. (1993). *Beck Depression Inventory Manual*. New York, NY: Harcourt Brace.

Bennink, J., Gussak, D., & Skowran, M. (2003). The art therapists' roles as primary therapists in a juvenile justice setting. *The Arts in Psychotherapy*, 30(3), 163–173.

Boothby, J. L., & Durham, T. W. (1999). Screening for depression in prisoners using the Beck depression inventory. *Criminal Justice and Behavior*, 26(1), 107–124.

Brewster (1983). *An evaluation of the arts-in-corrections program of the California Department of Corrections*. San Jose: San Jose State University.

Brown, M. (2002). *Insider art*. Winchester, UK: Waterside Press.

Butterfield, F. (2003, October 22). Study finds hundreds of thousands of inmates mentally ill. *New York Times*. Retrieved April 21, 2008, from http://query.nytimes.com.

California Arts in Corrections (1987). *Research synopsis on parole outcomes for Arts-in-Corrections participants paroled December, 1980–February, 1987*. Sacramento, CA: Author.

Day, E., & Onorato, G. (1989). Making art in a jail setting. In H. Wadeson, J. Durkin, & D. Perach (Eds.), *Advances in art therapy*, (126–147). New York: Wiley.

Day, E. S., & Onorato, G. T. (1997). Surviving one's sentence: Art therapy with incarcerated trauma survivors. In D. Author & E. Virshup (Eds.), *Drawing time: Art therapy in prisons and other correctional settings* (pp. 127–152). Chicago, IL: Magnolia Street Publishers.

DeWolfe, T. E., Jackson, L. E., & Winterberger, P. (1988). A comparison of moral reasoning and moral character in male and female incarcerated felons. *Sex Roles*, 18(9–10), 583–593.

Dissanayake, E. (1992). *Homoaestheticus: Where art comes from and why*. New York, NY: The Free Press.

Eyestone, L. L., & Howell, R. J. (1994). An epidemiological study of attention-deficit hyperactivity disorder and major depression in a male prison population. *Bulletin of the American Academy of Psychiatry and the Law*, 22, 181–193.

Fenner, L., & Gussak, D. (2006). Therapeutic boundaries in a prison setting: A dialogue between an intern and her supervisor. *The Arts in Psychotherapy*, 33, 414–421.

Fox, W. M. (1997). The hidden weapon: Psychodynamics of forensic institutions. In D. Gussak & E. Virshup (Eds.), *Drawing time: Art therapy in prisons and other correctional settings* (pp. 43–55). Chicago, IL: Magnolia Street Publishers.

Gantt, L., & Tabone, C. (1998). *The formal elements art therapy scale: The rating manual*. Morgantown, WV: Gargoyle Press.

Gibbs, J. J. (1978). Stress and self-injury in jail. Unpublished doctoral dissertation, State University of New York, Albany, NY.

Gussak, D. (1997a). The ultimate hidden weapon: Art therapy and the compromise option. In D. Gussak & E. Virshup (Eds.), *Drawing time: Art therapy in prisons and other correctional settings* (pp. 59–74). Chicago, IL: Magnolia Street Publishers.

Gussak, D. (1997b). Breaking through barriers: Advantages of art therapy in prison. In D. Gussak & E. Virshup (Eds.), *Drawing time: Art therapy in prisons and other correctional settings* (pp. 1–12). Chicago, IL: Magnolia Street Publishers.

Gussak, D. (2004). Art therapy with prison inmates: A pilot study. *The Arts in Psychotherapy*, 31(4), 245–259.

Gussak, D. (2006). The effects of art therapy with prison inmates: A follow-up study. *The Arts in Psychotherapy*, 33, 188–198.

Gussak, D. (2007). The effectiveness of art therapy in reducing depression in prison populations. *International Journal of Offender Therapy and Comparative Criminology*, 5(4), 444–460.

Gussak, D. (2009a). Comparing the effectiveness of art therapy on depression and locus of control of male and female inmates. *The Arts in Psychotherapy*, 36(4), 202–207.

Gussak, D. (2009b). The effects of art therapy on male and female inmates: Advancing the research base. *The Arts in Psychotherapy*, 36(1), 5–12.

Gussak, D. E. (2016). Art therapy in the prison milieu. In D. Gussak & M. Rosal (Eds.), The *Wiley-Blackwell handbook of art therapy* (pp. 478–486). Oxford, UK: Wiley-Blackwell Publishers.

Gussak, D., & Cohen-Liebman, M. S. (2001). Investigation vs. intervention: Forensic art therapy and art therapy in forensic settings. *The American Journal of Art Therapy*, 40(2), 123–135.

Gussak, D., & Ploumis-Devick, E. (2004). Creating wellness in forensic populations through the arts: A proposed interdisciplinary model. *Visual Arts Research*, 29(1), 35–43.

Hall, N. (1997). Creativity and Incarceration: The purpose of art in a prison culture. In D. Gussak & E. Virshup (Eds.), *Drawing time: Art therapy in prisons and other correctional settings* (pp. 25–41). Chicago, IL: Magnolia Street Publishers.

Harris, J. W. (1993). Comparison of stressors among female vs. male inmates. *Journal of Offender Rehabilitation*, 19(1/2), 43–56.

Human Rights Watch (2003). Rates of incarceration of the mentally ill. Ill-Equipped: U.S. prisons and offenders with mental illness. Retrieved from www.hrw.org/reports/2003/usa1003/index.htm.

James, D. J., & Glaze, L. E. (2006, September). *Mental health problems of prison and jail inmates* (NCJ No. 213600). Washington, DC: Bureau of Justice Statistics.

Kramer, E. (1993). *Art as therapy with children* (2nd ed.). Chicago, IL: Magnolia Street Publishers.

Liebmann, M. (Ed.). (1994). *Art therapy with offenders*. London: Jessica Kingsley.

Morgan, C. (1981). Developing mental health services for local jails. *Criminal Justice & Behavior*, 8(3), 259–262.

Nowicki, S., & Duke, M. (1974). A locus of control scale for noncollege as well as college adults. *Journal of Personality Assessment*, 38, 136–137.

Pardini, J., Scogin, F., Schriver, J., Domino, M., Wilson, D., & LaRocca, M. (2014). Efficacy and process of cognitive bibliotherapy for the treatment of depression in jail and prison inmates. *Psychological Services*, 11(2), 141–152. Doi: 10.1037/a0033378.

Rank, O. (1932). *Art and artist*. New York, NY: W.W. Norton.

Rubin, J. A. (1984). *The art of art therapy*. New York, NY: Brunner/Mazel Publishing.

Toch, H. (1992). *Mosaic of despair: Human breakdowns in prison*. Washington, DC: American Psychological Association.

Torrey, E. F., Zdanowicz, M., Kennard, A., Lamb, H. R., Eslinger, D., Biasotti, M. & Fuller, D. (2014). *The treatment of persons with mental illness in prisons and jails: A state survey*. Arlington, VA: Treatment Advocacy Center.

Warner, G. (n.d.). Do mentally ill inmates have access to adequate care? Retrieved March 9, 2005, from www.naminycmetro.org/inmate_healthcare.htm.

Watt, M. C., Frausin, S., Dixon, J., & Nimmo, S. (2000). Moral intelligence in a sample of incarcerated females. *Criminal Justice and Behavior*, 27(3), 330–355.

Winfree, L. T., Jr., Mays, G. L., Crowley, J. E., & Peat, B. J. (1994). Drug history and prisonization: Toward understanding variations in inmate institutional adaptations. *International Journal of Offenders Therapy and Comparative Criminology*, 38, 281–295.

Zingraff, M. T. (1980). Inmate assimilation: A comparison of male and female delinquents. *Criminal Justice and Behavior*, 7, 275–292.

Chapter 9

Music therapy clinical practice and research for people with depression

Music, brain processing and music therapy

Helen Odell-Miller, Jörg Fachner and Jaakko Erkkilä

Introduction

It is a startling fact that recently the World Health Organisation (WHO, 2016) declared that 350 million people of all ages suffer from depression. That is, clinically diagnosed depression; more severe than ordinary mood changes in response to daily life events, common to most people. Serious depression can affect our ability to work and to live life normally. Most surprising is that until the last decade little attention has been paid by music therapists to prioritising music therapy and depression from a clinical and research perspective. It is surprising, considering music's powerful capacity to change mood and music therapists' training and expertise in working with affect through musical interaction. Our view is that recently the picture is changing. This chapter provides an overview of current music therapy research, including brain research, supported by clinical practice and case studies, illustrating how music therapy works for people with depression and what is unique in this therapeutic approach.

As researchers and clinicians, we are interested in applying results of research to clinical work, and also to demonstrating how research springs from clinical work. There is a need to investigate more fully phenomena such as: how are language and music differentiated in their functions? What might be happening emotionally, physically, intellectually and socially if in a group, during a music therapy session for a person with depression?

Overview of research: approaches, models and techniques

Music therapy includes group and individual active and receptive (listening-focussed) music therapy techniques. It can assist with shifts in mood states, motivation and connectedness, and meaning (H. Odell-Miller, 2014). For example, a person with depression might develop a sense of active listening in a music therapy session, which in turn could move into musical interaction using musical instruments and singing, which later could be a focus for reflection upon the capacity for increased motivation, mood change and change in self-perception. A patient playing a wind instrument (recorder) might improvise with the therapist, who plays a musical accompaniment with keyboard, whilst listening, enabling the patient to find her own voice.

There is little literature and only a few randomised controlled trials (RCT) specifically focussing upon depression in mainstream adult mental health services (Albornoz, 2011; Erkkilä et al., 2011), which support anecdotal case-study findings that music therapy can reduce symptoms of depression. Whilst Albornoz (2011) studied the effects on depression of individual music therapy for adolescents and adults with substance abuse issues, Erkkilä et al. (2011) studied the effects of individual music therapy with adults suffering from depression. Albornoz's (2011) study was a small trial with 24 people randomised to twelve sessions of music therapy and standard care, or standard care alone. Significant differences were found between groups of observer-rated depression (but not self rated), with greater improvements seen in the music therapy group.

The larger study (n = 79) (Erkkilä et al., 2011) investigated individual free musical improvisation and standard care (which included sessions of psychotherapy, psychiatric counselling and medication, and standard care alone), for ten weeks, with music therapy delivered twice a week. Dual diagnosis and bi-polar disorder were not included, and adults were living in the community. At three month follow up patients receiving music therapy and standard care showed greater (statistically significant) improvement in depression anxiety and general functioning compared to the control group, who received standard care only. Improvements were also seen in alexithymia and quality of life sustained at six month follow up, but these were not statistically significant. Findings from the Cochrane Review (Maratos et al., 2008) suggest that music therapy is accepted by people with depression and is associated with improvements in mood. The conclusion called for high-quality trials evaluating the effectiveness of music therapy in depression, and these two studies are responding to the review. Recently, a new RCT trial was published (Porter et al., 2017), showing that active improvisational music therapy can also be beneficial for adolescents in reducing depression and raising self esteem.

For non-unipolar populations, such as those in prison, who are likely to also suffer from personality disorder and other mental illness, a research study (n = 200) with male prisoners in China found that music therapy reduced depressive symptoms (Chen, 2014; Chen et al., 2015). Results showed that group music therapy was effective for promoting offenders' self-esteem, anxiety, depression and social functioning. Effects of music therapy increased with the number of sessions. No significant effect was found in the comparison of different music therapy approaches and this aspect now needs further inquiry.

Carr et al. (2017) are running a UK NIHR (National Institute of Health Research) funded study; specifically looking at the effects of group music therapy using song writing and active improvisation; in a feasibility RCT trial for adults with long-term depression living in the community. This follows on from Carr et al. (2013) suggesting that community-based music therapy groups using active music-making for adults living at home with depression are needed. Moreover Carr's previous research (Carr, 2014; Carr et al., 2012) and other anecdotal case studies suggest that in addition to free improvisation using a psychoanalytically-informed approach (Odell-Miller, 2002; Odell-Miller, 2007), people with mental health problems including those with depression, may benefit from focussed music therapy approaches such as using song-writing and structured improvisation where the end product or aesthetic outcome are satisfying and helpful.

Odell-Miller's (2007) mixed methods study explored the nature of why and how music therapists link what they do to diagnosis. The unique aspects of how 23 music therapists worked across five established European music therapy services in psychiatric settings, was examined, using a purposive sampling survey. For people with depression, themes such as symbolic work, links between low self-esteem and the importance or not of the performance element in music therapy, emerged. Specific points were made that were different to those for people with psychosis. One centre with specialist training in a client-centred approach suggested that music structures should not be imposed, and may arise from the therapist's anxieties: as a result, patients may not feel properly understood. In contrast, Carr et al. (2017) recently found that a sense of musical structure in groups was reassuring, leading to the belief that there is more work to be done in this area.

Odell-Miller's (2007) study found that psychoanalytic symbolically-focussed approaches for people with depression were preferred; emphasising the importance of using counter-transference, to address issues. Not working in the counter-transference especially in individual work, could avoid working with the depression itself; thus reinforcing avoidance which is a common symptom of depression. Current psychological treatment for depression in the UK recommended by NICE (National Institute for Clinical Excellence) (NICE, 2016) is short-term cognitive behaviour therapy (CBT), but in 2017 guidelines will include psychodynamic therapies and couples therapy which could add to the argument that psychoanalytic approaches to music therapy may be useful. The emphasis upon CBT in the past may be partly because more studies with large numbers have been carried out with CBT, rather than looking at psychoanalytic approaches in the psychological therapies, including music therapy and depression. In the UK most recently, short-term therapy as delivered by Access to Psychological Treatments (IAPT) are found to have only temporary effect for some (NHS, 2017). Non-verbal emotionally accessible methods such as music therapy and other arts therapies are therefore indicated.

The literature emphasises an active engagement in music making, as people with depression need to actively drive forward the musical process, themselves. Moving in and out of music and words can encourage links with thoughts and feelings and enable resistances to be addressed. Previously, Odell-Miller (2002) demonstrated how powerful emotional, psychological and physical components of free improvisation can reveal the patient's inner world. The music therapy improvisational relationship, linked to verbal interpretation, was a strong tool for therapeutic change and for lifting depressive symptoms.

Opinion was divided in the research study about whether people with depression benefit from passive aspects of music, such as directed music – listening or listening with the therapist. Working symbolically, using role-play and 'as if' techniques were important, and as much use of music to encourage spontaneity as possible was stressed in individual work. In addition, points were made that free musical improvisation enabled people to face difficulties, as it was easier to tolerate deficits when improvising, than when using composed music.

Interestingly, no centres used group Guided Imagery in Music (GIM), a receptive technique where people listen to music and associate to images which emerge during the process, guided by the therapist; and only one centre used it for individual work. However, Meadows (2002), in his overview of the use of GIM for people with depression, cites four case studies (Bush, 1988; Holligan, 1992; Walker, 1993; Weiss, 1994) and suggests that in general GIM in these cases is used in order to 'lessen defences and help the client enter into unconscious psychic material' (p. 194). Meadows (2002) also draws attention to the different approaches therapists take to focussing upon imagery, either as a way of helping to create images of depression, or to help stabilise symptoms and therefore, not focus so much upon using imagery to confront the depression. Further evidence for GIM and its effect for depression can be found in McKinney and Honig (2016). Notably, GIM is so little used in the centres in this study, implying that in many European trainings, GIM training is not prevalent, or non-existent. Therapists appear unaware of the literature about its use. In some countries, such as in Scandinavia, GIM training for music therapists is becoming more frequent, and in the UK just starting to grow.

Erkkilä et al. (2011) used Improvisational Psychodynamic Music Therapy (IPMT) (Erkkilä et al., 2012). Only mallet instruments, djembe drums and electronic drums were employed. Therapist and client had identical instruments to ensure equal expressive possibilities between the improvisers. Later on, the name of the model was changed to Integrative Improvisational Music Therapy (IIMT), in line with changing trends in modern psychotherapeutic models; thus, reflecting influences from relational and integrative approaches, rather than purely from psychoanalytic thinking. The RCT study (Erkkilä et al., 2011) consisted of 20 twice-weekly sessions, 60 minutes each, for three months. Although psychodynamic thinking still forms the ground for the IIMT, approaches such as Resource Orientated Music Therapy (Rolvsjord, 2010) and supportive psychotherapy, which integrates psychodynamic, cognitive-behavioural and interpersonal views (Winston et al., 2004), have been incorporated. In short, integrative psychotherapy (Norcross & Goldfried, 2005), or psychoanalytically-informed music therapy (Odell-Miller, 2001), best describes the versatile theoretical background of IIMT, because music itself is a flexible and complex phenomenon, not easily linked to only one specific theoretical model.

Considerations around music and spoken language

In Figure 9.1 different experience-based core meanings are described, as they are understood in IIMT. Whilst music as a phenomenon represents an earlier, more comprehensive and penetrable world than spoken language, such as prosody, these two forms of basic communication have a common interface. Prosody refers to the musical features of speech (Fernald, 1989), where an adult talks to the baby, who cannot yet talk. So, a further question is about the meanings beyond language. For instance, the melody of speech may carry the most important message instead of the content of speech. Elsewhere researchers have found that when adults are talking to infants, speech is characterized with specific emotionality; that is the manner in which the adult is using their voice. However, for adult to adult conversation, the emotionality of speech is more repressed (Trainor et al., 1997). This shows that language becomes more abstract along with the increase of verbal skills and, thus, diverges from its musical root, and from embodied cognition. It is clear that this process serves to insure the conveyance of precise meaning, and it facilitates the control of self-expression. When we are conversing, conveying the meaning of language in this manner, we are operating within the blue area displayed in Figure 9.1. So, how successfully, based on language, can we as humans deal with our inner sensations, conflicts, crises and traumas?

Some individuals have more advanced language skills than others, and some conditions such as psychiatric disorders, can directly affect one's abilities to express and understand via language. In psychotic speech there are disturbances of how thoughts, sentences and words are connected (Kuperberg & Caplan,

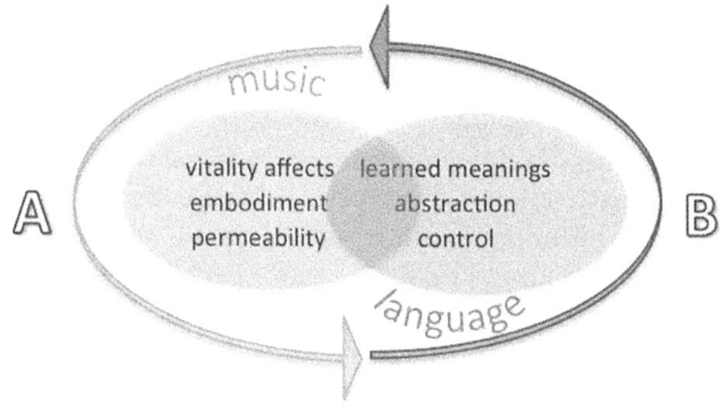

Figure 9.1 Theoretical diagram for IIMT.

2004). According to DeLisi (2001), people with chronic schizophrenia tend to use less clausal speech and fewer words than their family members, and then patients whose illness has been recently diagnosed.

For people with depression speech is often affected, speech and may increase the occurrence of negative emotions (Murray et al., 1993); sometimes causing psychomotor regression (Flint et al., 1993). Also typical to depression is slowed speech and increase of silent episodes (Hoffmann et al., 1985). In IIMT (or any equivalent music therapy approach), it is possible to 'skip' the verbal process using words and enable non-verbal interactions to take place in response to music.

Even when verbal language is not disturbed, it is not always the most optimal medium for complex and spontaneous emotional expression characterized by images, metaphors, associations, bodily sensations and symbols (Erkkilä, 1997; Erkkilä et al., 2012). Here we approach one of the fundamental differences between music and language, which is embodiment, or embodied cognition. When language is distanced from drives and emotions by creating an abstract system for precise conveyance of meaning, music is closely tied to primitive, comprehensive meaning formation, which connects abstract thoughts and mental representations to instinctual drives (see Perlovsky, 2015). According to Perlovsky (2015), in animals, all the experiences are embodied, and emotions penetrate their every movement. The creation of human language enabled a more abstract form of knowledge and experience to be communicated. Perlovsky (2015) argues that the price of this development, typical only to human beings, is a tendency to separate our bodily experiences from our mental life. In other words, language does not automatically become embodied or assimilated with cognition and emotion. For this reason, our psyche is not as harmonic as in animals. Interestingly emotional release was reported in Odell-Miller's (2007) study as important by interviewed music therapists. Encouraging self-expression is not necessarily the most beneficial thing for a person suffering from psychosis, who may need to use music to help organise and calm their mind instead. This is markedly different to working with people with non-psychotic disorders. For the person with depression, music can function as an active motivator, and through talking and interpretation and symbolic meaning, patterns of thinking and feeling can change.

We now proceed to explore more specifically, the significance of music therapy, for emotion and frontal brain processing in depression.

Emotion and frontal brain processing in depression

People with depression have difficulties in expressing and processing emotion (Punkanen et al., 2011), and, given the frequent comorbidity with anxiety (Aina & Susman, 2006), are more likely to act in a withdrawn and anxious manner in social interaction (Davidson et al., 2000). People with depression tend to use rumination and expressive suppression as strategies to regulate their emotions (Joormann & Gotlib, 2010). Negative emotions seem to be processed dominantly in the right frontal cortex and a concept explaining affective disorders links the withdrawal behaviour of people with depression to increased right frontal activity, that is, pathological asymmetric frontal processing of emotion (Henriques & Davidson, 1991).

One way to measure frontal processing is looking at the different frontal EEG values and there is some evidence that Frontal Alpha Asymmetry (FAA) and Frontal Midline theta (FM Theta) might serve as biomarkers for depression and anxiety. The alpha range indicates how much 'work' the brain requires to process mental tasks and indicates relaxation. Frontal asymmetries on the alpha range also indicate different emotional processing. The left site of the frontal cortex is expected to show more activity when processing positive and the right site when processing negative emotions. The theta range is an indicator of emotional processing and attention; FM theta is an indicator for anxiety levels (Mitchell et al., 2008).

There is some evidence that music therapy improves depression, and that music listening might change FAA in people with depression (Field et al., 1998; Jones & Field, 1999; Tornek et al., 2003). These results indicate an immediate influence of music listening on frontal processing in depression. The aim of Fachner et al.'s (2013) study, which was linked to Erkkilla et al. (2011), was to find out whether these effects were lasting, and could be observed in an additional resting EEG recording.

This was different to taking observation during or directly after listening, as in the study with mothers with depression (Field et al., 1998). In the later study (Fachner et al., 2013), observations were taken after a course of 20 bi-weekly active music therapy sessions and results pointed to fronto-temporal changes, in particular changes in frontal alpha asymmetry and in frontal theta power, which means that there is different activity in the left and right site (on alpha) and the middle part (more theta power) of the frontal cortex after music therapy. These changes in the EEG biomarkers indicate the difference between both groups and between the pre and post music therapy treatment (Jörg Fachner et al., 2013).

Fronto-Temporal changes in the alpha and theta range of the resting state EEG indicate that music therapy had an influence on emotional processing and expression of the patients and indicate neural reorganisation. Fronto-temporal areas have broadly been investigated in research on common areas of music and language processing (S. Koelsch, 2012). Emotional modulation of limbic structures, activation of the perception–action mediation in premotor areas, and intentional processes of social cognition in frontal and temporal areas are discussed as possible neuroscientific concomitants of music-therapeutic action (S. Koelsch, 2009).

At intake participants in aforementioned RCT trial (Erkilaa et al., 2011), all of whom had a diagnosis of depression perceived emotions in film music excerpts representing sadness and anger, differently from healthy non-depressed controls; that is, they detected anger and fear more often (Punkanen et al., 2011). Non-verbal expression of emotional content through music creation, and subsequent verbal reflection of its personal meaning, is part of the therapeutic relationship established during music therapy (Erkkilä et al., 2012). About 70% of the therapy sessions were used for verbal reflection and 30% for improvising, therefore fronto-temporal changes may demonstrate that doing music therapy initialised neural reorganisation in areas which were busy with processing music and language in manifold ways. At the same time, clients were offered a context to experience and embody a playful means of emotional expression, supporting reduction of anxiety and depressive withdrawal from others. Interestingly, FM theta values (FM theta is discussed as a biomarker for anxiety) correlated with decreases of anxiety scores (of the HADS-A – Hospital Anxiety and Depression Scale-Anxiety Subscale) in the music therapy group.

In the RCT trial in question (Erkkilä et al., 2011) 79 adults diagnosed with a depressive disorder were included. Resting EEG and psychiatric tests (MADRS; HADS-A) were administered at intake and after three months. FAA was calculated at three electrode pairs (Fp1-Fp2, F3-F4, F7-F8), and FM theta (F3/4, Fz). EEG (see Table 9.1) was transformed into z-scores (compared to a normative EEG database). A normative database allows to compare the individual EEG rest recordings against healthy matched controls in a given age range. This allows a neuro-metric assessment of the deviations (z-scores) from normal functioning pre- and post-intervention (John et al., 1988; Ridder & Fachner, 2016; Thatcher et al., 2003). Correlations between EEG and psychiatric tests were examined statistically. Psychometric properties of FAA and FM theta were also explored.

Here we now focus on one case from the table, to explore whether changes in EEG measures and psychiatric tests are congruent with clinical case descriptions by the attending music therapist and to shed further light on the relationships between EEG measures, clinical assessments and processes in therapy.

As pointed out above a basic principle of music therapy, and specifically the approach used here, is to encourage and engage a client in expressive musical

Table 9.1 Test results, FAA and FM Theta Changes (z-scores) for Anna. Note: Alpha asymmetry z-scores are based on a normative database. Alpha asymmetry was calculated as 200* (L – R)/(R + L), which means that positive asymmetry values indicate greater amplitude (less activation) in the left hemisphere. Reference electrodes were linked ears.

Scores for Anna	*pre*	*post*	*change*
Depression (MADRS)	31	9	−22
Anxiety (HADS)	8	2	−6
FAA: z(Fp1-Fp2)	0.11	−0.39	−0.50
FAA: z(F3-F4)	0.42	1.24	0.82
FAA: z(F7-F8)	0.94	1.48	0.54
FM theta: M(z(F3), z(Fz), z(F4))	0.58	0.95	0.37

interaction (Erkkilä et al., 2008). The starting point for improvisation might be free (without an agreed topic, theme or title for the improvisation), or referential (based on an agreed topic, theme or title). The dialogue between verbal discussion and improvising is based on spontaneous and intuitive process so that sometimes an idea for improvisation may emerge from discussion, and sometimes a topic for discussion may arise from improvisation. As a non-verbal, symbolic and emotional tool, improvisation often triggers emotionally loaded experiences such as associations, images, metaphors and memories (Erkkilä, 1997).

Anna's case

Anna,[1] a 30-year-old academic woman at the start of music therapy, suffered from several episodes of depression since her late teenage years. These episodes provisionally interrupted her studies and part-time work in the family company. Her depressive illness caused social isolation and relationship difficulties. Anna was communicative in one to one situations, but somewhat unsociable when more people were present. Her non-verbal expression was rather scant. She did not express her emotions overtly, in particular negative emotions, although she could laugh and smile when the mood took her. She tended to control her emotions, but had the capacity to recognize and understand emotions. Anna had not played musical instruments or sung since her early school years, but was a passionate music listener, preferring Finnish rock bands. Undoubtedly, she was musical.

Anna was immediately capable of rich, verbal dialogue in sessions. Her verbal expression was open, soft, analytic and decisive and not highly emotional. Sometimes she was rather outspoken, within a safe context. There were no clear turning points in her verbal expression in the course of therapy. The first two sessions seemed rather unconstructive from the music/improvising point of view. Her playing was careful, fragile and mechanical – definitely not overtly expressive. From the third session onwards a clear change in Anna's musical expression took place. Improvisations became more intense and 'loaded'; interaction improved and she began to enjoy playing music. Later, her musical expression expanded into a more creative, relaxed, dynamic and playful mode. She started to make more frequent connections between music and emotions. Her purposefulness, courage and feeling of safety in playing increased as well. The improvisations triggered both images and emotions.

Anna's understanding of the meaning of improvisation in dealing with themes arising in the music therapy process, improved. In the first two sessions she described feeling fearful, melancholic and empty. From session three, she was more able to deal both with positive and negative emotions. At the midpoint, and thereafter, Anna often reported that she felt serene and peaceful, which was better than she could have imagined, considering the severity of her illness and difficulties. Serenity and peacefulness were more or less present for the rest of the therapy. The first two sessions were much more based upon processing problem- orientated themes such as working on her problematic relationships with close family and friends. The personal traits that supported her depression appeared to be her mechanical behaviour and inability to throw herself spontaneously into situations. Later on the sessions were more resource -orientated and positive but Anna was still able to express difficult feelings and negative emotions. In middle to late stages of the therapy, she began to consider the future and how to live life fully. She wanted to become more open to her emotions, and to solve the conflicts between her and her close friends and family. Anna was doubtful about whether her own resources were sufficient to do this on her own, which was often a topic in sessions. The ending of music therapy was often discussed, which she described as her tendency to prepare herself in advance for the unavoidable.

Therapist's analysis of Anna's clinical improvisations

According to the protocol of Erkkilä et al.'s study (2008) the musical outputs of the sessions were analysed as well. Therefore, all the improvisations created were saved on a computer hard disc both as MIDI and digital audio to be analysed by computational music analysis tools, specifically designed for analysing music therapy improvisations. In the analysis of the improvisations for Anna, the computational tool called Music Therapy Toolbox (MTTB) was employed (Erkkilä, 2007). By MTTB, several musical features can be extracted from MIDI data. In the analysis of Anna's improvisations only electric vibraphone improvisations were included for the sake of data coherence and because the vibraphone was most often played in this client's therapy.

In general, Anna's improvisations sounded relatively calm, and often unresponsive to the therapist's musical interventions. She mainly continued in her own way of playing, whilst the therapist seemed to vary his music much more than the client. These variations in the therapist's playing were identified through musical density, pitch, pulse clarity, and articulation. Through variation the therapist influenced the client to vary her music as well. In Bruscia's (1987) listing of multiple musical interventions, this could fall into the category of 'introducing the change'. However, the calm quality of the client's music did not mean that her music was non-communicative. She often commented upon the therapist's musical role and responded to the therapist not so often musically but at least verbally, after improvising.

In a memorable episode in session five, the therapist intentionally took a dominant, more forceful, musical role, thus reflecting the behaviour of the client's friend; which often irritated her. After the improvisation the client said she noticed the therapist's provocative musical role, but just like in real life, she did not let herself be provoked on the behavioural level. Instead, she tended to hide this kind of provocation without visible responses, which sometimes further instigated the other to continue the unpleasant behaviour. Furthermore, the client often connected emotional images to improvisations and clearly benefitted from dealing with her mental processes through music, in a symbolic way. In other words, her music was not far from her as a person but through music, and by discussing her images triggered by the music, she gained insights about herself and her behavioural patterns. One could say that a clinical improvisation is a self-portrait which can be considered after completion for learning new things about oneself, seeing oneself from a new angle and from symbolic distance.

The client's music and expression evolved and changed, in its own way, during the therapy process, especially in pitch. In music, melody is often at the highest pitch because it is meant to be recognised. Bruscia (1987) describes melody in clinical improvisation as a specific expression of emotion. While at the beginning of the process, the client did not often vary the pitch, later on, she varied it more (although less than the therapist). The interplay with the therapist in terms of melody also increased. This might refer to increased self-expression, self-confidence and emotional openness. In general, the client played louder in the melodic phrases (higher velocity ≈ higher 'volume') than the therapist. In music therapy, volume may refer to energy and size of psychic objects. The louder the volume, the more energy and size, whatever they symbolize at a given time. To the therapist, the client's tolerance for, and tendency to, higher velocity (volume) in comparison to the therapist, reveals something about the client's inner strength, and internal, emotional pressure, which was searching for expression. Signs of repression and the client's higher velocity could be explained by the therapist's professional intervention – playing softer than the client gives more space ('voice') to her.

In the first two sessions, the client said that she was so preoccupied with her own illness and related concerns that she had developed a strategy to ignore other peoples' problems and worries. Her behaviour had been more withdrawn over a long period. The first signs of a change in her behaviour, showing she was interested in building new relationships, with the therapist and close friends and family, occurred in session three. Here she appeared to feel joy and expressed this in relation to a newborn baby in her family circle. Interestingly, she was now able to deal with negative feelings towards her close family and friends, and expressed these feelings to them, which afterwards she was both worried and pleased about. Therefore, she did not avoid challenging and conflict-ridden situations anymore, but was able to tolerate them. During sessions 7–15 again new aspects of relationship- building behaviour emerged when Anna's social life became more active. She even thought about starting a family. She understood the meaning of dealing with negative emotions and was stronger when facing them, thus showing better control and regulation of her emotional life. In sessions 16–20 she was adjusting to her new lifestyle and appeared to be in a good mental space and in a better mood, generally participating in more activities

EEG and psychometric data corresponding to the therapeutic process

For this client in the RCT study, the Montgomery Asberg Depression Ratings Scale (MADRS) scores improved from very high to sub-clinical; the Hospital Anxiety and Depression Scale-Anxiety subscale (HADS-A) scores were already sub-clinical and improved more (Table 9.1). FAA z-scores presented again a mixed picture. At F7-F8 they were indicative of a somewhat depressed person, but Fp1-Fp2 and F3-F4 were close to zero, indicating normality. However, only Fp1-Fp2 indicated some improvement over time, whereas F3-F4 and F7-F8 indicated deterioration.

The frontopolar cortex is involved in decision making, reward processes and anticipation of possible outcomes of concurrent plans (Koechlin & Hyafil, 2007). Here, a frontopolar FAA might represent this process as outlined from the therapist above. FM theta indicated no impairment at outset and further improvement over time. We explored topographically where changes in alpha and theta bands were located by subtracting pre/post means and showing the topographic power differences from pre- to post-mean (Figure 9.2). In the theta band, we can see increases in amplitude (red) occurred in frontal and midline areas. Overall the tendency was towards increase, as would be expected in clients moving towards recovery. In the post-mean Anna displayed increased FM theta power (Table 9.1). In the alpha band, the greatest changes seemed to take place in the parietal-occipital region and frontal alpha power increased.

Discussion

Narratives of therapy processes are neither objective nor unbiased. Therapists are naturally expected to have a tendency to see positive changes in their clients.

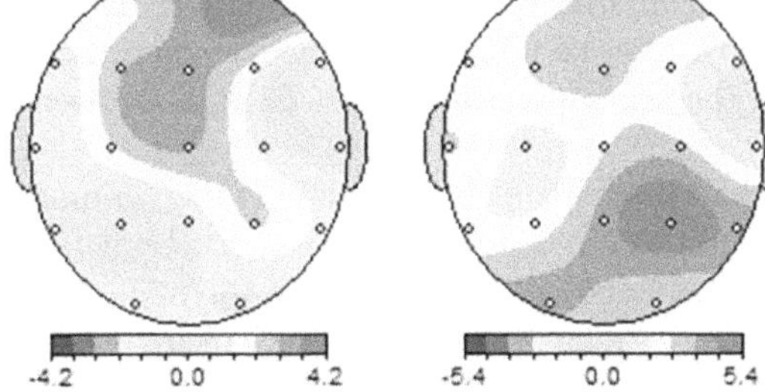

Figure 9.2 EEG pre/post Absolute Power Differences. Note: Figure shows the difference mapping of the pre- and post-power values separately for alpha and theta, i.e. the post values were subtracted from the pre-values and the differences are mapped here.

The focus here was not to show how well clients improved through music therapy but to examine how their apparent improvement as described by their therapist matched the various quantitative measures. Since the narratives were written without knowledge of the quantitative data, the extent of a potential positive bias in the narratives should be independent of the changes seen in brain functions, so that the relationship between the sources of information should not be manipulated. For a biological process to be seen as a valid marker it must reflect not only the pathological processes involved in the clinical condition but also the way the treatment is supposed to work (De Gruttola et al., 2001). Therefore, we explored the individual therapy processes as seen by the music therapist and compared the qualitative, narrative outcomes of these cases to the quantitative data collected. The case analysis revealed that psychiatric tests appear to more clearly reflect the clinical impression given by the free descriptions (Jörg Fachner et al., 2010). FAA and FM theta z-scores were typically within the normal range, and when deviations from the normal range occurred these were indicating changes in the left and also the right frontal cortex. However, an increase in alpha asymmetry showed that the left and right frontal cortex processing changed and together with the frontal theta, indicate a different emotional state after therapy. Topographical examination of brain maps suggested that change processes vary greatly between individuals and therefore shed some light on intra-individual brain processing changes in the therapy process.

In summary, we found evidence of some relationship between EEG measures and psychopathology, but the correlation is far from deterministic, and there seem to be many other factors that are influencing the values of FAA and FM theta as well (Gold et al., 2013). The fronto-temporal changes in Fachner et al. study (2013) may indicate that the emotional process targeted in music therapy helped the clients to express and differentiate the underlying emotional tension, anger and anxiousness of their withdrawal in music and discussion with the therapists. F7 and F8 reflect activity in both sites of the fronto-temporal cortex and in Anna's case they reflect her work on negative emotional processing as discussed above. Frontal shifts of brain activity after the therapy intervention indicate that the therapy work leaves a trace in the frontal processing of emotion.

On a more general level discussing the value of these biomarkers for therapy intervention (Fachner et al., 2010) we can see that both FAA and FM theta have an empirical basis from previous research to support their use. It might be that certain aspects of depression and/or anxiety are more closely related to FAA and FM theta than others. Given that an important basis for the theory on FAA comes from emotion research, it might be, for example, that FAA is more related to emotional than to cognitive aspects of depression. An established distinction in the measurement of anxiety is between state and trait anxiety. Given that EEG recordings reflect current mental processes at the time of the recording, this distinction might be useful to investigate in order to distinguish instantaneous EEG changes as reported in the studies from Field et al. (1998), Tornek et al. (2003) and Sammler et al. (2007) from lasting changes of brain activity as seen in Fachner et al. (2013). These different aspects of the biomarkers utilised may help to understand and what is driving the outcome therapy interventions and how individuals respond.

Conclusion

In music therapy, we think that through connecting, and utilising the core qualities of music and language – instinctual and abstract – the music therapist can meet a client in a manner which is suitable to meet his or her needs, problems and disorders by adjusting and regulating the context of encounter. With some clients, it is important to start within the musical area A (Figure 9.1) if, for instance, a client's language is disturbed or inhibited. With many clients from our depression RCT trial (Erkkilä et al., 2011), the process started in this area because they might have difficulties in verbal communication. As the process developed, many clients become more talkative as the consequence of music triggered mental processes – emotional images, for instance. Thus, in IIMT, the interplay between instinctual (music) and abstract (language) is an essential feature and quality of therapeutic working. This is supported by respondents in Odell-Miller's (2007) study and elsewhere. De Backer (2008), for example, described similar processes in improvisational music therapy for people with psychosis, who also had depressive symptoms.

From a psychodynamic or psychoanalytic point of view, the basic process of IIMT can be illustrated also by the concepts of 'conscious', 'pre-conscious' and 'unconscious' (Erkkilä et al., 2012). An example is shown through the musical domain of IIMT (Figure 9.1) which is very close to the concept of the pre-conscious, whereas for the language domain the concept of conscious is perhaps more characteristic. So, music therapy typically consists of movement between pre-conscious and conscious ≈ music and language ≈ instinctual and abstract ≈ emotional and logical as demonstrated by a synthesis of RCT research results, theory, literature, case studies and the growing body of music therapy research.

Implications for practice are that for people who find accessing pre-conscious or unconscious processes difficult, music therapy and musical process can find another means of access (H. Odell-Miller, 2001). In psychoanalysis, unconscious processes are also explored through words and thinking, so it is important not to define which area of the brain is exactly responsible for this process, but music therapists should be mindful of the links between neuroscience, psychological and developmental processes in their practice, as these links offer a window into the particular mind-body interaction initiated in therapy processes.

Note

1 Pseudonym is used and disguised details for participants.

References

Aina, Y., & Susman, J. L. (2006). Understanding comorbidity with depression and anxiety disorders. *The Journal of the American Osteopathic Association*, 106(5 Suppl 2), S9–14.

Albornoz, Y. (2011). The effects of group improvisational music therapy on depression in adolescents and adults with substance abuse: a randomized controlled trial. *Nordic Journal of Music Therapy*, 20(3), 208–224. Doi: 10.1080/08098131.2010.522717.

Bruscia, K. E. (1987). *Improvisational models of music therapy*. Springfield, IL: C.C. Thomas.

Bush, C. A. (1988). Dreams, mandalas, and music imagery: Therapeutic uses in a case study. [Printed]. *Arts in Psychotherapy*, 15(3), 219–225.

Carr, C. (2014). *Modelling of intensive group music therapy for acute adult psychiatric inpatients*. London: Queen Mary University of London.

Carr, C., d'Ardenne, P., Sloboda, A., Scott, C., Wang, D., & Priebe, S. (2012). Group music therapy for patients with persistent post-traumatic stress disorder – A pilot randomised controlled trial. *Psychology and Psychotherapy: Research and Practice*, 85, 179–202. Doi: 10.1111/j.2044–8341.2011.02026.x.

Carr, C., Odell-Miller, H., & Priebe, S. (2013). A systematic review of music therapy practice and outcomes with acute adult psychiatric in-patients. *PLoS ONE*, 8(8), e70252. Doi: 10.1371/journal.pone.0070252.

Carr, C., O'Kelly, J., Sandford, S., & Priebe, S. (2017). Feasibility and acceptability of group music therapy vs wait-list control for treatment of patients with long-term depression (the SYNCHRONY trial): Study protocol for a randomised controlled trial. *Trials*, 18(1), 149. Doi: 10.1186/s13063-017-1893-8.

Chen, X. (2014). Music therapy for improving mental health problems for offenders in correctional settings (PhD thesis). Aalborg University.

Chen, X., Hannibal, N., & Gold, C. (2015). Randomised trial of group music therapy with Chinese prisoners:impact on anxiety, depression and self esteem. *International Journal of Offender Therapy and Comparative Criminology*, 60(9), 1064–1081. Doi: 10.1177/0306624X15572795.

Davidson, R. J., Marshall, J. R., Tomarken, A. J., & Henriques, J. B. (2000). While a phobic waits: Regional brain electrical and autonomic activity in social phobics during anticipation of public speaking. *Biological Psychiatry*, 47(2), 85–95. Doi: 10.1016/S0006–3223(99)00222-X.

De Backer, J. (2008). Music and psychosis. *Nordic Journal of Music Therapy*, 17(2), 89–104.

De Gruttola, V. G., Clax, P., DeMets, D. L., Downing, G. J., Ellenberg, S. S., Friedman, L., . . . Zeger, S. L. (2001). Considerations in the evaluation of surrogate endpoints in clinical trials. Summary of a National Institutes of Health workshop. *Controlled Clinical Trials*, 22(5), 485–502. Doi: S0197–2456(01)00153–00152 [pii]

DeLisi, L. E. (2001). Speech disorder in schizophrenia: Review of the literature and exploration of its relation to the uniqely human capacity for language. *Schizophrenia Bulletin*, 27(3), 481–496.

Erkkilä, J. (1997). Musical improvisation and drawings as tools in the music therapy of children. *Nordic Journal of Music Therapy*, 6(2), 112–120.

Erkkilä, J. (2007). Music Therapy Toolbox (MTTB) – An improvisation analysis tool for clinicians and researchers. In T. Wosch & T. Wigram (Eds.), *Microanalysis in music therapy* (pp. 134–148). London: Jessica Kingsley.

Erkkilä, J., Ala-Ruona, E., Punkanen, M., & Fachner, J. (2011). Perspectives on creativity in improvisational, psychodynamic music therapy. In D. Hargreaves, D. Miell, & R. MacDonald (Eds.), *Musical imaginations: Multidisciplinary perspectives on creativity, performance and perception* (pp. 414–428). Oxford: Oxford University Press.

Erkkilä, J., Gold, C., Fachner, J., Ala-Ruona, E., Punkanen, M., & Vanhala, M. (2008). The effect of improvisational music therapy on the treatment of depression: Protocol for a randomised controlled trial. *BMC Psychiatry*, 8, 50. Doi: 1471–1244X-8–50 [pii]10.1186/1471–1244X-8–50.

Fachner, J., Gold, C., Ala-Ruona, E., Punkanen, M., & Erkkilä, J. (2010). Depression and music therapy treatment – Clinical validity and reliability of EEG alpha asymmetry and frontal midline theta: Three case studies. In S. M. Demorest, S. J. Morrison, & P. S. Campbell (Eds.), *Proceedings of the 11th International Conference on Music Perception and Cognition (CD-ROM)* (pp. 11–18). Seattle: University of Washington – School of Music.

Fachner, J., Gold, C., & Erkkilä, J. (2013). Music therapy modulates fronto-temporal activity in the rest-EEG in depressed clients. *Brain Topography*, 26(2), 338–354. Doi: 10.1007/s10548–10012–10254-x.

Fernald, A. (1989). Intonation and communicative intent in mothers' speech to infants: Is the melody the message? *Child Development*, 60(6), 1497–1510.

Field, T., Martinez, A., Nawrocki, T., Pickens, J., Fox, N. A., & Schanberg, S. (1998). Music shifts frontal EEG in depressed adolescents. *Adolescence*, 33(129), 109–116.

Flint, A. J., Black, S. E., Campbell-Taylor, I., Gailey, G. F., & Levinton, C. (1993). Abnormal speech articulation, psychomotor retardation, and subcortical dysfunction in major depression. *Journal of Psychiatric Research*, 27(3), 309–319.

Gold, C., Fachner, J., & Erkkilä, J. (2013). Validity and reliability of electroencephalographic frontal alpha asymmetry and frontal midline theta as biomarkers for depression. *Scandinavian Journal of Psychology*, 54(2), 118–126. Doi: 10.1111/sjop.12022.

Henriques, J. B., & Davidson, R. J. (1991). Left frontal hypoactivation in depression. *Journal of Abnormal Psychology*, 100(4), 535–545. Doi: 10.1037/0021–0843X.100.4.535.

Hoffmann, G. M., Gonze, J. C., & Mendlewicz, J. (1985). Speech pause time as a method for the evaluation of psychomotor retardation in depressive illness. *British Journal of Psychiatry*, 146, 535–538.

Holligan, F. (1992). Case study: Guided imagery and music. *The Australian Joural of Music Therapy*, 3, 27–36.

John, E. R., Prichep, L. S., Fridman, J., & Easton, P. (1988). Neurometrics: Computer-assisted differential diagnosis of brain dysfunctions. *Science*, 239(4836), 162–169.

Jones, N. A., & Field, T. (1999). Massage and music therapies attenuate frontal EEG asymmetry in depressed adolescents. *Adolescence*, 34(135), 529–534.

Joormann, J., & Gotlib, I. H. (2010). Emotion regulation in depression: Relation to cognitive inhibition. *Cognition & Emotion*, 24(2), 281–298. Doi: 10.1080/02699930903407948.

Koechlin, E., & Hyafil, A. (2007). Anterior prefrontal function and the limits of human decision-making. *Science*, 318(5850), 594–598. Doi: 318/5850/594 [pii]10.1126/science.1142995.

Koelsch, S. (2009). A neuroscientific perspective on music therapy. *Annals of the New York Academy of Sciences*, 1169, 374–384. Doi: 10.1111/j.1749–6632.2009.04592.x.

Koelsch, S. (2012). *Brain and music.* Oxford Wiley-Blackwell.

Kuperberg, G., & Caplan, D. (2004). Language dysfunction in shcizophrenia. In R. B. Schiffer, S. M. Rao & B. S. Fogel (Eds.), *Neuropsychiatry* (2nd ed., pp. 444–466). Philadelphia, PA: Lippincott Williams and Wilkins.

Maratos, A. S., Gold, C., Wang, X., & Crawford, M. J. (2008). Music therapy for depression (review). *The Cochrane Database of Systematic Reviews*, (1), CD004517. Doi: 004510.001002/14651858.CD14004517.pub14651852.

Mitchell, D. J., McNaughton, N., Flanagan, D., & Kirk, I. J. (2008). Frontal-midline theta from the perspective of hippocampal "theta". *Progress in Neurobiology*, 86(3), 156–185. Doi: 10.1016/j.pneurobio.2008.09.005.

Murray, L., Kempton, C., Woolgar, M., & Hooper, R. (1993). Depressed mothers' speech to their infants and its relation to infant gender and cognitive development. *Journal of Child Psychology and Psychiatry*, 34(7), 1083–1101.

NHS (2017). Adult improving access to psychological therapies program. Retrieved from www.england.nhs.uk/menmtal-health/adults/iapt.

NICE (2016). Depression in adults: Recognition and management. Retrieved from www.nice.org.uk/guidance/cg90.

Norcross, J. S., & Goldfried, M. R. (Eds.). (2005). *Handbook of psychotherapy integration*. New York: Oxford University Press.

Odell-Miller, H. (2001). Music therapy and its relationship to psychoanalysis. In Y. Searle & I. Streng (Eds.), *Where analysis meets the arts* (pp. 127–152). London: Karnac Books.

Odell-Miller, H. (2002). One man's journey and the importance of time: Music therapy in an NHS mental health day centre. In A. Davies & E. Richards (Eds.), *Music therapy and group work*. London: Jessica Kingsely.

Odell-Miller, H. (2007). The practice of music therapy for adults with mental health problems: The relationship between diagnosis and clinical method. (PhD), Aalborg University, Aalborg.

Odell-Miller, H. (2014). The development of clinical music therapy in post-war Britain as a profession in mental health practice: Music, health and therapy. In S. Goodman & V. Bates (Eds.), *Medicine, health and the arts in post war Britain*. London: Routledge.

Perlovsky, L. (2015). Origin of music and embodied cognition. *Frontiers in Psychology*, 6. Retrieved from Doi: 10.3389/fpsyg.2015.00538.

Porter, S., McConnell, T., McLaughlin, K., Lynn, F., Cardwell, C., Braiden, H.-J., . . . the Music in Mind Study, G. (2017). Music therapy for children and adolescents with behavioural and emotional problems: A randomised controlled trial. *Journal of Child Psychology and Psychiatry*, 58(5), 586–594. Doi: 10.1111/jcpp.12656.

Punkanen, M., Eerola, T., & Erkkilä, J. (2011). Biased emotional recognition in depression: Perception of emotions in music by depressed patients. *Journal of Affective Disorders*, 130(1–2), 118–126. Doi: 10.1016/j.jad.2010.10.034.

Ridder, H. M., & Fachner, J. (2016). Objectivist case study research. Single-subject and small-n research. In B. Wheeler & K. Murphy (Eds.), *Music therapy research* (3rd ed.). Dallas: Barcelona Publishers.

Rolvsjord, R. (2010). *Resource-orientated music therapy in mental health care*. Barcelona Publishers.

Sammler, D., Grigutsch, M., Fritz, T., & Koelsch, S. (2007). Music and emotion: Electrophysiological correlates of the processing of pleasant and unpleasant music. *Psychophysiology*, 44(2), 293–304. Doi: 10.1111/j.1469–8986.2007.00497.x.

Thatcher, R. W., Walker, R. A., Biver, C. J., North, D. M., & Curtin, R. (2003). Quantitiative EEG normative databases: Validation and clinical correlation. *Journal of Neurotherapy*, 7, 87–105.

Tornek, A., Field, T., Hernandez-Reif, M., Diego, M., & Jones, N. (2003). Music effects on EEG in intrusive and withdrawn mothers with depressive symptoms. *Psychiatry*, 66(3), 234–243.

Trainor, L. J., Clark, E. D., Huntley, A., & Adams, B. (1997). The acoustic basis of infant preferences for infant-directed singing. *Infant Behavior and Development*, 20, 383–396.

Walker, V. (1993). Integrating guided imagery and music with verbal psychotherapy. *Journal of the Association for Music and Imagery*, 2 111–121.

Weiss, L. (1994). Accessing the inner family through guided imagery and music. *Journal of the Association for Music and Imagery*, 3, 49–58.

Winston, A., Rosenthal, R., N., & Pinsker, H. (2004). *Introduction to supportive psychotherapy*. Washingon, DC: American Psychiatric Publishing.

World Health Organisation (2016). Retrieved October 31, 2016 from www.who.int/en/.

Chapter 10

Phototherapy in the treatment of patients with depression in a clinical setting

Development and evaluation through a randomised controlled trial

Kathrin Seifert

Introduction

Photography has been perceived as a socially multi-faceted, broad and universally employed medium that fulfills diverse objectives and functions. Although the first clinical applications of photography had already been shown publicly ten years after the invention of the Daguerreotype process in 1839 (Spitzing, 1985), the medium has seen relatively little practical application within the therapeutic field. Since then, various photo-therapeutic movements have emerged, particularly in England and North America.

Almost every form of photographic technology is employed in contemporary art, not only analogue and digital processes, but also collage and a combination of processes, mixed media as well as multimedia. All of these techniques also have a great potential for phototherapy in identifying themes, and processing and transforming personal material.

In this chapter, the use of photography will be explored within the context of phototherapy. A particular model developed within a multimodal treatment clinic will be described and some results relating to its value in decreasing symptoms of depression will be reported and discussed.

Some key theoretical ideas relating to photography

The invention of the Daguerreotype process sparked controversial philosophical discussions and texts in cultural anthropology and social criticism. The American pragmatist Charles Sanders Peirce (1986) was the first who analysed photography as a sign system. According to his semiotic theory, photography was perceived in its materiality, meanings and functions (Geimer, 2009). Referring to Sassure's (1857–1913) image semiotic questions, the structuralist Roland Barthes (1980) analysed pictures of amateur photographers under a phenomenological perspective and developed first eidetic approaches (Barthes, 1989). The communication-theorist Vilém Flusser (1983) analysed the medium photography under the critical of culture and society perspective. Flusser worked on the potential and limitations of a technologically-driven world of images and the interdependencies of image and script (Flusser, 1992). Walter Benjamin (1936) underlined the criteria of singleness, of uniqueness and of presence as mandatory characteristics of art but did not recognise these attributes in photography. However, he believed that authenticity can be achieved with photography because it is an aesthetical process connected with the outside world. (Benjamin, 2006). Susan Sontag (1977) discussed the relation between photographical aesthetisation of objects and replication of reality, and questioned the imperative of truthfulness and embellishment. Sontag's (1977/1995) contribution to the discussion of photography reveals an important insight that can also be applied therapeutically. She argues that photography contributes to the "aesthetisation of everyday life" (Sontag, 1995: 160). Photography can accommodate the strong desire for beauty, peace and clarity in times of trouble (Schwering, 1995). This aesthetic perception is also a universal quality for Schurian (1986) that is psychologically and therapeutically valuable.

The emergence of phototherapy

Developments in photography over three centuries have facilitated the emergence of phototherapy. This relatively new discipline established itself particularly well in the Anglo-American settings, with significant proponents such as Jerry Fryrear (1983) and Judy Weiser (2004). Since then, the therapy has also developed in other countries and now enjoys wide applications in the treatment of children, young people and adults. The practice can be broadly differentiated into three forms: Phototherapy (Weiser 1993/2004), Therapeutic Photography (Spence, 1995) and Photo-Art-Therapy (Corbit et al., 1990/1992). The first form was developed by Weiser through five specific therapy programmes: for the purposes of self-reflection, self-communication, the production of self-images, the production of family albums and for the use of photos in group sessions as self-projection. The second form views photography as a means of documentation of people and experiences for the purposes of biographical research. The third one is oriented towards art therapy and uses photography as an artistic medium (Weiser & Krauss, 2009).

The positive effects of phototherapy have been investigated in several studies with differing parameters.

Spire (1973) developed the PSIC methodology (Photographic Self Image Confrontation) for patients with a chronic schizophrenic psychosis. Twelve female patients were confronted twice a week with a Polaroid self-portrait. This approach was evaluated by qualitative and quantitative means such as structured interview, self-observation (according to Gough, 1965), ongoing process diagnostic and the Draw-A-Person test. At the end of the project most patients stated the following positive effects: they developed a positive picture for their personal future, showed evidence of a corrected body schema, developed a passion for photography and discovered their personal identity.

In a study with three test subjects, Walker (1986) was able to demonstrate that ambiguous photos evoked more associations than those with clear imagery. Those associations were used within the psychoanalytic treatment and supported the development of a stronger insight of the patients. Glover-Graf and Miller (2006) evaluated the use of photography within a multi-modal ambulant group therapy of five patients addicted to drugs. The results showed that all patients had experiences of abuse and all were able to talk about client-specific topics such as abuse, trust, etc. Ziller and Smith (1977) worked on the use of photography as an approach to phenomenological psychology (Merleau-Ponty, 1962; Speigelberg, 1970; Giorgi, 1970) and explored differences of perception in several application areas. The results revealed that the gender and the perception of the physical environment self-perception of the study participants influenced the content and use of their photographs.

Phototherapy in the treatment of depression

Based on the positive experiences reported in the literature, when it came to treating depression, it became important to employ a sound treatment methodology which was evaluated by both qualitative and quantitative means. Maier's and Wagner's gene-environment interaction model (2005) was applied. The model assumed multiple factors that could lead to depression. Those factors could be endogenous (genetic) and exogenous (psychosocial).

The main symptoms of a depression are low mood, anhedonia (loss of pleasure) and loss of energy (Härter et al., 2007). All types of depression – specific and concomitant disease – were included in the study.

According to van Elst (2010), patients with depression show a reduced perception process on a primary level. As a result, promoting stimuli of perception became an important consideration for the photo-therapeutic treatment model developed. As the following section shows, particularly relevant seemed to be the work of Schurian (1986) who argued that aesthetic perception entails sensing and processing of perceptual stimuli, making therapeutic intervention possible.

Phototherapy research study

The aims of the intervention that targeted the treatment of depressive disorders were based on the effects achieved by the application of photography in every-day educational and learning processes. These included:

- to enhance perception
- to stimulate action
- to increase the willingness to learn new subjects
- to create connections to cognitive and emotional processes
- to dialogue during photography and when viewing the results
- to heighten awareness of the aesthetic possibilities in every-day life. (Seifert, 2013)

The emphasis on treating patients with depression through phototherapy was twofold: increasing the patient's capacity to act and making their experience as hands-on as possible without raising the aesthetic bar too high, as is sometimes the case in other forms of art therapy (see for example Dannecker, 2006; Wheeler, 2009). Moreover, engaging in phototherapy enabled patients to combine their biographies with everyday aesthetic experiences in new ways.

The "formative evaluation" (Wichelhaus, 1989) of the project permitted the development of the main thesis. The study was integrated into the patient's overall treatment programme, i.e. combined with medicinal and behavioural treatments (Hautzinger, 1984) as well as complementary movement, and occupational, dance and sports therapies.

Maier and Wagner's (2005) gene-environment interaction model, which ranked the causes of a patient's depression as multifactorial events, lied at the heart of this complex approach to treatment. Schurian (1986) posits the theory that active psychological and motivational factors behind aesthetic processes can be activated through photo-therapeutic processes when treating the patient.

This led me to the formulation of the following hypothesis:

Phototherapy is suitable for reducing the severity of symptoms in depressive patients; uni-polar depression was selected as the specific criterion for this study.

In our previous research we found that reduction in depressive symptoms occurs through:

1 The intensification of visual perception
2 The aesthetic-figurative codification through which psychic factors (emotion, cognition and self-awareness) are communicated and the resources of pro-social actions stimulated
3 Reduction or removal of the central symptoms of the illness, such as low spirits, joylessness and apathy
4 A combination of cognitive attitudes and emotional experiences initiating a process of reflection in which the clinical picture, stage of the illness and environment are all involved
5 A confrontation with biographical content, for instance the choice of motive on an aesthetic and symbolic plane, which opens up new possibilities for communicating experiences and future perspectives with oneself and others (Seifert, 2013).

Development of a phototherapy model

The photo-therapeutic treatment method used in the study was art therapy-oriented. The first step was to carry out a search of existing literature on the subject of phototherapy and art therapy in the treatment of depression. Multiple databases such as Medline, Web of Science, DigiBi, Judy Weiser and Bio Publications were used. The identified literature was synthesised to guide the treatment methods (Seifert, 2015).

Several theoretical background works on photography (including Cohnen, 2008), communication theory (Bense, 1969; Wichelhaus, 1989), and core psychological (Hautzinger, 1984; Seligman, 1979) and depression-specific texts (Härter et al., 2007; Maier & Wagner, 2005 and others) were all incorporated into the development of the photo-therapeutic treatment model.

The model was designed for a range of different applications and needs and could be adapted to the client, situation and institution on an individual basis. For this study, the specific circumstances of a psychiatric clinic were observed, hence many group activities as well as the possibility of individual therapeutic treatment became available. Although this enabled a high degree of flexibility in terms of treatment, it also led to fluctuations in group size and participants over a longer period. Therefore, the phototherapy model was carried out within the framework of this project-oriented therapy.

The group size, however, still had to remain constant and manageable at six–nine patients. The therapeutic objectives in the project-oriented therapy sessions were aimed to provide photographic skills without narrowing the level of artistic freedom for personal experimentation and interpretation (Seifert, 2013).

Despite the differing durations, the fluctuations in the therapy group and the varying severity of illness, a structured therapy programme was employed and developed as a three-phase model: stabilisation phase, exposure phase and integration phase. Each phase is built progressively upon the previous one and may call for different time periods and methods for its completion (Reichelt, 2008).

Stabilisation Phase: During the stabilisation phase, patients are first familiarised with the project and introduced to photographic techniques. Besides technical photographic skills, the figurative possibilities of photography, composition and aesthetic forms of expression are also investigated in order to stimulate motivation and interest in the task ahead. At the same time, rules of aesthetics are taught and nurtured for the purpose of capturing the strong emotional stimuli encoded in visual objects (Wichelhaus, 2000). In the emotionally engaged, heightened awareness brought about by the photographic work, some patients are confronted with their particular personal circumstances.

The first therapy sessions also serve as a stabilising factor, since the sessions themselves are structurally organised and lead to developing a "coping strategy" (Hautzinger, 2003). Also initiated here is the atmosphere of trust, acceptance and social interaction that will be strengthened and deepened in the following sessions.

Exposure Phase: autonomy and self-representation in symbolically encoded form are in the foreground of the exposure phase. Through photography, patients find motifs and designs to help them process their biographical themes, themes which in themselves can be conflict-ridden. The medium opens up new vistas for finding the solution to personal and general problems.

Integration Phase: the integration phase is concerned with the exchange of experiences and insights arising from the previous processes and the visual results. In addition to dialogue and discussion, a refinement of the artwork with

Phase	Explanation
1 Stabilization Phase – Stimulating action, – Object perception, – Aestheticization	Learning and testing, Experimenting and playing, Aesthetic and sensory experiencing.
2 Exposure Phase – Stimulating resources, – Confronting conflicts, – Codification	Finding and forming one more personal motifs, e.g. through the selection from the experiential world (photography), transformation and distancing. Codification of interior psychic states through visual media (iconic, indexical, symbolic). Collages, Photoshop.
3 Integration Phase – Acceptance, recognition, – Communication, – Expansion.	Reflection on and communication of the elements of form and content. Recognition of the design as part of one's own mental constitution, Transformation using additional artistic media, language, painting etc.

Figure 10.1 Model of the phases of a photo-therapeutic-clinical treatment (minimum of eight sessions of 75 minutes each) (Seifert, 2013).

mixed media, as well as individual and group exhibitions, are all possible. Therapeutic processes are thereby deepened and creative processes accelerated. The patients are encouraged to view their current life issues from new perspectives and to develop their own solutions (Seifert, 2013).

Research methodology

A small Randomised Controlled Trial (RCT) design was adopted to test the efficacy of the outlined photo-therapeutic treatment model with quantitative as well as qualitative methods employed (Seifert, 2013). The work was preceded by a pilot study to test the suitability of the outcome measures (Seifert, 2013) and the final design was based upon these results. Since the sample size was relatively small, the research methodology was modified accordingly. Both standardised observational and self-completed questionnaires were used. Likert-type questionnaires were also developed and tested in pilot study groups to capture psychological changes and those related to aesthetic perception (Seifert, 2013), while participant observations and photographs from the process were recorded for the group as a whole and for each individual separately.

Permission to undertake the study was granted by the Bonn University Clinic (Ltd. No. 112 /08).

Quantitative methods

1 HDRS-scale (pre-post-test): a third-party observational assessment of the effects of phototherapy was carried out by the attending doctor before therapy and a day after its conclusion. The Hamilton Depression Rating Scale (HDRS-scale; Hamilton, 1960) is a significant instrument for measuring the reduction or disappearance of depressive symptoms.
2 Evaluation of Visual Material (pre/post- test): a non-standardised questionnaire to determine and evaluate changes in aesthetic perception and the potentially connected intensification of emotion was developed based on visual material. The participants' receptivity to the material and related impressions was surveyed before and after the tests. The material, produced by the pilot groups, drawn from the fields of architecture, sculpture and painting and consisted of a pair of pre- and post-test images. Each pair contained similar pictures motif with small differences intended to reduce the memory effect after the test (Seifert, 2013).
3 Process questionnaire: in addition to the third-party evaluation with the HDRS- scale, a self-evaluation was also used. Likert scales of multiple items were developed to survey the emotional factors of joy, pride, relaxation/ peace, curiosity, expectation, sadness and disdain in the reception of the visual material.
4 Closure questionnaire: finally, a participants' questionnaire relating to the efficacy of the phototherapy project with regards to six categories was developed: motivation, memory, emotion, self-awareness, interaction and individual motif identification (Seifert, 2013).

Various interdependent tests, such as the T-test, ANOVA and McNemar's test, were employed to calculate the therapeutic effects using artistic visual materials in the pre- and post-study surveys (Seifert, 2013). Of particular note here is Bühl's codification system (2008), in which variables as well as principal characteristics can be captured, entered into the SPSS computer system and evaluated. With help of ANOVA, the therapeutic effects of the sample were calculated according to the age and gender of the subjects.

Qualitative methods

Participant observations took place for each session. Observations were recorded soon after the completion of each sessions by the therapist/researcher. Compliance to the model, group dynamics and comments for each individual were included in these records. Copies of all photographs used within sessions were made. Both participant observations and photographs were analysed thematically using thematic analysis.

Participants

In order to be able to carry out a RCT, the patients first had to be assessed for the severity of their depression and the clinical picture of their overall mental illness, for example depression and psychosis, depression with a cerebro-organic disorder (F06. ICD10) or depression within a bipolar disorder. The inclusion criteria were: 1) adults with unipolar depressive disorder HDRS ≥7; 2) participation in the project consisted of at least eight sessions. Of the eighty potential participants, only thirty-eight were found to be suitable to be part of the study and randomly allocated to the intervention and control groups. To guarantee the parity between the intervention and control groups a socio-demographic evaluation was conducted. The differences in the participants' gender distribution, age and educational level yielded by the evaluation appeared to be marginal. It was therefore, assumed that the ratio of 20:18 participants between the therapy and control groups played only a negligible role on the validity of the results (Seifert, 2013).

Some quantitative results

HDRS-scale (pre/post- test)

The effect of the photo-therapeutic treatment, measured by the attending doctor using the HDRS-scale, was considerable and revealed a clinically relevant result. Seventeen of the twenty patients (85%) in the therapy group experienced a reduction in depressive symptoms of between 4 to 26 points, with an average value of 9.05 points on the HDRS-Scale. In comparison to the results of the "standard" treatment measures on patients in the control group, the differences displayed here were statistically relevant. The average value in the control group was only 8.25 points, a significantly lower effect indicated by statistical tests (T-test) as shown on Figure 10.2.

Evaluation of visual material (pre-post-test)

Figure 10.3a shows values related to the patients' self-assessment in the fields of receptivity and perception of encoded visual material. The emotional factors measured here show a significant improvement in peace/relaxation and improvement in curiosity and an increase in positive expectations. These factors were evaluated through proprietary questionnaires based on visual material from the pre/post- test. Interestingly, independent variables such as age and gender presented no distinguishing features within the therapy and control groups.

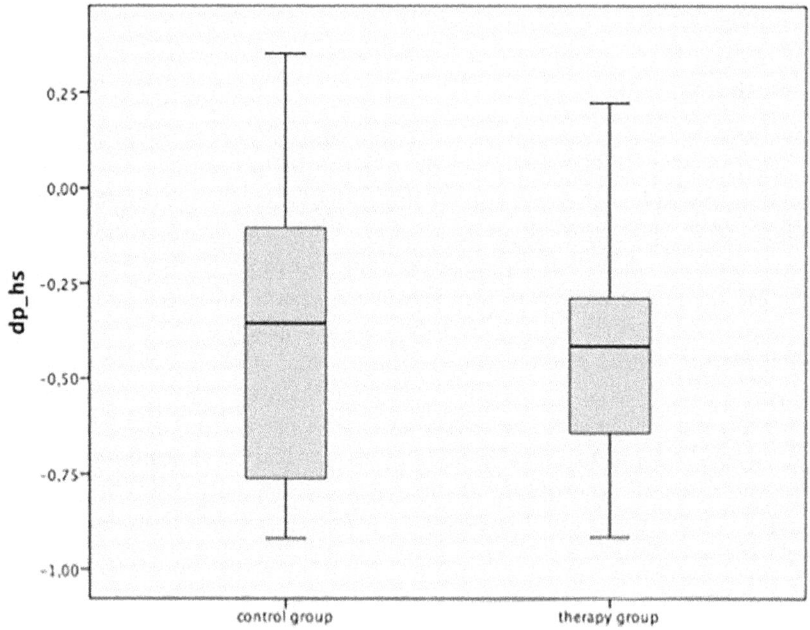

Figure 10.2 Boxplots of Hamilton depression (HDRS) scale scores of the control (left) and the therapy group (right) measured before and after therapy. There was an improvement of 4–26 points in seventeen of the twenty patients (85%) in the therapy group. This result represents an average improvement of 9.05 points comparing to an average of 8.25 points in the eighteen patients of the control group.

A significant improvement in cognitive abilities in the reception of visual material with high artistical expression was recorded (see Figure 10.3b). Data for these calculations were obtained in the pre/post- test from patients evaluating the third image pair. Based on these evaluations, the reception ability of the patients to an image of high artistic expression ("*Kornfeld mit Krähen*", van Gogh) was measured. The numbers of thoughts while looking at the image was significantly higher compared to the control group which had not participated at the developed photo-therapeutic treatment.

An increase in cognitive ability in the therapy groups for women and men of all ages was assessed. An increase in the cognitive abilities amongst young women was particularly high. The result provided evidence that allowed us to accept the study hypothesis. In comparison to the patients with depression who did not receive the intervention, patients in the therapy group experienced an improved receptivity and ability to relax through the intensification of visual perception and artistic challenges. The high receptivity of young female participants was particularly notable.

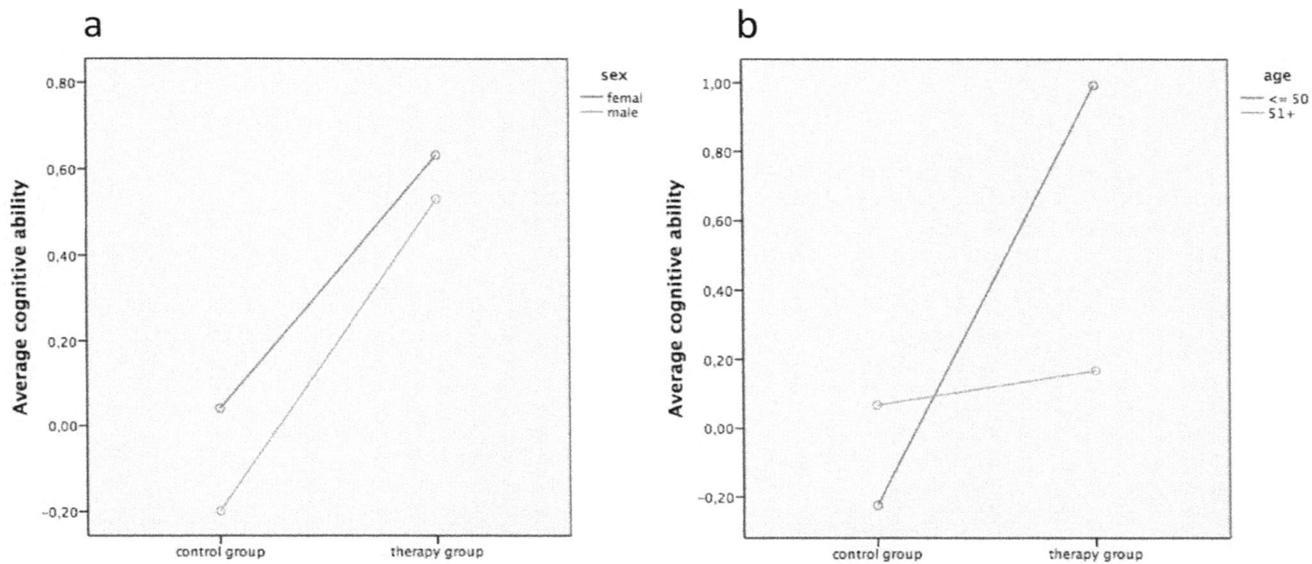

Figure 10.3 1) Change in cognitive ability according to the gender of the participants in the therapy and control groups; 2) Changes in cognitive ability according to the age of participants in the therapy and control groups (Seifert, 2013).

Process questionnaire

The process questionnaire including five categories was administered in an interview. These categories were related to curative effects, which are built upon aesthetic relevant experiences and a reduction in depressive feelings. These experiences were stimulated by the treatment model. By reflecting on the selected motifs, the patients became aware of their current preoccupations, wishes and feelings and were able to recognise and evaluate their positive and negative memories. This procedure was revisited and consolidated during discussions in therapy sessions and the conclusions were made available for further phototherapy work. The combination of verbal and non-verbal activities, facilitating an intense actualisation of conflicts and problems, was of particular benefit to those patients unwilling, or unable, to speak openly as a result of their depression. The aestheticisation of the mental motifs in the creation process created perspectives that bordered on transformation. The material result was photographic motifs imbued with personal meaning for the patients. The motifs were further processed so that the personal content became more visible in the final version. The patients were taught artistic techniques to accomplish this. This process was accompanied by an awakening of activity and statements like "I can create beautiful pictures; I can confront my problems through pictures" (Seifert, 2013).

Closure questionnaire

In the closure questionnaire activities, emotional and communicative behavior, interaction, memory processes, discussions and immersion, all played a part in the self-assessment. The questionnaire included also a section on artistic work for the participants. Artistic work within the framework of the phototherapeutic project was understood to mean the selection, the photography and the shaping of an individual motif by aesthetic means, in order to transform or endow it with new meaning. The overall quantity of data was reduced to three factors through the use of factor analysis (Rost, 2007):

1 Emotion, motivation, self-awareness.
2 Group behaviour (including communication and interaction) and memory (including sensory impressions and introspection)
3 Selection and forming of motifs (Seifert, 2013).

The results of the factor analysis on the self-assessment form were visualised using the sun-ray technique (See Figure 10.4). Each triangle stands for an individual participant of the therapy group and their self-assessment. The upper point of the triangle refers to the factor of emotion, motivation and self-reference, the left point refers to the evaluation of the motif and the right

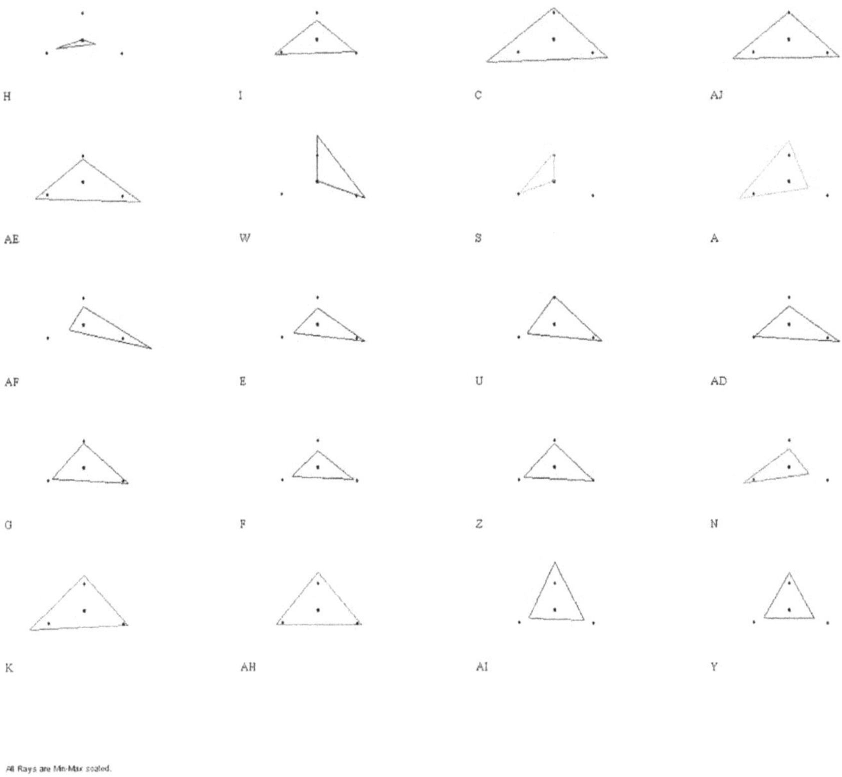

Figure 10.4 Graphic representation of the factor analysis in self-assessment a sun-ray questionnaire (Seifert, 2013).

point to the factors of memory and group-reference. The black points mark the mean value of all the factors and tell us how highly the patients rate the success of the programme on average. For example, the evaluation of the complex factors was similar for participants H and C, although H rated the therapy programme as least effective, whereas C rated the efficacy of the therapy as very high across all categories.

According to their self-evaluation, almost all the participants – with the exception of participant H – reported that they benefited in the fields of group behaviour and memory (Seifert, 2015). There follows an individual case study drawing on both quantitative results but also results from the participant observations and photos collected that illustrates the process of the work and elaborates on the practical implementation of the photo-therapeutic model.

Case study: study participant K (30 years old)

Although suffering from dysthymia and a recurrent depressive disorder, the patient took part in the phototherapy project regularly (ten times) and with great enthusiasm. Her pre-test HDRS-scale evaluation, carried out by the attending doctor, registered a value of 25 points, indicating severe depressive characteristics.

K's particular interest in the process of art therapy sprang from her study of art history. Photography as a form of art therapy held a particular attraction. She quickly got to grips with the technical possibilities of photography in the stabilisation phase and, without hesitation, progressed to the exposure phase by looking for motifs. At first, she photographed the motifs and people of her surroundings, then motifs and details in the city. Later she illustrated shells, relics of her childhood spent on a tropical island, which she brought to the project herself (see Figure 10.5a).

This biographical reference prompted interpretations that saw K counterpoise her positive memories of childhood with the present and an aesthetic reworking of the past. The theme of childhood became an occasion for dialogue with other project participants who also found themselves on the track of biographical clues. She developed a particularly close bond with participant I, who was grappling with childhood issues arising from his migrant background. Born and raised in the Arab world and then moving to Germany in his youth, he had experienced a range of ethnic and cultural problems.

K found many points of reference here, not only of a verbal nature, but also in the creation of her visual work. Moving from photography to photo-collage, she put her historical knowledge of the medium, derived from Dadaism and

a b

Figure 10.5 Participant K a) "Shells from my Childhood", digital photograph, 21x29.7 cm. b) digital photo-collage, 21 x 29.7 cm

the work of John Heartfield (1891–1968), to practical use. A typical technique was the inclusion of profound texts alongside semi-satirical pictorial elements. For example: *Baudelaire de, Des Fleurs du Mal est bordé Mon chemin* (*Of Baudelaire, Flowers of Evil bordered My path).*

In her second work she photographed the cover of a sketch pad. On the right-hand side two vultures can be seen rising up in startled flight. On the lower-left hand side a wolf howls at the birds. In the vacant area on the upper-left the artist had mounted a circular cut-out photograph of participant I, a blurred figure seen against a reflective window pane that functioned as a mirror. The work was completed with a legend, a quotation from Friedrich Nietzsche: "*Wenn du lange in den Abgrund blickst, blickt der Abgrund auch in dich hinein*". ("When you gaze long enough into the abyss, the abyss will gaze back into you") (Figure 10.5b).

K's third work is equally caustic and enigmatic. Here she photographed a portrait of Salvador Dali with pointer, index finger raised. Over the image of Dali's finger she has placed her own, their fingertips touching. She has integrated the logo of Germany's *Arbeitsamt* (job centre) and written below: "*Alle Richtig Gut Einschränken*". ("Limit everyone well"). While the first collage deals with depression, the second places the problem of unemployment firmly in the foreground.

Viewing all three works in order, there appears to be references to looking into the past (childhood), the present (the clinic, depression) and the future (work, creativity), an interpretation confirmed by the patient's conversations during therapy and her comments to other participants. The triptych of images offsets K's disappointment about her work life with her empathy for another patient and delicate childhood memories.

K utilises light and shadow on an aesthetic level to create contrast in her photography as well as in her collages. Influenced by her familiarity with art history, she has worked with symbolically and emotionally charged illustrations. The dramatic text passages deepen the content and composition of her work, articulating the artist's hopes and mental state in a highly contradictory form.

Significant changes in K's depression score, which sank from 25 to 13 points, were confirmed by the patient's self-assessment and her evaluation by the third-party observer. The result was a significant improvement in cognitive ability in the fields of aesthetic perception and visual reception. Not only did K experience improvements in her memory and social interaction, she also developed a keen creative motivation from the activities and a strong emotional connection to the form and content of her work. At the same time, the process seems to have contributed to her sense of relaxation and relief.

Conclusion

The study was developed in response to formative work by Michael Scriven (Wichelhaus, 2007) and conducted in a clinical setting. It was based on a philosophical groundwork on the theory and artistic applications of photography, comprehensive research on older and newer concepts, models and the uses of phototherapy domestically and abroad. The study was carried out in a medical and psychotherapeutic context. Going further, the leading principle behind the study was the practical experience of art therapy combined with a broad knowledge of artistic processes, and art-therapeutic methods and structures. This led to the three-phase treatment model.

Various assessment techniques were employed to record the efficacy of phototherapy through a pre/post- test and process analysis. A wide range of evaluation instruments served to safeguard the reliability of the results. The results of the control and test groups were compared. A clinically relevant reduction in the severity of depressive symptoms could be determined amongst patients who underwent the photo-therapeutic treatment. Here mechanisms were based on the combination of aesthetic perception and experiences with biographical content.

Through design activities, patients initially experienced an emotional distance to their personal problems. There then began a "dynamisation of psychological problems" (Seifert, 2013), an important process in addressing the inertia of patients with depression. In a further step (see Integration Phase/ model of phases of phototherapeutic-clinical treatment) resources were activated, without which this "dynamisation of psychological problems" would not come about. The clinical relevance of the photo-therapeutic programme developed for this study was underpinned by multiple factors:

1 The high flexibility of the methods (from a low to high-threshold) which can be adapted to the situational and clinical requirements – as well as the artistic ability – of patients with depression
2 The complex and holistic approach of combining different spheres of life, activities, learning, social interaction, play and artistic creation with discussion and reflection
3 The strengthening of identity by self-reflection and positive interaction with others.
4 The promotion of proactivity

The present small trial shows that depressive patients in the inpatient area can be treated with the phototherapeutic programme presented here. Further research is necessary to achieve validity, to support the effects and to confirm the basic mechanisms of action of phototherapeutic action.

References

Barthes, R. (1989). *Die helle Kammer: Bemerkungen zur Photographie. (Erstausgabe 1980).* Frankfurt/M.: Suhrkamp Verlag.

Benjamin, W. (2006). *Das Kunstwerk im Zeitalter seiner technischen Reproduzierbarkeit.* Frankfurt/M.: Erstausgabe Suhrkamp Verlag, 1936.

Bense, M. (1969). *Einführung in die Informationstheoretische Ästhetik: Grundlegung und Anwendung in der Texttheorie.* Reinbeck b. Hamburg: Rowohlt Verlag.

Bühl, A. (2008, elfte aktualisierte Ausgabe). SPSS 16. *Einführung in die moderne Datenanalyse.* München: Pearson Studium Verlag.

Cohnen, T. (2008). *Fotografischer Kosmos: Der Beitrag eines Mediums zur visuellen Ordnung der Welt.* transcript Bielefeld: Verlag.

Corbit, I. E., Fryrear, J. L., & Landarten, L. (1992). *Photo art therapy: A Jungian perspective.* Springfiel, IL: Charles C. Thomas.

Dannecker, K. (2006). *Psyche & Ästhetik: Die Transformationen der Kunsttherapie.* Berlin: Medizinisch Wissenschaftliche Verlagsgesellschaft OhG.

Flusser, V. (1992). *Für eine Philosophie der Fotografie. (Erstauflage 1983).* Göttingen: Hubert & Co. Verlag.

Fryrear, J., & Krauss, D. (1983). *Phototherapy in mental health.* Springsfield, IL: Charles C. Thomas Publisher.

Geimer, P. (2009). *Theorien der Fotografie. Zur Einführung.* Hamburg: Junius Verlag.

Giorgi, A. (1970). *Psychology as a human science.* New York: Harper & Row.

Glover-Graf, N., & Miller, E. (2006). The use of phototherapy in group treatment for persons who are the chemically dependent. In *Rehabilitation counseling bulletin* (pp. 166–181). Austin/Texas: Verlag PRO-ED, Inc.

Gough, H. G., & Heilbrun, A. B. Jr. (1965). *The adjective check list manual.* Palo Alto, CA: Consulting Psychologists Press.

Hamilton, M. (1960/2005). *A rating scale for depression.* Weyer, C.I.P.S. (Hrsg.) (deutsche Version), Göttingen: Beltz-Verlag.

Härter, M., Bermejo, I., & Niebling, W. (2007). *Praxismanual Depression: Diagnostik und Therapie erfolgreich umsetzen.* Köln: Deutscher Ärzteverlag.

Hautzinger, M. (1984). Veränderungsverläufe depressiver Symptomatiken bei kognitiver Verhaltenstherapie. In M. Hautzinger & R. Straub (Hrsg.), *Psychologische Aspekte depressiver Störungen* (S. 243–267). Regensburg: Roderer.

Hautzinger, M. (2003). *Kognitive Verhaltenstherapie bei Depressionen* (6., überarbeitete Aufl.). Weilheim: Verlagsgruppe Beltz.

Maier, W., & Wagner, M. (2005). Genetische Faktoren. In M. Perrez & U. Baumann (Hrsg.). *Lehrbuch. Klinische Psychologie – Psychotherapie.* 3. überarbeitete Ausgabe (pp. 188–211), Bern: Verlag Hans Huber.

Merleau-Ponty, M. (1962). *Phenomenology of perception.* London: Routledge & Kegan Paul LTD.

Peirce, C. S. (1986). Semiotische Schriften. (Hrsg. Kösel, C.; Pape, H.). Frankfurt: Shurkamp Verlag.

Reichelt, S. (2008). *Prozessorientiertes Malen als traumatherapeutische Intervention: Ein Beitrag zur ressourcenfundierten Bewältigung von Extremerfahrungen in Kindheit und Adoleszens.* Regensburg: Roderer Verlag.

Rost, D. H. (2007). *Interpretation und Bewertung pädagogisch-psychologischer Studien: Eine Einführung. (zweite Auflage).* Weinheim, Basel: Beltz-Verlag.

Schurian, W. (1986). *Psychologie Ästhetischer Wahrnehmungen: Selbstorganisation und Vielschichtigkeit von Empfindungen, Verhalten und Verlangen.* Opladen: Westdeutscher Verlag.

Schwering, J. (1995). Wahrnehmung in der Melancholie (endogene Depression). In *Psychiatrische Praxis* Bd. 22, (S. 254–256). Stuttgart: Georg Thieme Verlag.

Seifert, K. (2013). *Kunsttherapie bei Patienten mit unipolaren Depressionen im klinischen Bereich: Entwicklung, Durchführung und Evaluation eines fototherapeutischen Behandlungsmodells.* Köln: Claus Richter Verlag.

Seifert, K. (2015). Studie zur Anwendung und Evaluation eines fototherapeutischen Behandlungsmodells für Patienten mit unipolaren Depressionen in der klinischen Versorgung. *Zeitschrift für Musik-, Tanz- und Kunsttherapie*, 26(2), 88–102.

Sontag, S. (1995). *Über Fotografie. (Amerikanische Originalausgabe 1977)*. Frankfurt/M.: Fischer Taschenbuchverlag.

Speigelberg, H. (1970). One human uses of phenomenology. In F. J. Schmith (Ed.), *Phenomenology in perspective*. The Hague: Nijhoff.

Spence, J., & Salomon, J. (1995). *What can a woman do with a camera? Photography for woman*. London: Scarlett Press.

Spire, R. H. (1973). Photographic self-image confrontation. *American Journal of Nursing*, 73(7), 1207–1210.

Spitzing, G. (1985). *Fotopsychologie: Die subjektive Seite des Objektivs*. Weinheim und Basel: Beltz Verlag.

Van Elst, Ludger Tebartz (2010). Trübe Aussichten: Die Netzhaut depressiver Menschen reagiert schwächer auf Kontraste. In: Gehirn & Geist (Eds.), *Das Magazin für Psychologie und Hirnforschung*, Nr.7–8, Heidelberg: Spektrum der Wissenschaft, Verlagsgesellschaft.

Walker, J. (1986). The use of ambiguous of artistic images for enhancing self-awareness in psychotherapy. In *The arts of psychotherapy* (vol. 13, pp. 241–248). USA: Ankho International Inc.

Wheeler, M. (2009). Photo-psycho-praxis. *European Journal of Psychotherapy and Counseling*, (11)1.

Weiser, J. (2004). PhotoTherapy techniques in counseling and therapy – Using ordinary snapshots and photo-interactions to help clients heal their lives. *The Canadian Art Therapy Association Journal*, 17(2), 23–53.

Weiser, J. Phototherapeutische Techniken in Beratung und Therapie. Verfügbar unter: Retrieved March 14, 2017 from https://phototherapy-centre.com/german.

Weiser, J., & Krauss, D. (2009). Picturing phototherapy and therapeutic photography: Commentary on articles arising from the 2008 international conference in Finland. Rouledge Verlag (11/1), 77–99.

Wichelhaus, B. (1989). *Semiotische Grundlagen der Themenbildung. Kunstwissenschaftliche Grundlagen der Themen-Generierung auf semiotischer Basis*. Aachen: Alano-Verlag.

Wichelhaus, B. (2000). unst als Medizin – Kunstraum" Krankenhaus. *Zeitschrift für Musik-, Kunst- und Tanztherapie*, 11(3), 146–152.

Wichelhaus, B. (2007). Formative Evaluation in der Kunsttherapieforschung. In P. Sinapius & M. Ganß (Hrsg.). *Grundlagen, Modelle und Beispiele kunsttherapeutischer Dokumentation* (S. 179–186). Frankfurt/M.: Peter Lang Verlag.

Ziller, C., & Smith, D. E. (1977). Phenomenological utilization of photographs. *Journal of Phenomenological Psychology*, 7(2), 172–182.

Part III

Arts therapies with those experiencing depression in later life

Chapter 11

Art therapy with the older person

One life, many losses

Jane Burns

Introduction

Depression is a complex condition that is difficult to define and is interconnected with other mental and physical disorders (Zubala et al., 2014). The black dog institute (2012) state that "the most common type of depression in later life is a non-melancholic depression which is linked to psychological factors, personality characteristics and stressful life events" (p. 2). Key amongst the psychological factors contributing to depression is loss, or more precisely the impact of multiple losses of family, home and a deterioration in health experienced by many older people.

This chapter will first consider the society's construct of loss in light of the images of ageing that surround us in the media. Following this, research and clinical data will be drawn upon to consider the psychological consequence loss has on the person. Faced with such a loss the potential of counseling or therapy for the person becomes ever more relevant. Acknowledging this, the second part of this chapter will draw from my PhD study in the use of arts therapies (art, drama, dance movement and music therapy) (Burns (2009) and will focus on the role art therapy can play in supporting the person to express and process feelings of loss. It is argued that the sensory, stimulatory touch of the art materials can offer a safe and contained way to help the person unlock and work through feelings of grief triggered by multiple losses.

Methodology

The methodology underpinning the findings reported here is interpretive description, a Canadian qualitative methodology (Thorne et al., 2008). Interpretive description advocates a pluralistic approach for understanding the complex dialogue between clinical and research knowledge.

The study involved thirty-one semi-structured interviews with arts therapists from art therapy, music therapy, dramatherapy and dance movement therapy, participant observations of thirteen care settings and formal and informal interviews with ten medical/care staff who work with the arts therapists. The descriptive map was analysed using template analysis (King, 1998) and was interpreted using an integrative interpretive analysis (Heidegger, 1927; Smith 2004).

In this chapter, I will highlight findings relating to *art* therapy, while I will refer to case examples from my own clinical practice as an art therapist. These examples will act as illustrations of the key points made in the text. Links with the literature will be made throughout.

Constructs of loss

Ageing in itself is not a prerequisite to feelings of *loss*. Loss is part of life and happens to us all throughout the life cycle. What is interesting is society's view of *loss* as it pertains to the older person. Society's understanding of what constitutes the 'remaining' capabilities of the older person once milestones like retirement and free bus passes come along is often very skewed. A scroll through Google Images of the older person highlights juxtaposed views on ageing – ranging from either photographs of very actively engaged older people epitomised in one image I saw of an eighty-year bikini-wearing woman, mid-star jump, doing beach aerobics, contrasted with a photograph of an isolated, hunched-over, wheelchair-bound older lady staring hauntingly into the camera. You feel her pain! Her loss! Tyler (2002) talks about a society which does not want to 'get too close' to someone like her for fear of how this reminds us of the fragility of our own life and ultimately our own mortality.

Pressure to successfully negotiate Erik Erikson's (1994) life-stage eight 'ego integrity vs despair' to the satisfactory conclusion that 'life was generally ok' falls short for many people due to an accumulation of factors which may or may not be age-related. Feelings of loss for anyone at any age often begin with an event which triggers some sort of life transition such as a change of routine brought about by loss of work, family or friends. For some older adults, retirement or moving from the family home into smaller accommodations, a small deterioration in health alters the status quo and leaves the person feeling more vulnerable and less assured about everyday certainties. Self-confidence ebbs away as doubts and anxieties emerge. The person may be reminded of other losses that they have experienced (Waller, 2002)

Research has indicated that a period of significant life transition can trigger depression and feelings of social isolation (Greaves & Farbus, 2006). Older adults in Nimrod's (2007) study who chose to keep actively involved in social activities in their extended leisure time were found to have a greater sense of wellbeing than those who reduced their active involvement. Moreover, those who sought new challenges found "a positive association between innovation and wellbeing" (Nimrod, 2007: 107). Proactive involvement in creative arts can help to counteract any negativity they experience (Burns et al., 2008). Furthermore, research by Burns et al. (2008) looking at the impact of the arts on the wellbeing of those recently retired found that unless the person actively went out and engaged in some form of meaningful activity shortly after retiring then there was the possibility that the person might never engage, thereby potentially putting their wellbeing at risk. Many of the fifteen participants in this qualitative action-research study spoke of how quickly confidence erodes once retired and how easy it is to withdraw from friends and family. Losses such as those mentioned previously and in particular the loss of a loved one such as a spouse may catapult the person into a state of numb passivity and ultimately the detachment of depression which can be difficult to return from without appropriate therapeutic support.

Unsurprisingly the experience of *loss* for the older person living with a cognitive impairment such as dementia is often magnified particularly when the person moves into residential care. The loss of family and home and all that is familiar may bring about a state of such heightened stress and anxiety for the person that she may continually seek out her lost parent. The imprint of mother (or whoever is the significant attachment figure) and the importance of the parental relationship (Bowlby, 1997) leaves such an indelible mark on us that at times of stress that Miesen (1999, 1992) suggests the person who has dementia may continually seek out this parent figure, even if he or she is no longer alive. Miesen (1999, 1992) terms this 'parent fixation', where literally the person becomes completely focused on finding and resurrecting the lost parent. The following case example illustrates this 'parent fixation'.

Case Example 1

One lady, called Grace [pseudonym], I worked with attended a dementia day unit very close to her parental home. She was referred to art therapy to help reduce her anxieties about finding her parents. Grace spent most of her time in the unit waiting by the front door for an opportunity to dash out and cross the road to visit her parental home, despite both parents having long since been deceased. In art therapy, I listened to Grace telling and re-tell stories about her golden-haired mother, pipe-smoking father and naughty younger sister. Each session I saw her draw pictures of her family and the home she lived in. Once Grace's life-story was being heard and her images viewed she didn't have the same desire to run out the door.

Evans (2004) notes that where there has been a particular disruption in the early attachment relationship such as an early parental separation from the child might denote a particular vulnerability to depression in later life. Negative psychosocial feelings of alienation and isolation from others lead to depression. Evans (2004) notes the volume of losses that an older person may experience can trigger a bereavement reaction which for those with ambivalent or insecure attachment issues can be particularly difficult. Evans (2004: 49), for example, observes that the 'de-cathexis' that is required to let go of the lost object and to make room for new relationships is more difficult when there is no expectation that any new relationships are possible.

Bruce et al. (2002) mixed method study looking at the quality of life of people with dementia in residential settings found that "people with dementia need different kinds of support for their efforts to seek meaning and make sense of what is happening to them". During their two-year study the researchers followed the lives of ninety-three people living in residential care using a range of methods including interviews, rating scales and questionnaires. The authors concluded that the residents "attempted to make sense of and actively respond to the world around him/her", their "emotional wellbeing was fragile and easily threatened by what otherwise might seem small events and trivial interactions", and they needed "time to talk, and listeners who can tune into the manner in which they talk about their difficulties and acknowledge that they have significant problems to cope with" (Bruce et al., 2002: 10).

In the care setting medical/care staff do not always have time to listen to the person in their charge as they are under pressure to look after the day-to-day needs of many people. Psychologically, it can be hard for staff to cope with the overwhelming losses that their clients project upon them. Without adequate supervision, it is perhaps easier to retreat into the practice of 'doing' tasks rather than 'holding' the relationship as advanced by Kitwood (1997) in his model of Personhood, which promotes the right of each person who has dementia to expect to have love, occupation, attachment, comfort, inclusion and identity.

Key practices of art therapy with the older person

Aware of late 1980s society's care culture in which a malignant standardization of care was offered to people with dementia, one that penetrated the care culture suppressing the person's unique experience of dementia and devalued the person's right to be treated as an individual, Kitwood (1997) acknowledged the importance of the therapeutic relationship. He felt that the therapeutic relationship had the potential to offer the person a different kind of relationship "one that is more tolerating, accepting and stable than normal relationships" (Kitwood, 1997: 98). He commented that through the relationship the person with dementia may feel a sense of self-worth and through involvement in a different type of relationship like this the person can learn "new action schemata" which can be transferred to other relationships, in other contexts. Kitwood (1997: 99) observed that for a person who has dementia "therapeutic change can endure but there is no point at which therapeutic work is done". He suggests that the person requires the constant replenishment of the six psychological concepts of Personhood.

Garner (2004) has written that psychodynamically-orientated psychotherapists have to adapt practice to suit the needs of the person. She noted that in verbal psychotherapy the psychotherapist may take on the role of narrator helping the person to remember the stories and words that they have used. Empathetic listening is an important part of the work because through listening attentively to the person, symbolic and metaphoric themes may emerge from his/her stories which may direct the therapist to how the person is feeling. Casson (1994) notes through these stories that the person can maintain a sense of identity, remember him/herself as an active person who coped with situations in certain ways.

In one of the earliest papers on group psychotherapy with older adults, Lakin (1988) suggests that psychotherapists need to pay attention to the physical and psychological capabilities of their clients by offering them shorter but more regular sessions. In my PhD research (Burns, 2009) I found that a regular session of up to one hour per week (session duration depended on the person's assessed needs in terms of desire and capacity to stay present in the session) was perceived by arts psychotherapists as being enough to sustain a meaningful therapeutic interaction. In terms of attending either group or individual art therapy there can be a justification for people experiencing extreme loss to be offered either (or often starting individually and moving into the group); both types of therapy appear to have a place. Individual therapy is important for people who Abraham (2004) and Lakin (1988) consider might require personal support, who are frightened and paranoid, perhaps have difficulty with interpersonal relationships. The following case example illustrates this point.

Case Example 2

Jill, who was 55 years old had recently been diagnosed with early onset Alzheimer 's disease, was referred to art therapy because she was finding the group culture of the day unit difficult. Jill had spent her life caring for her children and husband. On arrival she would retreat into a chair in the corner of the unit's living room and hardly move from the seat despite the best efforts of the staff to encourage her engagement in the unit's activities. Staff wondered if some individual art therapy might be preferable for Jill. I invited Jill for an initial first session to see how she would get on.

Jill arrived at the make-shift art room (a converted relaxation room with existing laser projector and fiber optics). As I invited her in she darted, without saying a word, straight to the window and stood looking out over the suburban landscape before then turning to come and sit at the table. On the table was a small selection of art material (paints, pencils, paper and some textiles). I introduced myself and spoke a little about art therapy careful not to overload Jill with information. I invited Jill to try the materials but she seemed too absorbed in her own thoughts, somewhat nervously pulling at her sleeve. Slowly I took a piece of paper from the pile and filled a palette with some blue, red and green paint, using a brush I very slowly began to paint a mandala. Jill watched the repetitive action of me loading the paint and putting it on the paper. She reached out to touch the palette and withdrew her hand. She then stood up and went to the window. I asked her what she saw and she said 'worms'. She came to the table and picked up a sheet of white paper and pointed at the blue and red paints. I loaded them into the palettes, Jill picked up the brush and began to create figure 11.1.

As Jill worked, I was struck by the depth and fluidity of line in the blue background and the red central shape. These contrast sharply with the choppy lines to the bottom right of the image. I asked Jill about the image and she said, "it's a picture of fire and worms".

Jill's work was potentially symbolic of the paranoia she was experiencing as part of her dementia. Her hypervigilance at the window hinted at a potential threat. It is not uncommon for clients new to therapy to find it anxiety provoking but I wondered if Jill's image spoke also about the temporal loss of her husband and children as she adjusted to spending daytimes with strangers in the unit.

Individual work was appropriate for Jill, she needed somewhere away from the group to express her feelings of anxiety and loss. The image contained her feelings in a way that was tolerable for her to view and give name to them.

Figure 11.1 Jill's picture "of fire and worms".

For many other older people healing and solace can be found in the company of others in the form of group art therapy. Rusted et al. (2006) and Lakin (1988) comment on the importance of group work in providing important social connections to enable the, often, isolated person, to remain socially involved with a group of like-minded people. In an early paper on psychodynamic groups with older clients, Linden (1953) agreed that the person can be lifted out of his/her isolation by taking part in the group, but only if it is a group in which the person feels motivated and happy to participate. Group success requires careful planning (Burns, 2009). All too often therapists are faced with a situation where group membership is often determined by who is in the residential/ward lounge at the time the therapist arrives. Offering an introduction session in the lounge can be a useful starting point for meeting potential referrals. Longevity of the group with a potential meaningful outcome for group members does depend on the art therapist carefully assessing the different needs of each person and most importantly that person's readiness to take part in the group process, to engage with other group members and with the art materials. Loss can leave a person in such a state of numbed detachment that it can be difficult for that person to reach out and connect with other people. The image, as Jill's work suggested, can act as a powerful container of the person's unspoken loss, a loss when viewed by other group members may spark a light of recognition about their own situation. Thus, a shared emotion, embodied in the image of one person, can have a cathartic effect on many.

Images containing death symbols such as figures of deceased relatives, coffins, tombstones and religious symbolism often appear and are discussed together often through use of 'black' humour. For example, one group I worked with kept an ongoing discussion of the best funerals they had attended with highest marks given to music played and buffet choices. As a young therapist at the time I was slightly shocked by the frivolity of joking about funerals like this. I wondered if it showed a lack of psychological depth and understanding within the group. I soon understood that expressing feelings of loss to others is both powerful and painful and humour used as a defense mechanism was just one way in which such losses could be safely explored.

One aspect of the tolerating relationship art therapists aim to foster with their older clients is the desire to encourage independent choice-making and freedom to explore the art materials (Burns, 2009; Harlan, 1990). The assumption is that the more directive the therapist is the more she dominates the session thereby suppressing the 'voice' of the person and perpetuating biomedical cultural norms that things are still 'done to us' rather than 'with us'. The reality in practice is not so simple and in fact in my research I found that art therapists skillfully mediate between more directive and non-directive elements within both individual and group sessions (see table 11.1). Orientating the person at the beginning of the session to time and place "Welcome! It's Friday afternoon

Table 11.1 Arts Therapies Session Structure (Burns, 2009).

Structure		*Method*	*Process*
Beginning	Phase One	Check-In	Orientating
	Phase Two	Art Form Warm Up	Engaging
Middle		Main Activity	Connecting
			Expressing
End	Phase One	Art Form Close	Reflecting
	Phase Two	Goodbye	

and we are here at the art therapy session" and then to other group members "Jean, I notice you are wearing a dark blue jumper today and Mandy has chosen to wear pink."

Small connecting statements can help to orientate the group or individual client to the room, to other people (if in a group) and then to the art materials. Findings from Burns' 2009 research study indicated that many therapists engage the person or group in a small art exercise warm-up, a checking-in using the materials, a conversation on paper where two people turn to dialogue with each other via the art materials or drawing mandalas. The two starting phases supported the move into the main activity which was largely non-directive and by which time the person or group feel more confident about working independently with the art materials. The end of the session was signaled by a chance for the participants and therapist to sit back and look at the artwork. Those able to speak might offer a reflective comment about their work (or others' work if in a group) while more non-verbal participants might just rely on sensory tactile exploration of the images through touch.

Mediating the relationship between directive and non-directive approaches can support vulnerable older clients who may feel too exposed by a solely non-directive approach or equally too controlled by a dominate therapist. Assaults on ego strength such as the multiple losses that some older people have experienced by the time they come to art therapy require the art therapist to modify and adapt conventional practice in this way. An example of this can be found in the third case example presented here.

Case Example 3

I was working as a sessional art therapist in a new state-of-the-art dementia unit. I was passing by the dining area when I noticed Susan, a care worker, gingerly putting down a bowl of soup in front of a very petite older woman who I later discovered was 92 years old. Susan said, "no Betty please don't nip". Speaking to Susan during handover she told me that staff were finding it difficult to cope with Betty's constant nipping and scratching every time they went near her. I asked Susan if she knew why Betty was doing this. She said 'no'. Betty wasn't from Scotland and had no relatives in this country so they were unable to check with the family about possible triggers. Betty had been seen by a doctor to determine (as far a possible) that she wasn't in any pain. I was curious about Betty's desire to scratch staff, which on the surface could be interpreted as attacking towards the staff but also could speak of an unmet need. Was Betty's desire to make physical contact with someone/something – a need to leave a mark?

The next week I went back and asked Betty and her key worker if she would like to attend art therapy. Betty seemed quite curious about the box of materials I had with me. Once consent was given it was agreed Betty would come to an introduction session.

I was sitting at the table when Betty was brought to the room, in her wheelchair, by Susan. Betty joined me at the table and promptly fell asleep for 10 minutes. It was the after-lunch time-slot so no real surprise. I sat quietly beside her sorting the material box. Betty awoke and said, 'what's that'? I reminded her she was in the art room and talked a little about the small selection of art materials (pencils, paint, brushes, textiles, paper and easy-form clay) in front of her. As I moved my hand to illustrate the various materials she made a lunge forward to grab my right hand. I didn't want to recoil in fear but rather to try and stay in the moment. As Betty's nails were about to reach the surface of my hand, my fight or flight response kicked in and I reached for the box of pencils which sat half way between Betty and myself. I offered it to Betty to take a pencil. Betty stopped her hand in mid-air and grabbed hold of a rogue felt-tip pen that had found its way into the box and looked at it carefully. She then rolled it between her fingers and pulled the top on and off. After a few moments she said 'paper'. I pulled a sheet of A5 white paper from the pile and put it in front of her. She didn't bother about my hand as I placed the paper in front of her. She then appeared to hunch over the paper and began to use the felt-tip with what seemed like great determination. I couldn't see what she was drawing but the force of some of her movements against the table left the air filled with small screeching sounds. She then let out a huge guttural cry, like wounded animal. She then promptly fell asleep, hands over the image. I suddenly felt a huge wave of sadness come over. I felt overcome with homesickness. I felt I had to take a few deep breaths to stop the tears from flowing. Betty awoke just as the session ended and as Susan came in the room to collect her. We didn't get time to acknowledge and reflect on the image. So, I told Betty that I would keep her image safe and looked forward to seeing her the next week. She gave me a small nod as she left the room.

When finally, I looked at the image Betty had literally etched into the paper the words 'home' and 'want to go home' over and over again, sitting beside one of words 'home' was a small half drawn building with three walls and what looked like a single-branched tree. When I met with Susan later that day I asked her if the team had considered that Betty's behavior might be related to her feelings of loss. Susan said that staff had possibly perceived Betty's attacks as her rejection of them and they had concluded she wished to be left alone. I felt the opposite was true that instead Betty needed someone to hear her story, to learn of the land she came from and to witness her pain at being parted from it.

When working with an older person who has experienced multiple losses important considerations are the issues of transference and countertransference. Hepple (2004) discussed how often the transference dynamic is overlooked by psychotherapists when they work with older people, particularly those who have dementia.

> To overlook the possibility for transference, to neglect the memory traces of adult sexuality, to disregard the vestiges of a former reasoning, judicious, and responsible ego, denies any therapy the goal of personality rehabilitation and reintegration.
>
> (Hepple, 2004: 155)

In the transference relationship the art therapist is forced to confront his/her own feelings about death and mortality (Burns, 2009). The therapist's feelings may mirror those experienced by the person she is working with, feelings such as loss, helplessness and anger (Waller, 2002, Wilks & Byers, 1992). Wilks and Byers (1992) comment on the complexity of the countertransference.

> It is often hard to keep aware of the value of the work. Our clients convey a sense of futility and helplessness which makes us feel helpless in countertransference. I think that this is one reason why the care of elderly people with severe memory loss is often seen by professionals as one of the least attractive areas of work.
>
> (Wilks & Byers, 1992: 95)

In my own research (Burns, 2009), I found that only five out of the thirty-one arts therapists I interviewed actually wanted to work in this area. They were there because jobs in other, more desirable, clinical areas such as adult mental health or work with children were unavailable. One therapist reported that she began working in the field during her training but due to ill health she missed the allocation of placements. As a result, she was given the last one available which was on a continuing care ward. She said she was initially 'devastated' and thought she would not get on well with this client group. She did not feel ready to work with older clients. Spaniol (1997) talks about therapists' feeling 'culturally incompetent' to work with older clients when a big part of society is focused on youth and beauty. Working with people at the end of their lives requires the therapist to work through their feelings of 'futility and helplessness" so that they tolerate the multiple losses encountered in the transference dynamic of the people they work with.

Interestingly, all the therapists I interviewed did not want to leave the clinical field once they had begun the work. They found the work challenging but also very rewarding. All spoke of it being a privilege to bear witness to person's memories and life-narratives. Wadeson (2000) talks about feelings of love that may be evoked as the relationship mirrors other positive relationships. Wadeson (2000) comments on the deep sense of attachment and love the therapist may feel towards her "grandparent". Unless worked through in supervision, the deep attachment felt by the therapist may spill over into a tendency to infantilise the older person (Linden, 1953). Unlike working with children who are in a state of dependency waiting for the development of independence, the older person has already led an independent life and is now in a state of forced, or 'hostile, but anxious and fearful' dependency as a consequence of the degenerative disease (Linden, 1953: 155). The person needs therapeutic support from a not-too-controlling therapist; otherwise dormant infantile patterns, related to dependency may be re-awakened.

When the balance is correct, the relationship between therapist and the older person should offer her an 'increased control' over her life according to Falk (2002: 68). In an art therapy session the person is able to select and use the art materials in the way she chooses thereby offering her "an opportunity to organise their experience in their own way without expectations from others" (Falk, 2002: 68). Exploring this issue further, Falk (2002) writes that the images created can act as a strong 'holding-memory' in the sense that week on week clients could remember the symbolic images they had created. Falk's (2002) explanation of this feature of the work is that, through the image the person is able to "move from an exterior space that was perceived as muddled and full of dread, to an interior space, over which they had some sense of control (Falk, 2002: 120). The notion of the art form 'holding' the person was also observed by the art therapists I interviewed; images were often remembered long after the name of the art therapist or carer had been forgotten. Furthermore, the awakening of the person's sensory world by the stimulatory touch (Kahn-Denis, 1997) of the art materials provides a powerful link to the unconscious state and may support the person to work through her losses.

Conclusion

Loss enters all of our lives at some point. What perhaps separates early from later life loss is often the multitude of different types of loss the person may have experienced by reaching an old age. It is, therefore, perhaps hard to think of a time when therapeutic support is more needed. Helping the person traverse the emotional wilderness of loss (and ultimately, if left unattended, depression) is a role that the art therapist can help with. The symbolic, metaphorical quality of the image offers a non-verbal more tolerating way of viewing and ultimately processing the loss(es) the person has experienced.

Art therapists can attend to the needs of their clients by paying careful attention to the person's unique experience of dementia and to consider how sessions may need to be adapted to provide the correct level of direct and non-directive support to facilitate creative exploration and engagement.

References

Abraham, R. (2004). *When words have lost their meaning Alzheimer's patients communicate through art.* London: Praeger.

Black Dog Institute (2012). Depression in older people. Retrieved from www.blackdoginstitute.org.au/docs/DepressioninOlderPeople.pdf. Accessed on 24th February 2016.

Bowlby, J. (1997). *Attachment and loss.* London: Pimlico.

Bruce, E. M. A., Surr, C. B. A., Tibbs, M. A., & Downs, M. (2002). Moving towards a special kind of care for people with dementia living in care homes. *Nursing Times Research*, 7, 335–347.

Burns, J. (2009). An interpretive description of the patterns of practice of arts therapists working with older people who have dementia in the UK. PhD thesis, Queen Margaret University.

Burns, J., Oliver, S., & Karkou, V. (2008). The Older Persons' experiences of creativity in relation to wellbeing: A collaborative research project. Royal Bank of Scotland Centre of Older People's Agenda. Queen Margaret University.

Casson, J. (1994). Flying towards neverland. *Dramatherapy*, 16 (2–3), 3–7.

Erikson, E. H. (1994). *Identity and the life cycle.* W.W. Norton & Company; Rev Ed edition.

Evans, S. (2004). Attachment in old age: Bowlby and others, in talking over the years. In S. Evans & J. Garner (Eds.), *A handbook of dynamic psychotherapy with older adults.* Hove: Brunner-Routledge.

Falk, B. (2002). Holding memory. In D. Waller (Ed.), *Arts therapies and progressive illness.* Hove: Brunner-Routledge.

Garner, J. (2004) Dementia. In Evans, S. and Garner, J. (eds.). *Talking over the years. A handbook of dynamic psychotherapy with older adults.* Hove: Brunner-Routledge.

Greaves, C. J., & Farbus, L. (2006). Effects of creative and social activity on the health and well-being of socially isolated older people: Outcomes from a multi-method observational study. *Journal of the Royal Society for the Promotion of Health*, 126(3) May, 134–142.

Harlan, J. (1990). Beyond the patient to the person aspects of autonomous functioning in individual with mild to moderate dementia. *The American Journal of Art Therapy*, 28 (4), pp. 99-106.

Heidegger, M. (1927). Translated as Being and Time by John Macquarrie and Edward Robinson. Oxford: Basil Blackwell, 1978.

Hepple, J. (2004). Psychotherapies with older people: An overview. *Advances in Psychiatric Treatment*, 10, 317–337.

Kahn-Denis, K. B. (1997). Art therapy with geriatric dementia clients. *Art Therapy Journal of American Art Therapy Association*, 14(3), 158–160.

King, N. (1998). Template analysis. In Cassell, C. & Symon, G. (eds.) *Qualitative methods and analysis in organizational research*, Thousand Oaks, CA: Sage Publications.

Kitwood, T. (1997). *Dementia reconsidered*. London: Routledge.

Lakin, M. (1988). Group therapies with the elderly, issues and prospects. In B. Maclennan, S. Saul & M. Baku-Weiner (Eds.), *Group psychotherapy for the elderly*. New York: International Universities Press.

Linden, M. E. (1953). Group psychotherapy for institutionalized senile woman: Study in gerontologic human relations. *International Journal of Group Psychotherapy*, 3, 150–170.

Miesen, B. M. L. (1992). Attachment theory and dementia. In G. Jones & B. M. L. Miesen (Eds.), *Caregiving in dementia research and application*. London: Routledge.

Miesen, B. M. L. (1999). *Dementia close-up*. Hove: Routledge.

Nimrod, G. (2007). Expanding, reducing, concentrating and diffusing: Post retirement leisure behavior and life satisfaction. *Leisure Sciences*, 29, 91–111.

Rusted, J., Sheppard, L., & Waller, D. (2006). A multi-centre randomized control group trial on the use of art therapy for older people with dementia. *Group Analysis*, 39(4), 517 536.

Smith, K.. (2004). Art therapy and older people. In S. Evans & J. Garner (Eds.), *Talking over the years: A handbook of dynamic psychotherapy with older adults*. Hove: Brunner-Routledge.

Spaniol, S. (1997). Art therapy with older adults: challenging myths: Building competencies. *Art Therapy Journal of American Art Therapy Association*, 14(3), 158–160.

Thorne, S. (2008). *Interpretive description*. Canada: Left Coast Press.

Tyler, J. (2002). Art Therapy with older clients clinically diagnosed as having Alzheimer's disease and dementia. In Waller, D. (ed.) (2002) *Arts Therapies and Progressive Illness*. Brunner-Routledge. Hove.

Waller, D. (2002). Difficulty in being. In D. Waller (Ed.), *Arts therapies and progressive illness*. Hove: Brunner-Routledge.

Wadeson (2000). *Art therapy practice*. John Wiley and Sons: New York.

Wilks, R., & Byers, A. (1992). Art therapy with elderly in statutory care. In D. Waller & A. Gilroy (Eds.), *Art therapy a handbook*. Buckingham: Open University Press.

Zubala, A., Karkou, V., & Gleeson, N. (2014). Description of arts therapies practice with adults suffering from depression in the UK: Qualitative findings from the nationwide survey. *The Arts in Psychotherapy*, 41(5)

Chapter 12

Dramatherapy in working with people with dementia

The need for playfulness in creative ageing as an antidote for depression and isolation

Sue Jennings

Introduction

This chapter concerns the anxiety and depression that affects older people when they are under pressure to maintain self-control of their bodies and to keep alert and memorise with their brains. It also discusses the many losses suffered by older people and the decreasing attachments of close relationships and familiar surroundings.

The chapter proposes that changes of attitudes are needed in a world that has an increasing number of people living into old age (Schweitzer & Bruce, 2008). In a country like the UK where little value is put on older people, (Walker, 1985), there is a need to shift perspectives and place significance in older age as a source of experience, maturity and wisdom (Jennings, 1998). The chapter also proposes an approach called 'Creative Ageing' (Jennings, 2006) which has become adapted into a philosophy and training known as 'Creative Care' (Jennings, 2012; Allan, 2013). It emphasises that dramatherapists need in depth training in working with dementia and are also uniquely placed to address attachment issues with older people through dramatic playfulness and process (Marshall, 2013), especially those who are in institutional care.

Bodies, age and activity

Ageing people are subject to enormous pressure to be clean and tidy. There is distaste for normal bodily functions, and an increasing fear of loss of control, or 'disgracing oneself'. This of course means big business for continence pads and pants, waterproof bed sheets and aprons. However, the loss of control or the *fear* of losing control, both contribute to the anxiety and depression amongst older people. Weight control and plenty of exercise can assist the delay of incontinence. The physical movement involved in therapy approaches such as dramatherapy and dance movement therapy and activities such as drama games, yoga, creative dance and a host of other approaches encourage flexibility, coordination, balance, self-confidence, social relations and many more benefits.

Older people by and large do not want to sit still and watch TV or doze in the chair until the next cup of tea or visitor. As described in the projects below, participants could not wait to be active and involved. An inspiring source for me was this idea of being able to 'weave lives back together' through creative activity (Futterman Collier, 2012). There is often a misapprehension that older people want to be 'quiet' and nursing staff tell me that they do not want to be troubled. This can be so engrained to make one staff member say that residents were not affected by family members not visiting.

Brains and age

As people get older there is some slowing down of thought processes and maybe lapses of memory. This may be part of normal ageing and not necessarily a sign of dementia. However, forgetfulness can cause anxiety from families that the person is deteriorating mentally or developing dementia. The person themselves can feel this anxiety from others and also wonder if they are 'losing it'.

> *A personal example illustrates this when I attended a GP surgery for a visiting appointment in a town where I used to live. There was a familiar name on the board and I asked to see this doctor. When I went through I had never seen this doctor before and it was a man, not a woman. He looked at me with a look of, how shall I say, disbelief and impatience, rather than reassurance and kindliness. Then the penny dropped: the name was the same as a doctor from my own surgery. I felt stupid.*

Older people may be treated like children who are still learning control and developing their brains. As a consequence of this, decorations and materials in care homes are often more reminiscent of a day nursery rather than an adult environment (Chalfont, 2008). In addition, instead of trying to understand clients who protest, they are called 'difficult'.

The Creative Care approach suggests that maintaining playfulness and a healthy regard for the arts, contribute to a feeling of wellness in everyone, not only older people (Jennings, 1998). Research now exists (Killick & Craig, 2012, Katz, 1999) that demonstrates that music and movement make the largest contribution to maintaining brain functions, compared with cross-words, brain games and Sudoku.

Attachment and age

The vast majority of literature on attachment refers to children and teenagers, with a sparse amount on attachment in later life (Cicirelli, 2010). Bowlby (1958), Spitz (1947), and Ainsworth (with Bowlby (1979), who are the early pioneers of attachment understanding, observed and worked in many infant and child settings.

Bowlby in his later writing (1979), commented on the wider context of attachment: "Attachment behaviour is any form of behaviour that results in a person attaining or maintaining proximity to some other preferred or differentiated individual" (p. 154).

Older people may have suffered loss of their spouse or siblings, and in some situations, loss of children (Crimmens, 1998). This loss is not necessarily through death but also children moving overseas where contact is maintained through means such as Skype, which is difficult for people with dementia. There are also couples where one person has developed dementia and their partner is unable to care for them, or have been deemed to be unable by authorities. As well as loss of attachment relationships there is also loss of the family home and familiar surroundings. Loss of favourite objects, such as the special vase that was given as a wedding present all contribute to the overall need for grieving, which, if not addressed will contribute towards depression. Additionally, many people have to leave behind pets which they may have had for many years. People also have routines: their daily walk to the shop or park, the arrival of post, many regular occurrences that structure their day and keep them orientated in experience and anticipation.

In private care homes, residents are able to take some possessions with them and even furniture if they have a private room. However, most people do not have this possibility and suffer the shock of major losses from which many of them do not recover.

In the training of care workers, I have found that they grasp the understanding of attachment very quickly, once they have looked at their own losses. The training has led to a deeper insight and a more flexible response towards people who are elderly and confused.

> *One example illustrates this when staff began to be fed up with the constant calling out from one resident, late at night. They tried locking her in so she banged on the door and shouted even louder. One of the care workers unlocked the door and asked her what she would like and she replied: "Oh can I go for a walk, I would love that". He proffered his arm and then gently walked with her down the corridor and at the corner she said: "That was lovely, but I think it is time to go home now". They returned to her room and she went to bed and slept deeply until the next morning.*
>
> *In the care home where the Shakespeare Project took place, described below, the staff attended a training workshop before we undertook the programme. It included the sensory, rhythmic and dramatic playing (even though it had to be conducted in a large conference room with an immovable table!). We then progressed into storytelling and I used small mouse finger puppets and 'squeezy hearts'. Participants were invited to create a story of how the mouse found his or her heart. They created delightful stories in pairs which they shared in the group. One woman began to quietly cry. She then said: "I have realised that I have lost my heart too and need to find it again for my work here". There was a profound moment of silent shared*

empathy, as everyone could acknowledge how easy it is to lose sight of one's heartfelt contribution to difficult care work.

Dramatherapy and playfulness in practice

I was fortunate enough to have been awarded a Churchill Fellowship (2012–2013) for researching the arts and older people that enabled me to travel to Czech Republic, Romania and Malaysia. The Fellowships support people to gather best practice in other countries, and in my situation also made it possible for me to gather attitudes towards ageing and variations in care provision (for full report see Jennings, 2013). I was able to raise some extra funding for a follow-up visit to Malaysia and continued my journey to Singapore. I presented a training programme of Creative Care for the Alzheimer's Society including: sensory, rhythmic and dramatic play and storytelling.

Ongoing group work with older people needs the constant awareness that people are likely to die during the life of the group. And it can be that the visiting dramatherapist needs additional training to deal with ongoing losses which many of the group members seem to accept as part of their life routines.

As Allan (2013) points out, when working with people with dementia, it is necessary to maintain 'repetition, repetition, repetition' on the one hand and not to lose sight of spontaneous creativity on the other (Booker, 2011). It is extremely important to acknowledge individual creative needs and tastes in music (Rio, 2009), activities and stories (Killick, 2013), as well as bringing a disparate group of people together who have few current attachment relationships. It is extremely difficult to maintain a cohesive group as people are taken out for medication or baths or visitors, and the dramatherapist needs to be able to hold the integrity of the group despite the comings and goings. Groups can be cancelled suddenly as a free activity person is coming to demonstrate aroma-therapy, tap dancing or flamenco castanets. Outings and parties may also take place and the dramatherapist has not been informed. Unless care staff have some training in what dramatherapy is about and the importance of consistency as part of an attachment philosophy, it can be lumped together with other activities as something to keep people busy! It is possible that busyness is one way to avoid addressing depression. Activities rather than process depression, they may emphasise it. Furthermore, the dramatherapist ends up feeling they have to pull new rabbits out of hats (Labbett, 2004)!

Methodology

The broad principle for this project was the application of a model of Neuro-Dramatic-Play, as the core of dramatherapy process. It was unusual in this sense that it was an intensive intervention that was intended to challenge the status quo of inertia, lack of activity and depression. NDP is the applicant of the earliest principles of dramatic interaction that commence before birth and continue for six months after birth. The developmental sequence consists of sensory, rhythmic and dramatic play. The programme was designed by sixteen mature NDP students as part of their practicum. The programme was evaluated through their observations of the NDP group work in terms of the residents' reactions, involvement, interaction and understanding.

Project 1: 'Fun in the Forest', A Midsummer Night's Dream in Penang, Malaysia

Background

As part of the Malaysian training programme in Neuro-Dramatic-Play (NDP; Jennings, 2011), participants worked with groups of older people including people with dementia. We were fortunate enough to be welcomed into one care home in Penang and encouraged to work on a large ward for female residents.

There were minimal activities apart from TV and I was told that few residents had visits from family members. When I was given my initial tour of the ward I asked about family contacts and the staff member said that there was little or no contact for most people. She said: "But we are happy enough". An elderly woman tugged at my blouse and said tearfully: "Is my son coming today?" The staff member took her own finger and put it on the lips of the older woman and said: "Ah, ah, we don't talk about that, do we?" I personally found this lack of attachment insight very distressing, but felt powerless to do anything apart from offering training.

We explained our proposal to work with dramatherapy on the ward with our group of sixteen volunteers (dramatherapy students from Penang, including psychologists, therapists and teachers) and that we would like as many people as possible to join in, including staff. There were the typical interruptions with visitors dropping by from a volunteer pool, some food needed to be finished and one woman was being given a blanket bath without any screens. Nevertheless, the dramatherapy volunteers would need some steely resolve and we needed to show what was possible.

A Midsummer Night's Dream

This endearing play by Shakespeare has themes that are relevant for everyone (see Box 12.1). The play contains some of the most beautiful poetry that has ever been written, and the constant rhythm of the language provides a sense of security for the exploration of the several stories: human folk; non-human 'spirits'; people of the court and people of the market; squabbling teenagers and arguing families; disputes over children, loyalty, friendship, rivalry and competitiveness! One reason that I regularly use this play in particular in practice is that it addresses most human experience and also is strongly rhythmic, both through the verse and through the structure of then play itself. Rhythm can create security through awareness of heartbeats, rhythmic music, clapping games and so on. I have been impressed by the research of Kelly Hunter (2014) who has done some unique work with children and teenagers on the autistic spectrum through the rhythm in Shakespeare's plays. In the context of this project, rhythm was one of the three main 'ingredients' of the approach used.

> **Box 12.1 *A Midsummer Night's Dream* by William Shakespeare**
>
> A Midsummer Night's Dream *by William Shakespeare is a play which covers a vast array of human dilemmas. It opens with an argument over a motherless teenager about whom she should marry. She and her boyfriend run away to the forest and promptly get lost. Meanwhile the duke is getting married and the work-people from the market go to the forest to rehearse their play for the wedding. In the forest there is another conflict amongst the fairy-folk. Conflict, transformation and mistaken identity all create a dynamic between the three worlds of the court, work-place and fairies. Everything works out in the end and people marry the right person, the play is performed and the fairies give their blessings.*

Session structure

The students had worked at scenes from the play and we brought costumes, masks and pretty cloths, as well as percussion instruments. Large clothes of varied fabric enabled us to change the environment to something magical. We divided the large ward into eight groups with eight–ten people in each group, some in their beds and others in wheel chairs. I had given a talk to care staff beforehand, so there was some understanding of our activities. We found the staff tended to be shyer about joining in than the residents! We used the three stages of NDP:

Sensory Play: hand massage with hand cream, shoulder massage which then developed into flowing and swaying movement. Silk scarves and Chinese flowing fans were used to enhance movement in a gentle way.

Rhythmic Play: we clapped familiar rhythms and sang songs; some people were pleased to use the musical instruments. We gently beat rhythms on backs and courage people to clap not only their hands but also thighs and chests. We felt for our heart beat and felt the pulse in each other's wrists. Chanting is also helpful for people to re-establish their 'rhythm of life'.

Dramatic Play: we used simple drama games with cloths to play hide and seek, and told simple stories with sound effects. Hand puppets grabbed many people's attention and they enjoyed the cuddly animal puppets and stroked them against their cheeks.

Integrated project

The whole ward was used as our theatre for playing short scenes from *A Midsummer Night's Dream*. The residents became very involved as they contributed ideas. They concealed runaway lovers under cloths and showed a mischievous sense of humour! For once the ward and the people in it looked less institutionalised and there was colour and glitter in fabrics and fans. Everyone clapped for the final wedding procession which took place round the beds and throughout the ward. People were alert and involved and the care staff notice this too and were surprised that people had responded!

We repeated a similar progression in an open area with people who were more mobile. They could walk with sticks or frames and used to socialise in a small café area. Unlike the large ward, the people wore their own clothes instead of uniform cotton pajamas. Generally, there was a greater sense of freedom and more social interaction. We gathered in five groups with eight people in each group plus three students per group.

The groups became involved very quickly and they were able to create more complex movements. We created our own moving forest, starting gradually as a breeze, and then building up to vigorous storm. The group then developed voice work and breathing. We then created the storm noises of the forest and allowing the 'moving forest' to be very angry and then to calm slowly and be a gentle breeze. This proved so important for people to be able to express angry feelings rather than feel they had to smile at everything!

We shared the story of *A Midsummer Night's Dream* and role-modelled some scenes. Then a woman in her eighties said that she wanted to play Titania. She had her costume and flowers and retinue of attendants all dressed up. The woman spoke in Hokkien and I had simultaneous translation in my ear. In essence, what I understood through the translation was she wanted to speak to Oberon, another resident, and tell him he was not having the little Indian Boy. Oberon, also in his eighties was somewhat non-pulsed at this as he arrived with a rose to give Titania. Titania told him there was no way he could have the boy and basically to b— off!

Reflections

General observations from students:

- All the older people reacted to the activities.
- Most of the participants joined in the activities: massage, movement and rhythmic play.
- Several older people initiated their own responses to the play such as hiding people.
- Some of the older people wished to dwell on the physical activities that involved touch.

- They noted a sense of adventurousness.
- They noticed that staff found it more difficult to let go of daily routines such as: bathing, feeding and visitors.
- Staff fed back that they were surprised at the level of involvement by the older people.
- Staff also admitted that they found the creative involvement difficult and held back.

Everyone had shared a very creative time in an endearing way, and full of interaction and reaction. We were surprised at the adventurous of some of the older people and their level of involvement in the process. Several staff thought there would be no involvement by the older people on the ward. We could only wonder at the meaning for the woman playing Titania of her confrontation with Oberon. It was obviously significant for her as she insisted on this role and this scene. However, Oberon had plenty of support from his 'mates' in the forest.

It was very encouraging that several of the students elected to do their practice at the care home after the first round of programme was completed. This was the most positive outcome as I was worried that there could be yet another loss. The creative programme could have ended as suddenly as it had begun. Initially there had been doubts about working with this population and the fear that 'no-one will do anything'. Instead, the project had role-modelled a process approach, rather than activities, and the students saw the importance of continuing the work.

Project 2: the lion dance project: a roaring success!

Background

The Lion Dance Project grew out of an initiative that started in Singapore in 2013 and culminated in a UK project six months later. In Singapore, at the Alzheimer's Disease Society, twenty-five carers, teachers and activity workers participated in a range of creative and stimulating ideas including messy play, hand massage, 'play dough', transitional objects and attachment, movement and storytelling. Group members developed creative ideas using very simple props such as silk scarves for movement and sensory touch-communication, and a drum for rhythms, movement and sequencing. Quite spontaneously, one member began to beat the 'Ta, Ta, Taa' rhythm of the Chinese Lion Dance. A group began to respond, again spontaneously, and move to the rhythm. They wove their way through the room, with scarves on their backs to simulate the costume!

It was magical and seemed to respond to a core rhythm in all the Chinese participants. The training course concluded with exploration of traditional rituals and stories, such as those enacted in the Lion Dance. In particular, people responded to the idea of 'overcoming the monster' which I think works both at a practical and physical level as well as a metaphorical one. What bigger monster exists than the one of encroaching dementia, reminiscent too of Winston Churchill's name of 'Black Dog' for his chronic depression.

One of the outcomes from this programme was the wish by two participants to set up a drama project in a day centre for men and women with dementia. They designed a series of development sessions during Chinese New Year which would incorporate traditional rituals and special food.

I began to research the dance and stories, finding that lions were not even native to China. Forms of the dance had travelled from outside China, and the performances are now firmly established at weddings, festivals and other celebrations. The Lion mask and costume contains two people, who as well as being very acrobatic, chase away any dangerous forces, (reminiscent of the dangerous monster Nian who was chased away by the Lion in Chinese mythic history). In those groups where they have used the Lion Dance there has been amazing engagement by participants who seemingly were able to come out of their dementia and respond. One group reported that they enjoyed throwing screwed up paper balls to overcome the monster and drive it away.

A schema began to emerge in my mind of creating a project in a UK care home that focussed on the rhythm and the dance and culminated in a performance. I chose a care home in Somerset, where Alice Liddell, a UK dramatherapist, was already working and she would continue the ideas and respond to any overspill in the weekly groups.

We had a group of twelve carers, and twelve residents, at least half who had dementia. The carers attended for a preparation session beforehand and a post-group feedback session. The programme lasted for eight weeks.

Initial preparations

We started with the theme of China and some simple decorations, movement and rhythm. Immediately several group members had associations with China: one man had seen the Great Wall and described its construction (a nudge to bring in pictures and stories to the next session); someone else remembered the film *Inn of the 6th Happiness*. We built on this initial response and built up an environment with large sprays of jasmine and magnolia, and large fans and silk scarves. The fans were silk with various patterns and colours, used for extended movement as well as for hiding! We talked about Chinese horoscopes and red and gold decorations, and we kept coming back to a theme of silk that originated in China (Jennings, 2017a).

We progressed from brief stories to a longer story that is an important attachment story and enabled themes of promises and hasty judgements to be acknowledged (see Box 12.2). We found that the story provoked responses for discussion about families and acknowledgements of loss, both in staff and the residents.

During the telling of the story there was a lot of potential for movement, so we practised this as a warm up beforehand: clip-clop sounds, snorting, horse stroking, horse flying, horse movement, chair rocking. . . . Residents especially enjoyed the movements of the flying horse, although it is quite demanding physically.

Box 12.2 The story of the horse and the Mulberry tree

Long ago in ancient China there lived a family with mother, father and daughter, and mother's mother. One day bandits kidnapped the father as he was working in the fields and took him to their camp in the forest. They hoped the family would pay money to get him back again. At home the three women were very sad and did not know what to do. Grandmother sat in her chair very silent, mother cried and rocked, and Lee Ann, the daughter, spent time with the horse in the stable and wished she could do something.

After a few days, mother stood at the open window, wringing her handkerchief and said, 'If someone will rescue my husband, he shall have the hand of my daughter in marriage'. Immediately the horse came out from the stable and cantered away in a cloud of dust, mane and tail flowing.

Then next day the horse returned bringing the father on his back, and there was much celebration and laughter. The family had a special meal and everyone was content. The horse knocked with its hoof on the door; it repeated it several times until the father got really irritated. 'Why is that horse disturbing us?' he said, forgetting that he had just been rescued. And mother explained that she had promised Lee Ann as a wife to whoever rescued him. 'What nonsense!' said the father, and he went to the door and shouted at the horse, 'Go away or I shall get rid of you'.

The horse went back to the stable sadly, and later Lee Ann went out to look at the big mulberry tree in the garden. She went to the stable and stroked the horse who said 'Climb on my back and hold tight'. Whoosh, the horse sprouted wings and flew through the sky out of sight.

That evening, mother, father and grandmother came out into the garden, wondering where Lee Ann was. Then they saw her in the sky, a long way away, and she was waving to them and calling, 'Do not worry about me, I have been made Goddess of the Silk, so you must care for the mulberry tree', and with that she disappeared again. She was only seen once a year when it was the Festival of the Silk.'

The lion dance itself

We showed the group the two lion masks and then two carers put them on and moved slowly round the group. As they moved close to people, the fans were used to chase them away. The rhythm started 'Ta, Ta, Taa', with drums or clapping and the lions moved to the rhythm and then had a mock fight. We practised this for a couple of weeks before putting it together for a performance of the story. Residents also wished to try on the masks and growl and claw, and they were able to express angry feelings through the mask as well as chasing the staff who wore the masks. It is fortunate that the lion mask has a large enough aperture for the mouth that everyone can see through it and not feel claustrophobic.

We repeated the story of the Lion Dance and the importance of chasing away the monster, and the old story of Ni'an in Chinese mythology. We integrated all the elements of the flowers and decorations, fans and lengths of silk, Chinese scrolls and pictures. It culminated in an extraordinary performance with movement, rhythm, stories and the Lion Dance (Actionwork Films, 2014). Both residents and carers felt they had shared something very profound together, and each group felt more confident about 'being playful'.

Reflections

Observations from carers and therapists:

> The Trust that had given funding towards this project made it conditional on the participants filling in a questionnaire. We explained this to the carers who spent time with the older people, gauging their response where possible, and at times bringing actual feedback.

- All reported a feeling of involvement in the project.
- Individual older people reported an increased feeling of being able to communicate.
- Everyone reported a feeling of fun and laughter.
- One person said: 'Please come again, it helps us to remember'.
- Another said: 'I liked wearing the Lion mask, that was new'.
- Another said: 'It felt good to be angry and growl'.

The Lion Dance provided a structure of creative integration and right-brain play through movement, masks and story. It enabled older people and those with dementia, as well as carers to be playful and to show their feelings. An in-depth aspect of this is what I term 'the entranced experience' (Jennings, 2017b), when people become immersed in an art form and respond at a new level. The entranced experience enables people to enter dramatic reality at a profound level of immersion, and then a gradual return to everyday reality and the rhythm of ordinary life.

Concluding thoughts

There is no doubt that I have been changed by these experiences: working with older people and dementia with dramatherapy has given me a new perspective on the immense possibilities of working through a dramatherapy approach. However, I have been mindful of the need for more development of working models as our client groups expand in diversity. The participants in both *A Midsummer Night's Dream* and The Lion Dance all gained from the experience. This was reported back from the carers who filled in funders' questionnaires for pre- and post-group observations. People were more alert, there was greater interaction, there was a feeling of anticipation and overall less lethargy and irritability. There were changes in mood and relationships. Carers became enthusiastic that overall there was less 'misery' and people were friendlier to them and each other. These programmes show the important contribution that dramatherapy can make to the treatment of depression.

The experience also made me question the whole value system towards ageing populations. My research with the Temiar tribe in Malaysia (Jennings, 1998) established a value system where older people are respected because they have lived so long. They are seen to be wise and able to give advice and ideas. The older shaman is usually seen as a 'major healer', and many of the younger ones are often considered to be playing around! Similarly, with midwives, it is usually older midwives who are the most popular and requested to attend, maybe with a younger woman acting as a helper. However, the beliefs of this aborigine population in Malaysia do not always carry over to other racial and cultural groups.

The Creative Care approach which emphasises 'Creative Ageing' has been shown to bring about change in several older populations. The groups described in these projects, improved their communication and social interaction, and lifted their mood from the gloomy, depressive hopelessness to a more shared view of the world.

I am closing this chapter with a very human story that helps us re-think our attitudes and respect for older people.

> *I was asked to do a presentation at a newly opened day-centre for people with dementia in the north of Malaysia. It was attended by clinical and nursing staff, carers and people who were attending the centre. One of the carers talked over the head of a woman in a wheel chair and indicated to ignore her as she could not do anything. I gave a short talk and then introduced a short creative session which culminated in storytelling. I had in my hand a replica butterfly and a 'squeezy heart' and began to tell a story about the butterfly that had lost its heart. The woman in the wheel chair became increasingly animated and to the extent that the carer wanted to take her from the room. It became apparent however that she was pointing at my blouse; it had a large butterfly across the front. She was the only person who had made a connection between the story and my blouse. Interestingly, the head of the centre later told me that this woman began to join in all the activities at the centre. I suggest that the dramatherapy session was a turning point for her. She had been largely ignored by staff as being incapable of joining in any activities, yet she made the connections of butterflies in the story and on my blouse. And then she became more alert and involved, much to the surprise of the staff.*

References

Actionwork Films (2014). A roaring success with the Lion dance. Retrieved from http://youtu.be/bwtK_Trm9n4.

Ainsworth, M., & Bowlby, J. (1965). *Child care and the growth of love*. London: Penguin.

Allan, A. (2013). Repetition, repetition, repetition: A dramatherapist's perspective of working with a group with advanced dementia. *The Prompt*, November.

Booker, M. (2011). *Developmental drama: Dramatherapy approaches for people with profound or severe multiple disabilities, including sensory impairment*. London: Jessica Kingsley.

Bowlby, J. (1958). The nature of a child's tie to his mother. *International Journal of Psychoanalysis*, 39, 350–373.

Bowlby, J. (1979). *The making and breaking of affectional bonds*. London: Tavistock.

Chalfont, G. (2008). *Design nature for dementia care (Bradford Dementia Group)*. London: Jessica Kingsley (with University of Bradford).

Cicirelli, V. G. (2010). Attachment relationships in old age. *Journal of Social and Personal Relationships*, 27(2), 191–199.

Crimmens, P. (1998). *Storymaking and creative groupwork with older people*. London: Jessica Kingsley.

Futterman Collier, A. (2012). *Using textile arts and handcrafts in therapy with women: Weaving lives back together*. London: Jessica Kingsley.

Hunter, K. (2014). *Shakespeare's heartbeat*. London: Routledge.

Jennings, S. (1998). *Introduction to dramatherapy: Ariadne's ball of thread*. London: Jessica Kingsley.

Jennings, S. (2006). An exploration of creative ageing and social theatre. *Nursing & Residential Care*, 8(1), 29–31.

Jennings, S. (2011). *Healthy attachments and neuro-dramatic-play*. London: Jessica Kingsley.

Jennings, S. (2012). *Creative care (1): Creating an alternative pathway*. Wells: Healing Tree.

Jennings, S. (2013). To me fair friends you never can be old. Fellow's report for Winston Churchill Memorial Trust, Arts and Older People.

Jennings, S. (2015). *When the world fall apart: Working with the effects of trauma*. Buckingham: Hinton House.

Jennings, S. (2017a). *Creative care (2): Attachment and older people*. Glastonbury: The Healing Tree.

Jennings, S. (2017b). Creative and non-verbal methods for trauma recovery: The importance of the theatre of resilience. In B. Huppertz (Ed.), *Traumatized people: Psychotherapy seen through the lens of divers specialist treatments*. New York: Rowman.

Katz, M. (1999). The phonograph effect: The influence of recording on listener, performer, composer, 1900–1940. University of Michigan, ProQuest Dissertations Publishing.

Killick, J. (2013). *Playfulness and dementia: A practice guide*. London: Jessica Kingsley.

Killick, J., & Craig, C. (2012). *Creativity and communication in persons with dementia*. London: Jessica Kingsley.

Marshall, K. (2013). *Puppetry in dementia care: Connecting through creativity and joy*. London: Jessica Kingsley.

Labbett, S. (2004). NAPA: Steering the path from entertainer to reflective practitioner. In Perrin, T. (Ed.), *The new culture of therapeutic activity with older people* (pp. 218–228). Oxon: Speechmark Publishing Ltd.

Rio, R. (2009). *Connecting through music with people with dementia: A guide for caregivers*. London: Jessica Kingsley.

Schweitzer, P., & Bruce, E. (2008). *Remembering yesterday, caring today: Reminiscence in dementia care: A guide to good practice*. London: Jessica Kingsley.

Spitz, R. (1947). Grief: A Peril In Infancy (silent film). University of Akron.

Walker, B. G. (1985). *The crone: Women of age, wisdom, and power*. San Francisco: Harper.

Chapter 13

Dance movement therapy research and evidence-based practice for older people with depression

Iris Bräuninger

Introduction

Depression is a common mental disorder with approximately 350 million people affected worldwide and more women affected than men (World Health Organization WHO, 2016a, 2016b). Globally, the world's population is expected to nearly double between 2015 and 2050 for those over 60 years from 12% to 22% (WHO, 2016c). According to Kinzl (2013), depression with 7% of older people is one of the most frequent mental disorders in old age. A person affected by depression can experience real suffering and reduced quality of life, can feel sad, lose interest and joy, may feel guilty and without self-worth, may have sleeping problems, low appetite, and reduced concentration (WHO, 2016d). It is not unusual for symptoms of depression in older adults to be overlooked and therefore left untreated, contributing to other types of poor health. According to WHO (2016c) this leads to extensive use of medical services and increase healthcare costs. It is, therefore, important that depression is recognized and treated early. Some treatment options recommended by WHO (2016c) include psychosocial interventions and medication.

Effective treatments for the elderly and especially for women are urgently needed. Alternatives to medication are constantly being sought. One such positive alternative is dance. Dance combines sensorimotor rhythmic activities with cognitive, social, and affective dimensions and "requires learning of complex motor sequences, procedural memory, attention, visuomotor integration, synchronization in space and time (rhythm movements), and emotional expression" (Merom et al., 2016: 2). Dance is one of the basic components of dance movement therapy. In this chapter, dance movement therapy[1] will be discussed as a potential psychosocial treatment option for depressed older people (Bräuninger, 2015). Some definitions found for the discipline include the following:

> **Dance Therapy is a form of creative and body oriented psychotherapy. Key components of intervention are movement and dance in combination with verbal expression.** Psychological diagnostics are based on complex procedures of movement analysis. **Integrating**

> **emotional, physical and cognitive processes into a self-guided expression of life are a major objective.**
>
> (German Professional Organization For Dance Therapists BTD, 2016)

> **Dance Movement Therapy (DMT)** . . . offers individuals of all ages and abilities a space to explore what drives them, **assisting people to develop self-awareness and sensitivity to others** and also to find a pathway to feeling more comfortable in their own skin.
>
> (European Association Dance Movement Therapy EADMT, 2016)

DMT often works with resourcing clients and thus, it may become a treatment option for older people as it preserves the dignity, respects the individual's needs and improves social participation (Bräuninger, 2014, 2012). This chapter presents DMT research and evidence-based practice for older people with depression. The emotional, psychosocial, and recreational potential of DMT in the treatment of depression in the elderly are reviewed. Practical implications and potential applications of DMT for older people with depression are highlighted.

Dance and DMT research in older adults with depression

High quality DMT research into older adults with depression is rare. There is a need for research such as randomized controlled trials (RCTs) that evaluates the effectiveness and efficacy of DMT for children, young people, and adults with depression (Lelièvre et al., 2015; Mala et al., 2012; Meekums et al., 2015), and for older people with depression (Bräuninger, 2014, 2015). For this reason, an overview of current research studies and literature on the topic is presented here. This overview comes from a systematic literature search has been conducted using the EBSCOhost Research Databases (AgeLine; AMED; CINAHL; MEDLINE; PsycBOOKS; PsycINFO; PSYNDEX) and key word combinations of DMT, depression and older people. Additionally, other sources such as GoogleScholar, textbooks, and professional journals have been searched for literature in a non-systematic way. Inclusion criteria were elderly and older patients >60 years suffering from depressive symptoms, who participated in DMT or dance intervention. Primary outcome studies, secondary literature as well as reports by experts were included. Excluded were studies with an emphasis on dance interventions only without including DMT. The data base search revealed 42 records after duplicates had been removed. Additionally, 36 records could be identified through other sources. In total, 17 sources have been included in this narrative review.[2]

As a result of the literature review, two systematic reviews were found. One of them suggested that dance therapy may increase the quality of life (QOL) of the elderly, support self-management capacities in chronically ill patients, improve wellbeing and self-esteem (Strassel et al., 2011). The other proposed that DMT may be effective for depression and elderly patients (Koch et al., 2014). Two other reviews summarized the impact of dance and DMT interventions with older adults on mood and depression (Crumbie et al., 2015) and on health status (Marks, 2016). Of these, the first suggested that effective dance interventions might produce positive outcomes (Crumbie et al., 2015) and the second proposed that "dance therapy may be useful as a rehabilitation strategy for older adults, in general, as well as for elders with varying degrees of depression, regardless of strategy employed" (Marks, 2016: 61). Marks (2016) continues arguing that older adults with or without depression may benefit from dance-based therapy, while the quality of life of older adults with depression or depressive symptoms may improve by participating in dance-based activities (Marks, 2016).

A randomized controlled trial (RCT) examined the effect of a dance-based therapy program on depressive symptoms in nursing home older residents (Vankova et al., 2014). The study compared the DMT intervention group who received an Intervention Exercise Dance for Seniors (EXDASE) Program for 60 minutes once a week over a period of three months with the control group who did not receive the intervention. Results showed that depressive symptoms significantly decreased in the DMT group compared to the control group. The study by Cross, Flores, Butterfield, Blackman and Lee (2012) examined the effects of 30 minutes passive listening to music (music therapy group) compared to 30 minutes active observation of dance accompanied by music (DMT group) on 100 elderly depressed care residents. The Beck Depression Inventory and the Recognition Memory Test-Faces Inventory were applied in the pre-test and two post-tests (three days and ten days after the intervention). In the pre-test post-test comparison the DMT group showed significantly lower Beck Depression scores and the improvements in the scores lasted longer compared to the music therapy group. According to Cross et al. (2012), active observation of DMT may temporarily improve some moderate depressive symptoms and cognitive deficits in older adults. Finally, in an international Internet-based survey that was undertaken with 113 DMT practitioners from Austria, Germany, and Switzerland on DMT with the elderly, explored useful interventions for older people (Bräuninger, 2014, 2015). Analysis of practitioners' reports revealed that participants would most frequently address themes related to improvements in wellbeing, especially reduced anxiety and depression during DMT sessions.

Evidence-based practice for older people with depression

Evidence-based practice integrates individual clinical expertise with the best available external clinical evidence from systematic research (Sackett et al., 1996). Several authors emphasized that DMT for elderly patients with depression should be included in the treatment plan as a regular group therapy

(Bräuninger & Blumer, 2004; Kipp & Groß, 2004; Wolter & Kipp, 2007). DMT may be offered as a highly intensive daily treatment, as Kipp and Groß (2004) suggested, or as a semi-structured group once or several times a week. The group may start in sitting position to make members feel safe (Bräuninger & Blumer, 2004) and a wide variety of exercises should be provided in order to respond appropriately to the group's mood (Wolter & Kipp, 2007). Treatment goals for patients with depression include an increase of energy levels by offering joyful activities and sensorimotoric experiences (Bräuninger & Blumer, 2004).

The current overview included DMT research with patients over 60 years suffering from depressive symptoms. Summarising, the findings from the review of the literature suggest that participating in a DMT group with joyful activities and sensorimotoric experiences may result in reduced depressive symptoms, increased social participation and improved energy levels in older people with depressive symptoms. Further clinical recommendations can be found from the survey of DMT practitioners (Bräuninger, 2014, 2015).

Some recommendations

DMT experts working with older people (Bräuninger, 2014, 2015) reported that they would treat patients with depression most frequently with open DMT interventions such as

> improvisation (everyday movements), guided exercises (grounding/breathing exercises), Chace Circle and Circle Dances.... Lack of Energy can be treated by gaining awareness and by focusing on a movement's quality rather than its quantity. Awareness exercises may furthermore lead to inner calmness thereby increasing energy levels.
>
> (Bräuninger, 2014: 141–142)

Two dance therapists who participated in another international online survey with 54 practitioners (Koch et al., 2013) mentioned that authentic movement would be a contraindication in elderly psychiatric patients. Another colleague stated that relaxation, Sherborne's approach, and over-stimulation would be contraindicated. A different colleague recommended not using authentic movement or too much strong or sudden effort when working with older people.

Specific DMT settings and qualities and experiences in the therapist applicable to older people with depression have not been defined or empirically evaluated yet. The following recommendations are derived from results of the previously mentioned survey with DMT experts on their recommendations for working with older people (Bräuninger, 2014, 2015). However, these recommendations were not proposed for older clients with depression but for the general older clientele only.

The majority of experts recommended co-leadership in groups when working with the elderly. Some therapists proposed to build gender-mixed and non diagnoses-specific groups with ten–12 participants and to offer high frequency sessions. They described the therapy room as needing to be easily accessible with good light, good acoustics, a non-slippery floor without carpets but contrasting floor colours, and enough space available for walking aids. They referred also to the need for chairs to be stable, light with backrests and a few with armrests, and seats which are disinfected and washable. The use of props that offer a variety of different sensory experiences such as cushions, sticks, floor mats, and music from past decades were mentioned. DMT experts emphasized the importance of creating a special atmosphere for this clientele by sharing food and drinks with them after the sessions (Bräuninger, 2014).

Based on findings from the same survey, working with older people requires special qualities and experiences in the therapists. As they are challenged by being confronted by their own ageing, therapy work can enable them to explore this fully, gaining an acceptance of the biological, physiological, and psychological changes related to ageing. In an empathic and patient-centred approach, providing enough time and space, demonstrating an understanding of the medical conditions the clients may have next to issues related to ageing were highlighted as important. Regarding age, therapists are most likely younger than the clients and the latter being at the age of parents or grandparents. Experts discussed that this age difference may act as both a challenge to the therapeutic role as well as a resource for growing towards personal development.

In the following section, some evidence-based interventions, which seem to reduce depressive symptoms in the elderly, are illustrated using an example from the author's clinical experience. Corresponding literature as well as results of the Internet-based survey with expert practitioners offer research support for the choice of these interventions.

Case example: the tea dance

As a dance therapist in a psychiatric day clinic for people of age 50 and older I worked with clients who suffered from many psychiatric disorders, including depression. As suggested in the survey of practitioners (Bräuninger, 2014), it was important for me as a therapist to accept the role of being at the age of their daughters/sons. I also needed to accept that I was neither suffering from physical limitations nor had experienced war or flight.

DMT was offered twice a week in two different groups and clients were allocated to either one of the groups depending on their level of energy and diagnosis. Additionally, I offered a third DMT group to all patients, which was called the *tea dance* because at the end of the session there was tea, coffee, and cake. The following descriptions refer to this group.

The tea dance group took place each Wednesday afternoon in the main hall of the ward. Before the clients arrived, the room was prepared, tables pushed aside and the chairs arranged in a large circle creating a spacious dance floor in the centre. Staff members were invited to participate whenever their time allowed it. Assistant doctors and the senior doctor would sometimes join in. If available, one staff member served as a co-therapist, who picked up patients from their rooms and gave a hand during sessions for those who needed special attention or who needed to leave. At the time of the tea dance, the 'dancers' arrived in the dance hall and chose their seats in the circle. At the beginning participants were asked to signal by their outstretched arms their energy level at that moment. An upward lifted arm signalled high energy level, a half high-stretched-out arm meant medium energy level and an arm pointing down to the ground meant no energy. At the end of the session I would ask the same question again.

For a physical and emotional warm-up, the routine was to start with a short seated dance where the dancers could suggest any movement they wanted that were repeated by the group. Additionally, a task supporting cognitive training was included, for example "I'm packing my suitcase and I'm taking __ with me": one participant after the other repeated the words and gestures of the previous ones and added a new word accompanied by a movement gesture, which was then repeated by the group. The main part of the session involved engaging in couple dances or circle dances that aimed to provide group members with joyful and sensorimotoric activities thereby reducing their depressive symptoms and increasing their social participation and energy levels (Bräuninger, 2014, 2015). The dancers could request different dances and music styles. Most often, more women than men were present and women also danced with each other. There was some tension in the air when it was time for a choice of a partner. "Whom will I pick?" or "Who will pick me?" was the only thing that counted in that instance – and basic interactional dynamics appeared which created emotions of envy, suspicion, amusement, fun, and happiness. On request of participants, couples were dancing Slow Waltz, Tango, Cha-Cha-Cha, Foxtrott, Jive, Boogie-Woogie, Samba, and many more styles. Depression or specific psychiatric disorders diagnosed were not in focus once the participants began to dance. It was decided that a positive approach to their experience of being involved in the dance was going to be adopted (Bräuninger, 2015). The tea dance was a time to be alive, to share joyful moments, and to enjoy the company of others. There was no space for isolation. Instead, it was an afternoon of lightness and humour.

I remember an elderly lady with depression who as an adolescent during the war had been forced to flee. She arrived in Germany as a displaced person, got married, and later divorced. She was at the time living alone in her apartment, with only her sister nearby but with no other social contacts. She had been in and out of the clinic many times. I will call her Mrs Green. Mrs Green had admitted herself to the day clinic to seek support because of a suicidal crisis. She also gave hints that the situation in her apartment had become unbearable. (It turned out that the apartment was messy; Mrs Green could hardly find a place to sleep.) Mrs Green could be at times a challenge to the team, she would express her underlying depression, despair, and loneliness in an agitated manner and wanted things to be done her way. Interestingly, Mrs Green loved the tea dance and would always be the first to arrive and the first to choose a dance partner. If she got hold of me before the session, she would ask me to bring Slow Waltz or Tango music. She would not miss any of the sessions. Mrs Green contributed to the tea dance in a unique and wonderful way. She would impress everybody with her dance skills and would motivate others to join in the dance.

Generally, we would end the tea dance with a polonaise where the dancers lined up in pairs one after the others facing toward me, standing at the front, facing the row. The couples walked in moderate tempo through the hall adapting to the polonaise rhythm. When the first couple arrived in front of me, I would greet them and signal to separate and to walk off to the right and left, proceeding to the end of the hall where they would re-unite. When meeting at the end of the hall the couples would create a line of two couples/four dancers; these four dancers would then walk forward. I would separate them again into twos. In the last round, the couples would part and walk off separately to the right and to the left. When they would come forward again in couples, I would take the hand of the first dancer and the group would form a long line. We walked into and out of a line and ended in a big circle. Everybody would sit down in a chair and I would ask participants to signal their energy levels at the end of the session. Many times, the energy level in participants had risen compared to the beginning, and the faces appeared to be more vital and energetic. Mrs Green appeared to be relaxed and in a good mood. The tea dance was followed by tea and coffee with biscuits and cakes, which gave a chance for a relaxed chat.

When nurses, assistant doctors, and the senior doctor participated, the competencies often shifted and laid in the hands and feet of the older people, who led staff dancers. In that way, staff members could experience how many psychosocial competences became available to deeply depressed clients in an embodied way, that is by means of moving and dancing and taking on responsibility. Clients' moods could change into joyfulness and pride, and negative symptoms and low energy could change into active participation and competent leadership. In other words, the dance activities supported the clients' empowerment by clients being the teachers in the dance situation. Depressed patients could experience a degree of self-sufficiency and autonomy where they could still take the lead, overcome low energy and powerlessness, and be able to feel different emotions again (Bräuninger, 2014, 2012; Merom et al., 2016). The dance elements invited participants to interact with and adapt to others and share joyful moments. To perform the polonaise many competences were needed: the couples had to lead, everybody had to be well oriented in space and had to quickly form correct floor patterns (straight, angular, curved), thereby requiring a high degree of attention, being present in the moment, using concentration, and applying cognitive functioning. Thus, depressive thoughts and cognitive narrowing down could be interrupted. The dancers needed to become socially involved with others and adopt their own walking speed to that of their partners. Coming together as a couple, leaving the partner, meeting again in couples and groups – all those rituals related to the circle of life – getting involved, saying good-bye, ending, starting again.

DMT treatment goals for working with older patients with depression, according to DMT experts, are to reduce depressive symptoms, to increase the energy level, to change cognitive thought patterns, and to activate resources (Bräuninger, 2015). In order to achieve those goals, as demonstrated in the tea dance example, different dance techniques such as social dance, ballroom dance, and circle dance can be applied in DMT to promote the joy for life. Carefully set up, structured dance improvisation may serve an additional goal, which is to foster emotional expression. Imagination techniques may stimulate cognition as the example of "I'm packing my suitcase and I'm taking __ with me" showed. Furthermore, using mirroring techniques would serve to increase the self-trust amongst older people with depression (Bräuninger, 2015). Mrs Green appeared to be very relaxed when she was able to dance a Slow Waltz and she enjoyed the admiration which she received from the others. On the other side, she could take on support from her dance partner during the polonaise and did not feel ashamed of it.

Conclusion

This chapter provides an overview of DMT research and evidence-based practice for older people with depression. DMT seems to have important emotional, psychosocial, and recreational potential in the treatment of depression in the elderly. Practical implications and potential applications, interventions and tools, indications and contraindications, recommendation for the therapeutic environment, and the specific role and qualities needed in the therapist have been discussed. The possibility to include a recreational dancing style to DMT when working with older depressed clients has been proposed as it " can be readily used outside of the therapy room" (Haboush et al., 2006: 90). Dance movement therapists can easily apply and include recreational dance in a more generic way into the daily activities of older adults on the ward, in the nursing home facilities, or in any other care facilities for the elderly. Thereby, the acceptance to participate might be more easily achieved in older people as this DMT group approach uses recreational, ballroom, and social dance techniques which allows for a more flexible entry and a lower level of commitment. As the therapeutic container is more open, less secure, and more transparent, a great amount of knowledge and confidence is needed from the part of the therapist. An additional effect might be that dance techniques in DMT serve as a door opener for older clients with depression, who otherwise would not get involved in DMT groups, and for other professionals who could drop by and participate in the session, thereby slipping into another role and acquiring new perspectives.

Based on the overview of literature and on evidence-based practice, it is suggested that DMT seems to offer great potential for older people with depression to improve their behavioral, cognitive, emotional, physical, and social aspects of wellbeing.

Notes

1 The terms dance movement therapy, dance therapy, and dance movement psychotherapy will be used interchangeably throughout this chapter.
2 Bräuninger 2015, 2014, 2012; Bräuninger & Blumer 2004; Cross, Flores, Butterfield, Blackman, & Lee 2012; Crumbie, Olmos, Watts, Avery, & Nelson 2015; Kipp & Groß, 2004; Koch, Kolter, & Kunz, 2013; Koch, Kunz, Lykou, & Cruz 2014; Lelièvre, Tuchowski, & Rolland, 2015; Mala, Karkou, & Meekums, 2012; Marks, 2016; Meekums, Karkou, & Nelson 2015; Merom, Grunseit, Eramudugolla, Jefferis, Mcneill, & Anstey 2016; Strassel, Cherkin, Steuten, Sherman, & Vrijhoef, 2011; Vankova, Holmerova, Machacova, Volicer, Veleta, & Celko 2014; Wolter & Kipp, 2007

References

Bräuninger, I. (2012). Dance movement therapy group intervention in stress treatment: A randomized controlled trial (RCT). *The Arts in Psychotherapy*, 39(5), 443–450. Doi: 10.1016/j.aip.2012.07.002.

Bräuninger, I. (2014). Dance movement therapy with the elderly: An international Internet-based survey undertaken with practitioners. *Body, Movement and Dance in Psychotherapy*, 9, 138–153, Doi: 10.1080/17432979.2014.914977.

Bräuninger, I. (2015). Tanz-, Bewegungstherapie im Alter. In R. Lindner & J. Hummel (Eds.), *Psychotherapie in der Geriatrie: Aktuelle psychodynamische und verhaltenstherapeutische Ansätze* (pp. 173–184). Stuttgart: Kohlhammer.

Bräuninger, I., & Blumer, E. (2004). Tanz- und Bewegungstherapie [Dance and movement therapy]. In W. Rössler (Ed.), *Lehrbuch Psychiatrische Rehabilitation* (pp. 380–387). Heidelberg, Germany: Springer, Fachbuch Medizin/Psychologie.

Cross, K., Flores, R., Butterfield, J., Blackman, M., & Lee, S. (2012). The effect of passive listening versus active observation of music and dance performances on memory recognition and mild to moderate depression in cognitively impaired older adults. *Psychological Reports*, 111(2), 413–423. Doi: 10.2466/10.02.13.PR0.111.5.413–423.

Crumbie, V., Olmos, F., Watts, C., Avery, J., & Nelson, R. (2015). The impact of dance interventions on mood and depression in older adults. *Therapeutic Recreation Journal*, 49(2), 187–190.

European Association of Dance Movement Therapy EADMT (2016). What is dance movement therapy (30.11.2016)? Retrieved from www.eadmt.com/index.php?action=article&id=22.

German Dance Therapy Association BTD (2016). Dancetherapy (02.12.2016). Retrieved from www.btd-tanztherapie.de/BTDengl/_E_dancetherapy.htm.

Haboush, A., Floyd, M., Caron, J., LaSota M. A. & Alvarez, K. (2006). Ballroom dance lessons for geriatric depression: An exploratory study. *The Arts in Psychotherapy*, 33(2), 89–97. Doi: 10.1016/j.aip.2005.10.001.

Kinzl, J. F. (2013). Psychische Erkrankungen bei Frauen und Männern im Alter. *Zeitschrift für Gerontologie und Geriatrie*, 46(6), 526–531.

Kipp, J., & Groß, M. (2004). Tägliche Gruppentherapien für ältere Patienten in einer Klinik für Psychiatrie und Psychotherapie. *Gruppenpsychother. Gruppendynamik*, 40, 148–163.

Koch, S. C., Kolter, A., & Kunz, T. (2013). Indikationen und Kontraindikationen in der Tanz- und Bewegungstherapie. [Indications and contraindications in dance movement therapy: An inductive approach.] *Musik-, Tanz und Kunsttherapie*, 2, 87–105.

Koch, S., Kunz, T., Lykou, S., & Cruz, R. (2014). Effects of dance movement therapy and dance on health-related psychological outcomes: A meta-analysis. *The Arts in Psychotherapy*, 41(1), 46–64.

Lelièvre, A., Tuchowski, F., & Rolland, Y. (2015). La danse, une thérapie pour la personne âgée: Revue de la littérature. *Les cahiers de l'année gérontologique*, 7(4), 177–187.

Mala, A., Karkou, V., & Meekums, B. (2012). Dance/Movement Therapy (D/MT) for depression: A scoping review. *The Arts in Psychotherapy*, 39(4), 287–295.

Marks, R. (2016). Narrative review of dance-based exercise and its specific impact on depressive symptoms in older adults. *AIMS Medical Science*, 3(1), 61–76. Doi: 10.3934/medsci.2016.1.61.

Meekums, B., Karkou, V., & Nelson, E. A. (2015). Dance movement therapy for depression. *Cochrane Database of Systematic Reviews*, 2, CD009895. Doi: 10.1002/14651858.CD009895.pub2.

Merom, D., Grunseit, A., Eramudugolla, R., Jefferis, B., Mcneill, J., & Anstey, K. J. (2016). Cognitive benefits of social dancing and walking in old age: The dancing mind randomized controlled trial. *Frontiers in Aging Neuroscience*, 8.

Sackett, D. L., Rosenberg, W. M., Gray, J. M., Haynes, R. B., & Richardson, W. S. (1996). Evidence based medicine: What it is and what it isn't. *BMJ*, 312(7023), 71–72.

Strassel, J. K., Cherkin, D. C., Steuten, L., Sherman, K. J., & Vrijhoef, H. J. (2011). A systematic review of the evidence for the effectiveness of dance therapy. *Alternative Therapies in Health and Medicine*, 17(3), 50–59.

Vankova, H., Holmerova, I., Machacova, K., Volicer, L., Veleta, P., & Celko, A. M. (2014). The effect of dance on depressive symptoms in nursing home residents. *Journal of the American Medical Directors Association*, 15(8), 582–587.

Wolter, R., & Kipp, J. (2007). *[Movement in the group – A therapy for elderly depressed patients] Bewegung in der Gruppe – Ein Therapieangebot für ältere depressive Patienten*. Gießen: Psychosozial-Verlag.

World Health Organization WHO (2016a). Media centre. Depression (29.11.2016). Retrieved from www.who.int/mediacentre/factsheets/fs369/en/

WHO (2016b). Gender and women's mental health (02.12.2016). Retrieved from www.who.int/mental_health/prevention/genderwomen/en/

WHO (2016c). Media centre. Mental health and older adults (29.11.2016). Retrieved from www.who.int/mediacentre/factsheets/fs381/en/

WHO (2016d). Depression (01.12.2016) Retrieved from www.who.int/topics/depression/en/.

Chapter 14

Perspectives on research and clinical practice in music therapy for older people with depression

Jasmin Eickholt, Monika Geretsegger and Christian Gold

Introduction

As the most common mental health problem for older adults, depression has profound negative impacts on all aspects of the life, family, and the community (Schneider & Nesseler, 2011). In addition, physical frailty and co-occurring disorders like dementia present obstacles for the identification and assessment of depression (Buchanan et al., 2006). Treatment recommendations are dependent on the severity of depression, with some guidelines suggesting non-pharmacological treatments like psychosocial interventions or psychotherapy in minor depressive disorders and the combination with pharmacological therapy in mild to major depressive disorders (Buchanan et al., 2006; Schneider & Nesseler, 2011). Music therapy is one of these non-pharmacological interventions, where older people have the possibility to address their mental, social, and physiological needs in a nonverbal way, and they can get the opportunity to train daily competences and to enhance their quality of life (Eickholt, 2017a; Staudinger, 2002).

New circumstances in later life bring about new challenges and may facilitate depression; the reasons for these challenges are varied, including for example growing difficulties in fulfilling general tasks, transition into retirement, as well as the loss of related persons and social tasks (Hautzinger, 2000; Staudinger, 2002). With increasing age, physical frailties increase as well, geriatric disorders like dementia, circulatory disorders, and stroke occur more often (Buchanan et al., 2006; Schneider & Nesseler, 2011). The loss of one's own house or apartment and moving to a resident home or nursing home is often someone else´s decision and results in a new social state and role in society (Schneider & Nesseler, 2011). With the changing circumstances, their purposes in life may change as well (Hautzinger, 2000). In addition to personal changes and challenges in late life, the partner, family members, and friends may become ill and need caregiving. The physical and mental burden of caregiving is high (Vitaliano et al., 2003). The caregiver´s age, relationship to the care recipient, time spent caregiving, and education may be relevant to risk of depressive symptoms (Schulz et al., 2008). Caregivers with a history of depression also show a higher risk of recurrence of depression than non-caregivers (Russo et al., 1995; Schulz et al., 2008).

In music therapy, depressive symptoms can be addressed using various methods. Participants can bring the experience of social and individual physical and emotional loss, mourning for a deceased person, as well as coping with past experiences, including the acceptance of unused opportunities, into the music therapy session (Eickholt, 2017b; Staudinger, 2002). Participants can acquire unique experiences, which may enable them to engage in interaction and reduce isolation, improve mood, increase self-esteem, self-efficacy, and sense of belonging, and, where possible, reflect on current problems and central themes of their lives.

This chapter provides an introduction of principles and research in music therapy in older people with depression. Symptoms and domains addressed in music interventions are presented as well as music therapeutic methods commonly applied in clinical practice. By describing a specific working model, we illustrate one possible way of music therapy work in geropsychiatric departments, day care departments, and nursing homes.

Principles and research

Music therapy with older people with depression

Music therapy is a growing field that calls for dialogue and interrelations between research and practice. Music therapy uses knowledge from different disciplines including musicology, social sciences, medicine, and psychology, and it systematically takes individual circumstances and biographies into account.

Music therapy for people with depression is provided in in-patient settings, including nursing homes, mental and general hospitals, and in outpatient settings, including day hospitals and private practice. Depending on the aims, music therapy may be provided in groups, for example to reduce isolation and to meet social needs, or as individual therapy, for example for people in severe stages of dementia, as preparation for group therapy, or where therapy in groups is not possible. It has been argued that depressive symptoms can be decreased through singing, playing music and listening to music in individual and group music therapy (Werner et al., 2017;Verrusio et al., 2014; Zhao et al., 2016). In addition, studies suggest that music therapy can enhance or maintain emotional functioning, cognitive functions such as memory and attention, as well as quality of life, reducing anxiety, agitation, and medication use in depression and the common comorbid disease dementia (Ceccato et al., 2012; Fang et al., 2017; Ridder et al., 2013). Music provokes emotions, which are shaped by life experiences. The non-verbal character of music allows even the patients with severe physical or cognitive restrictions to participate (Muthesius et al., 2010). The goals of music therapy differ depending on the severity of depression, psychosocial conditions, and cognitive abilities. Music therapy aims may include mental stabilisation, handling negative experiences and current situations, increasing access to and awareness of feelings, enhancing self-esteem, self-expression, group integration, learning relaxation, and developing new goals in life.

Different interventions using music

Music is used in different ways with older adults. It may include the use of music in a therapeutic context, recreational use (e.g. in singing groups), and music education (e.g. in a choir or in instrumental lessons). Music interventions are supported by promising clinical research evidence and may also be cost-effective (Choi et al., 2008; Clift et al., 2016; Hanser & Thompson, 1994; Livingston et al., 2014). However, while several studies have demonstrated effects of music therapy, studies considering other uses of music are scarce. Music therapy and group singing (ranging from recreational group singing to more performance-oriented choir singing) are currently the most widely used and studied interventions (Clift et al., 2016). They can support associated specific psychological and social needs, such as expressing current feelings or being part of a group, by utilising instruments, voices, and interactions. Nevertheless, each of them has unique features in their focus and implementation. For example, the possibility to expose individual themes may be unique to music therapy. In contrast, the possibility to support social integration in a gentle and nonverbal way, instead of direct confrontation with emotionally difficult situations, may be unique to singing groups. A meta-analysis of 19 studies (Zhao et al., 2016) showed a significant decrease of depressive symptoms in music therapy added to standard care. In contrast, nine other studies in which music therapy without standard care was compared with standard care showed no significant decrease. The authors of the meta-analysis therefore recommend music therapy in addition to standard therapies, which may include medication and psychotherapy (Zhao et al., 2016). In addition, the extent of music therapy is also important, as the effects of music therapy on symptoms of depression seem to increase with the number of sessions provided (Gold et al., 2009). One study comparing interactive group music therapy and recreational group singing found that music therapy reduced the depressive symptoms of nursing home residents more than recreational singing (Werner et al., 2017). The authors concluded that the professional qualification of the provider may be of importance. However, choir singing has also shown beneficial effects on depressive symptoms (Clift et al., 2016, Skingley & Vella-Burrows, 2010). One study investigating a music therapy choir found a reduction of depressive symptoms in 54% of residential and day care residents (Ahessy, 2016). Another study found community singing to be associated with significant effects on quality of life for the singers, including reduced levels of anxiety and depression and improved mental health-related quality of life (Coulton et al., 2015).

Beside the use of music in music therapy and group singing, music education for older people comprises another field of using music, in an educational context. This newer field (also termed "music geragogics" after Wickel & Hartogh, 2015) includes music education for the elderly as well as working with individual biographies, using the positive effects of music for the individual to increase life satisfaction, support for handling life crises and reducing social isolation (Wickel & Hartogh, 2015).

Different types of music interventions may have different goals and may fulfil different needs. For example, for residents with severe depression, music therapy may support primarily individual needs; group singing may support primarily social needs; and music geragogics may provide an opportunity for self-fulfilment.

Symptoms and domains addressed in music interventions

Music may support older people with depression to evoke suppressed or latent feelings, to express their inner side in a nonverbal way, to become aware of distress caused by life events, and to experience relief. Several controlled studies and a Cochrane systematic review have documented effects of music therapy on depression symptoms (Maratos et al., 2008). The effects of music therapy may be especially strong in people with depression symptoms who also have dementia (Werner et al., 2017). Dementia and depression are highly prevalent and comorbid conditions in older people (Schulz et al., 2008; Blazer, 2003). Importantly, a two-way interaction may be observed: depression can cause cognitive impairment and increase the risk of developing dementia (Blazer, 2003), while depression can also result from dementia, particularly at its early stages.

Findings from neuroscience suggest that music-induced emotions and memories may be preserved even in advanced stages of dementia (Cuddy et al., 2015). Findings from emotion theory suggests that positive feelings tend to be located in the left and negative feelings in the right frontal lobe of the brain (Davidson, 1998). One study found a short-term attenuation of frontal asymmetries during listening to music, (Jones, 1999). A more recent study described increasing right lateral activities after a course of 20 music therapy sessions. The authors concluded that verbal reflection and improvising on emotions may induce a reorganisation in frontotemporal areas, reduce anxiety (Fachner et al., 2013), and contribute to emotional processing (Fachner & Wosch, 2016). In people with dementia, music therapy has also shown effects on depression, anxiety, agitation, quality of life, cognitive function, and daily activities (Guétin et al., 2009; Gómez & Gómez, 2015; Ridder et al., 2013). In summary, however, the evidence for the clinical efficacy of music in dementia and old-age depression still remains unclear (Vink et al., 2011), and high-quality trials evaluating the effects on depressive symptoms are still required (Zhao et al., 2016). Further systematic evaluation in international large-scale randomised controlled trials is needed, considering severity of depression, comorbidities, and socio-economic impacts, to examine the effects of music therapy under different conditions. Further research will support the best application of music therapy and contribute to developing guidelines for depression in later life.

Music therapy in clinical practice

Methods of music therapy

Among four basic types of music experiences (improvising, re-creating, composing, listening (Bruscia, 2015)), one main distinction within music therapy is between active and receptive music therapy. People with depression commonly lose the ability to enjoy. At the most basic level, music can be perceived receptively by hearing and feeling the vibration of sounds, which may invoke emotions and experiences from the past (Staudinger, 2002). Biographically reminiscent songs can also invoke previous positive emotions, when the participant currently experiences mostly negative feelings, and they can help to accept ambivalence. One subtype of receptive music therapy is regulative music therapy as developed by Schwabe (2012). Through listening to classical music, the patient learns to intensify the perception in the areas of thoughts, feelings, moods, body, and music. In the feedback that follows, the patient reflects on how he or she reacts in the concrete situation, in order to learn about his/her defence mechanisms, strategies, and background; she/he learns to accept what is unchangeable and how to influence what may be changeable (Schwabe, 2012). Another subtype of receptive music therapy is Guided Imagery and Music (GIM) as developed by Bonny (also known as BMGIM – Bonny Method of Guided Imagery and Music), where the patient reflects feelings, imaginations, body sensations, and memories that emerge while listening to classical music, and the therapist guides to relieve blockages and supports development with guiding questions (Bruscia & Grocke, 2002).

Whereas patients in receptive music therapy perceive and trigger emotion and experience by listening to preferred, biographically reminiscent music, patients in active music therapy make music actively, either by playing instruments or using the voice, for example in instrumental improvisations. The music may be described as a threshold – between the inner and outer, conscious and unconscious processes, individual and collective, silence and sound (Bunt & Hoskyns, 2002). The instruments may also provide a bridge between the past and the present and may facilitate discovering new ways of relating in the present, even though the past cannot be changed (Volkman, 1993). If the patient feels comfortable with the instrument and the rhythm, the improvisation can contain different topics, such as expressing current feelings and feelings of the past, their inside and outside, different scenarios associated with suffering and trauma, and empathic improvisations where patients listen to one another (Borczon, 2015). Playing with instruments may also support the development of relationships (Raglio et al., 2012).

The focus of instrumental improvisation can vary depending on the goals of therapy and on how well the group is integrated. Music-oriented instructions can help when an explicit focus on relationships is not yet possible in the group process. In addition to songs and rhythmic play, these musical forms may include canon (singing and repeating the same melody with different starting points) and rondo (repeating different musical forms or melodies in different order, e.g. ABACA). In a musical play with non-musical instruction, patients may for example develop a shared rhythm to adjust their own play to the group or to influence the group's play. The focus in these improvisations is the integration into the group and finding own strategies, behavioural patterns and relationships. Own emotions and the feelings of group members are perceived and reflected, as is the influence of the improvisation on the self. A non-musical, theme-based musical play can have various aims: the feeling in a situation or relationship, inside and outside of the group. As an example, frustration about the group work can be shown with loud drums. This feeling of anger towards the group may be representative of the missing possibility to be heard in one's own family. By playing this anger and getting the attention or support of the group, this feeling may change into a more positive feeling of relief. Using a harp can support memories and can help to relax, thereby enabling a new experience in a grief process (Rudloff & Schwabe, 1997).

Singing is an important method in the work with older adults because songs are connected with memories and feelings of the past. However, songs can also be used to reflect and express current feelings, which may decrease isolation, a common consequence of depression, by means of group integration (Hamberger, 2011). Especially in the generation of those who are in that age group today, talking about grief, feelings, and needs was not a typically learned skill (Buchanan et al., 2006; Schneider & Nesseler, 2011). Lyrics can provide an opportunity for that. Therapeutic songwriting can extend these possibilities by thematising feelings, wishes, conflicts, and experiences not yet coped with. During the songwriting process, the therapist can guide the patient from negative feelings to the remaining possibilities and the immanent hope. Subsequent feedback from within the group may uncover similar wishes and individual possibilities, and thereby support mutual understanding (Baker, 2015).

Working model

The working model we present in this section was developed in a geropsychiatric department and nursing home by the first author and was first published in a German handbook for depression in old age (Eickholt, 2017a). It has been successfully tested (Werner et al., 2017) and is shown here to illustrate one possible way of working in music therapy with this population.

Processes in music therapy are dependent on the type of institution, the institutional and individual framework conditions, and aims. The following procedure is an example of how the working model is applied for late life depression

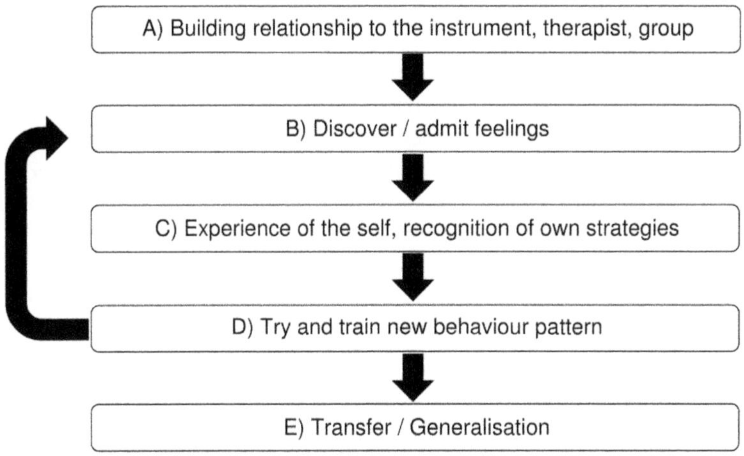

Figure 14.1 A working model of music therapy for late-life depression.

in a geropsychiatric department, a day care department, and with adaptations in a nursing home, in individual as well as in group therapy. Figure 14.1 shows the different phases during the process of therapy. The overarching objectives and detailed phases are adapted in relation to the duration of in-patient stay, individual conditions, and the duration the patient remains in each phase. In cases where complete recovery seems impossible during the in-patient stay, improvement of symptoms and quality of life should be considered a priority. The music therapy sessions are influenced by the mood and current situations, which are investigated at the beginning of the session. At the end of each session, experiences during the music therapy are ascertained and their relation to the current situation outside the music therapy is considered.

1 Building relationship to the instrument, therapist, group

Patients with depression are often diffident during the first sessions, voicing fear of doing something incorrectly. By joining the music therapy receptively, they can establish a connection to the group without having to become active. The fear of making mistakes may prevent them from playing openly. The sounds they make are often quiet, deciding for one instrument is difficult. At this stage, they may feel a strong need for "harmony" in the group and may block free improvisations where no concrete structure (such as a specific rhythm, tones, or reproduced music) is given by the therapist. Once patients have decided to choose a new or previously learned instrument with which they feel comfortable, they often stay with it for a while. Their perception remains in their own play, their own rhythm and melody, as opposed to communicating with the group. Furthermore, they may often seek confirmation of having played "correctly" (Hamberger, 2011: 78). For some clients, such a desire for harmony and confirmation or validation may be based on an orientation towards achievement and perfectionism. The main goal in this phase is to open up to the instrument, the therapist, and the group. First patterns of relationships and behaviour are identifiable. Exchanging experiences may disburden and strengthen the group integration and promote reciprocal support. The first feeling of disharmony can change towards verbal and mutual musical exchange, wider perception of the whole group, and support of a feeling of harmony and group cohesion.

2 Discover/admit feelings

In this second phase, patients learn to discover and admit positive and negative feelings. Patients may still be afraid to make mistakes or to show socially undesirable behaviour. Aggressive emotions are not accepted; they may have been suppressed for many years, and their existence is not allowed. The bass drum is often preferred, but played very softly. Often patients have not learned to accept and cope with aggressive emotions. Drums and gongs can help to release these suppressed feelings. Instrumental improvisation and regulative music therapy can help to discover emotions, to feel the body, and to perceive mutual interaction. In this phase, individual needs, such as the feeling of being needed and of having a direction in life, should be discovered. The patients learn about their feelings and needs, retrospection helps to process memories and grief. The therapist supports and accompanies the patients while they discover and admit their feelings in a safe frame. His/her role is to also offer stability to patients. The support offered during this process is very important. Especially when feelings and coping patterns from traumatic experiences may have existed for many years and become hardened, they can only gently be unravelled in musical plays and associated discussion.

Beside the use of instruments, another way to become aware of feelings is songwriting (Baker, 2015). Current topics such as worries about the family and wishes can be explored in a song. It is often the case that group members have similar feelings, even when the situations are different. Commonly group members suffer from their current situation and experience grief; conversely, they show the wish and hope to change the feelings. Writing a song supports the feeling of being taken seriously, to be understood, and to belong to a group.

3 Experience of the self, recognition of own strategies

Whereas patients typically describe somatic problems, they often appear unaware of the main symptoms of depression (Schneider & Nesseler, 2011). Awareness of depression can be very difficult, as this disease does not seem to exist for some patients. At this point, patients are encouraged to recognise and accept previous existing coping patterns and strategies. In order to identify them, different areas are explored (Hautzinger, 2000: 27):

- Existing strategies, behavioural patterns and processes which are conducive to burden or relief, reactions to stimuli and influences of mindset, conviction and motives
- Investigation of previous successful and failed attempts of self-management
- Benefit/function of disease and in-patient stay (e.g. expectation of external help, structure by fixed day structures, sense, and sympathy for patient stay), explanation of characteristics of the disease
- Underlying conditions for current and new coping strategies and resources (social, familial, partnership, as well as cultural and physical environment).

The therapist has to consider that especially older patients may have used particular behavioural patterns over decades; these patterns are familiar to them, even if they were not, or only partially, helpful, or, due to circumstances or declining capabilities, only temporarily helpful. It can be very difficult to learn about and accept one's own feelings and coping patterns. Familial, work-related or political circumstances might be a reason why the person could not consider their needs in the past and therefore, did not learn to take care of their own wellbeing. Losing responsibilities can lead to the loss of one's life's work. In addition, adverse experiences and traumata which were often suppressed as a way of coping can reappear. When the partner deceases, one's own role has to be re-defined. Besides coping with their own grief, older people are suddenly fully responsible for organising daily life, including taking care of finances, housework, cooking, or previously shared recreational activities. The aim in this phase is to improve introspection and to detect existing behavioural and avoidance strategies.

4 Trying and training new behaviour patterns

Previous strategies which have supported depression should be restructured by changing perception and behaviour. A patient who feels external pressure can experience autonomy in the protective frame of music therapy. For example, a patient who was advised to move into a nursing home and to give up her/his own home, which would limit their remaining abilities, decides not to follow that advice. In music therapy, he can re-establish his autonomy and abilities, at first with instruments, the way of playing them, choosing his own position in the group, and influencing group activities, and later in the autonomy of working out solutions. The interdisciplinary cooperation with medical doctors, psychologists, other therapists, and social workers supports the handling of topics through different approaches and media, so that previous strategies, the experience of autonomy and abilities, as well as possibilities, are worked out comprehensively and on several levels. New goals are based on individual resources and their possible applicability. To avoid overstraining, it is important to reflect this process together with the patient and to adapt it in relation to current circumstances. How a cognitive behavioural change can be processed in this phase is shown in the following example:

> *Adam described problems with taking care of his big flat and his garden, which was full of roses that he loved. His son had persuaded him to move into a smaller flat on the first floor, which had only a small balcony. Adam suffered from the loss of his roses and the fight with his son and he wanted to move back. The aim in the music therapy was to detect positive characteristics of the moving. In an instrumental improvisation, the garden was shown, the hard work was sounded with drums for cutting the hedge, the ocean drum reminded of the large amount of water given to the roses. The following play showed the possibilities of the balcony: Tiny and fine blossoms in colourful flowerboxes were played with a glockenspiel, hanging plants with a harp and the water with a rain stick. In the feedback, Adam reflected that the balcony was easier to keep and that he had more time and energy for this when the hard work of the garden ended. The group worked out which creations were possible and with what steps he would start between the sessions. Adam changed his view and was able to avoid getting involved in arguments with his son. In the next session, a new improvisation to his newly designed balcony confirmed his positive feeling in a melodious play.*

In songwriting, patients can describe their new strategies and thoughts in song lyrics, which can serve to intensify them and to detail the consequences for the future. In this phase of trying out new strategies, the perception of previous and newly learned behavioural patterns is constantly reflected. This reflection can guide back to phase B and support an extended self-perception and discovery of individual resources.

Another example of experimenting with new behaviour patterns is given below:

> *Amanda, a 70-year-old woman, describes a situation where she and her husband had a typical fight. She describes her own and her husband's behaviour and explains that she tried to avoid the conflict by saying nothing about what disturbed her. Sometimes the conflict situation would be solved in this way, but some situations were too serious, so that Amanda would become angry and would start to quarrel with her husband. A group member plays the situation together with Amanda in an instrumental role-play. During the role-play, Amanda changes her instrumental play from a reserved into a very intensive and accelerated way. In the feedback, the role-play partner, Amanda and the therapist reflect on her instrumental play. She finds out that it is difficult for her to give her husband the time to express himself when she is angry, and feels that her husband may react angrily because he does not feel respected. Together with the group she works out how she wants to react. In further role-plays,*

the role-play partner first plays her role, before she applies and trains her intended reaction herself. The instrumental improvisation changes now into a pleasant and respectful play. Transfer to daily life is practiced at first in easier situations; when she feels more secure, she uses the new behaviour pattern in more difficult situations.

Due to the inclusion of the role-play partner and the general play process, this example includes operant learning, developed by Skinner, and social cognitive learning, developed by Bandura, by describing and observing the intended behaviour pattern in another person (Schermer et al., 2016). Both of these aspects of behavioural therapy are integrated in a theme-based instrumental improvisation, according to Rudloff and Schwabe (1997).

5 Transfer/generalisation

Achievements in music therapy, such as awareness of existing strategies and development and training of new strategies, should be transferred and generalised into daily life. This conversion usually occurs in small steps, in which the abilities and possible overstraining are considered. A first step might be the imagination of a stressful situation and the new behaviour in a musical way; then the application in the daily life may follow as a second step. The aim of this process is that patients learn about their own strategies and possibilities by an extended perception of their current situation. Whereas psychiatry patients often go back to their home and reorganise their daily life depending on their individual needs, in the setting of a nursing home it is important to integrate the patient into the daily activities of the ward with consideration of individual requirements. Besides the planning of non-musical strategies in all areas of life and generalisation of the new behaviour pattern, recreational music activities can also be motivated by music therapy. Patients may learn an instrument (cf. musical education in elderly above) or start playing again; a membership in a senior choir can develop social networks and new life tasks. To be part of a group enables the use of abilities within society and supports autonomy.

Conclusion

The clinical working model of music therapy described here was evaluated in a pragmatic trial (Werner et al., 2017), which suggested that this type of music therapy might be more effective in reducing depression symptoms than recreational singing. The comprehensive and detailed description provided here illustrates the complex challenges and possibilities of music therapy for late life depression. Music therapy is typically customised to meet individual needs of patients. If conducted well, it can improve symptoms of depression and support individuals in coping with current problems. Therefore, it should be available in the care of older adults. Future research on music therapy should aim to examine processes and effects of music therapy and other music interventions for depression in older age. Understanding of the unique strengths of the different forms and working models of music interventions will be important to ensure their most appropriate and effective implementation.

Note: Parts of this chapter (in particular the figure and description of the working model) were previously published in German (ref. Eickholt, 2017a, 2017b) and are translated and reproduced here with permission from the publisher.

References

Ahessy, B. (2016). The use of music therapy choir to reduce depression and improve quality of life in older adults: A randomised control trial. *Music & Medicine*, 8(1), 17–28.

Baker, F. (2015). *Therapeutic songwriting: Developments in theory, methods, and practice*. Hampshire, NY: Palgrave McMillan.

Blazer, D. G. (2003). Depression in late life: Review and commentary. *The Journals of Gerontology: Series A*, 58(3), M249-M265.

Borczon, R. M. (2015). Music therapy for survivors of traumatic events. In B. Wheeler (Ed.), *Music therapy handbook* (pp. 379–389). New York, NY: Guilford Press.

Bruscia, K. (2015). *Defining music therapy* (3rd ed.). Gilsum, NH: Barcelona Publishers.

Bruscia, K. E., & Grocke, D. (2002). *Guided imagery and music: The bonny method and beyond*. Gilsum, NH: Barcelona Publishers.

Buchanan, D., Tourigny-Rivard, M. F., Cappeliez, P., Frank, C., Janikowski, P., Spanjevic, L., . . . Herrmann, N. (2006). National guidelines for seniors' mental health: The assessment and treatment of depression. *Canadian Journal of Geriatrics*, 9(supplement 2), 52–58.

Bunt, L., & Hoskyns, S. (2002). *The handbook of music therapy*. East Sussex, NY: Routledge.

Ceccato, E., Vigato, G., Bonetto, C., Bevilacqua, A., Pizziolo, P., Crociani, S., Zanfretta, E., Pollini, L., Caneva, P. A., Baldin, L., Frongillo, C., Signorini, A., Demoro, S., & Barchi, E. (2012). STAM protocol in dementia: a multicenter, single-blind, randomized, and controlled trial. *American Journal of Alzheimer's Disease and Other Dementias*, 27(5), 301–310.

Choi, A. N., Lee, M. S., & Lim, J. J. (2008). Effects of group music intervention on depression, anxiety, and relationships in psychiatric patients: A pilot study. *Journal of Alternative and Complementary Medicine: Research on Paradigm, Practice, and Policy*, 14(5), 567–570.

Clift, S., Gilbert, R., & Vella-Burrows, T. (2016). A review of research on the value of singing for older people. *A Choir in Every Care Home Working Paper 6*. London: Baring Foundation.

Coulton, S., Clift, S., Skingley, A., & Rodriguez, J. (2015). Effectiveness and cost-effectiveness of community singing on mental health-related quality of life of older people: Randomised controlled trial. *The British Journal of Psychiatry*, 207(3), 250–255.

Cuddy, L. L., Sikka, R., & Vanstone, A. (2015). Preservation of musical memory and engagement in healthy aging and Alzheimer's disease. *Annals of the New York Academy of Sciences*, 1337, 223–231.

Davidson, R. J. (1998). Affective style and affective disorders: Perspectives from affective neuroscience. *Cognition and Emotion*, 12(3), 307–330.

Eickholt, J. (2017a). Musiktherapie. In A. Fellgiebel & M. Hautzinger (Eds.), *Altersdepression. Ein interdisziplinäres Handbuch* (pp. 177–186). Berlin: Springer.

Eickholt, J. (2017b). Musiktherapeutisches Songwriting. *Musiktherapeutische Umschau*, 38, 17–27.

Fachner, J., Gold, C., & Erkkilä, J. (2013). Music therapy modulates fronto-temporal activity in the rest-EEG in depressed clients. *Brain Topography*, 26(2), 338–354.

Fachner, J., & Wosch, T. (2016). Neurowissenschaftliche Aspekte der Musiktherapie bei affektiven Störungen und bei Demenz. In W. Auhagen, C. Bullerjahn, & R. Georgi (Eds.), *Musikpsychologie – Musik und Gesundheit* (pp. 7–33). Göttingen: Hogrefe.

Fang, R., Ye, S., Huangfu, J., Calimag, D. P. (2017). Music therapy is a potential intervention for cognition of Alzheimer's Disease: A mini-review. *Translational Neurodegeneration*, 6(2).

Gold, C., Solli, H. P., Krüger, V., & Lie, S. A. (2009). Dose-response relationship in music therapy for people with serious mental disorders: Systematic review and meta-analysis. *Clinical Psychology Review*, 29(3), 193–207.

Gómez, G. M., & Gómez, G. J. (2015). Musicoterapia en la enfermedad de Alzheimer: Efectos cognitivos, psicológicos y conductuales [Music therapy and Alzheimer´s disease: Cognitive, psychological and behavioural effects]. *Neurología*, 32(5), 300–308.

Guétin, S., Portet, F., Picot, M. C., Pommié, C., Messaoudi, M., Djabelkir, L., . . . Touchon, J. (2009). Effect of music therapy on anxiety and depression in patients with Alzheimer's type dementia: Randomised, controlled study. *Dementia and Geriatric Cognitive Disorders*, 28 (1), 36–46.

Hamberger, M. (2011). *Musiktherapie im Alter: Demenz, Depression, Sterben und Tod.* Freising: Laubsänger.

Hanser, S. B., & Thompson, L. W. (1994). Effects of a music therapy strategy on depressed older adults. *Journal of Gerontology*, 49(6), 265–269.

Hautzinger, M. (2000). *Depression im Alter (Materialien für die klinische Praxis).* Weinheim: Beltz PVU.

Jones, N. A. (1999). Massage and music therapies attenuate frontal EEG asymmetry in depressed adolescents. *Adolescence*, 34(135), 529–534.

Livingston, G., Kelly, L., Lewis-Holmes, E., Baio, G., Morris, S., Patel, N., Omar, R. Z., Katona, C., & Cooper, C. (2014). A systematic review of the clinical effectiveness and cost-effectiveness of sensory, psychological and behavioural interventions for managing agitation in older adults with dementia. *Health Technology Assessment*, 18(39), 1–226.

Maratos, A., Gold, C., Wang, X., & Crawford, M. (2008). Music therapy for depression. *The Cochrane Database of Systematic Reviews*, 2008(1), CD004517.

Muthesius, D., Sonntag, J., Warme, B., & Falk, M. (2010). *Musik – Demenz – Begegnung: Musiktherapie für Menschen mit Demenz*. Frankfurt am Main: Mabuse.

Raglio, A., Bellelli, G., Mazzola, P., Bellandi, D., Giovagnoli, A. R., Farina, E., Stramba-Badiale, M., Gentile, S., Gianelli, M.V., Ubezio, M. C., Zanetti, O., & Trabucchi, M. (2012). Music, music therapy and dementia: A review of literature and the recommendations of the Italian Psychogeriatric Association. *Maturitas*, 72(4), 305–310.

Ridder, H. M. O., Stige, B., Qvale, L. G., & Gold, C. (2013). Individual music therapy for agitation in dementia: An exploratory randomized controlled trial. *Aging & Mental Health*, 17(6), 667–678.

Rudloff, H., & Schwabe, C. (1997). *Aktive Gruppenmusiktherapie für erwachsene Patienten – Theoretischer und methodologischer Kontext.* Crossen: Akademie für angewandte Musiktherapie Crossen.

Russo, J., Vitaliano, P. P., Brewer, D. D., Katon, W., & Becker, J. (1995). Psychiatric disorders in spouse caregivers of care recipients with Alzheimer's disease and matched controls: A diathesis – stress model of psychopathology. *Journal of Abnormal Psychology*, 104(1), 197–204.

Schermer, F. J., Weber, A., Drinkmann, A., & Jungnitsch, G. (2016). *Methoden der Verhaltensorientierten Sozialen Arbeit.* Aschaffenburg: Alibri.

Schulz, R., McGinnis, K. A., Zhang, S., Martire, L. M., Hebert, R. S., Beach, S. R., Bozena, Z., Czaja, S. J., Belle, S. H. (2008). Dementia patient suffering and caregiver depression. *Alzheimer Disease and Associated Disorders*, 22(2), 170–176.

Schneider, F., & Nesseler, T. (2011). *Depressionen im Alter: Die verkannte Volkskrankheit.* München: Herbig.

Schwabe, C. (2012). *Regulatives Musiktraining – Selbstentspannung mit Musik.* Crossen: Akademie für angewandte Musiktherapie Crossen.

Skingley, A., & Vella-Burrows, T. (2010). Therapeutic effects of music and singing for older people. *Nursing Standard*, 24(19), 35–41.

Staudinger, W. (2002). Das Leben ist wie ein Regenbogen: Musiktherapie mit alten Menschen. In W. Kraus (Ed.), *Die Heilkraft der Musik: Einführung in die Musiktherapie* (pp. 194–200). München: C. H. Beck.

Verrusio, W., Andreozzi, P., Marigliano, B., Renzi, A., Gianturco, V., Pecci, M. T., Ettorre, E., Cacciafesta, M., & Gueli, N. (2014). Exercise training and music therapy in elderly with depressive syndrome: A pilot study. *Complementary Therapies in Medicine*, 22(4), 614–620.

Vink, A. C., Bruinsma, M. S., & Scholten, R. J. (2011). Music therapy for people with dementia. *The Cochrane Database of Systematic Reviews*, 2011(4), CD003477.

Vitaliano, P. P., Zhang, J., & Scanlan, J. M. (2003). Is caregiving hazardous to one's physical health? A meta-analysis. *Psychological Bulletin*, 129(6), 946–972.

Volkman, S. (1993). Music therapy and the treatment of trauma-induced dissociative disorders. *The Arts in Psychotherapy*, 20(3), 243–251.

Werner, J., Wosch, T., & Gold, C. (2017). Effectiveness of group music therapy versus recreational group singing for depressive symptoms of elderly nursing home residents: Pragmatic trial. *Aging & Mental Health*, 21(2), 147–155.

Wickel, H. H., & Hartogh, T. (2015). *Musizieren im Alter: Arbeitsfelder und Methoden.* Mainz: Schott.

Zhao, K., Bai, Z. G., Bo, A., & Chi, I. (2016). A systematic review and meta-analysis of music therapy for the older adults with depression. *International Journal of Geriatric Psychiatry*, 31(11), 1188–1189.

Chapter 15

Assessment and therapeutic application of the expressive therapies continuum in music therapy

The case of Anna with cancer-related depression

Jana Duhovska, Vija Bergs Lusebrink and Kristīne Mārtinsone

Introduction

According to the National Cancer Institute, the lifetime risk of developing any type of cancer is 44% for men and 38% for women. A diagnosis of cancer, with the accompanying side effects from medical treatment, may result in extensive emotional, physical and social suffering (Irving & Lloyd-Williams, 2010; Gomez-Campelo et al., 2014; Schubart et al., 2014; Phillips et al., 2008). The actual experience of chemotherapy-induced side effects, such as nausea and vomiting, and their influence on psychological wellbeing varies widely in patients receiving the same cytotoxic agents. This suggests that non-pharmacological factors possibly play an important role in how patients experience or interpret physical symptoms during the treatment phase (Montgomery, 2000; Thune-Boyle, 2006 as cited in Bradt et al., 2016). It is therefore important that cancer care incorporates services that help meet patients' psychological, social and spiritual needs (Bradt et al., 2016).

Both medically and psycho-emotionally, there are several stages of survivorship from cancer, each of them characterized by specific needs to be addressed in the psychological domain. The newly diagnosed may be dealing with anxiety, fear of dying, treatment-related side effects and disruption in family and social roles (Allen, 2013). During an extended survivorship however, a period where patients finds themselves in remission or receiving maintenance therapy, cancer survivors enter a crisis of returning to *normal* life. Some of the issues that generally arise during this stage include the feelings of ambiguity related to the joy of being alive and fear of recurrence, adjusting to physical and psychosocial changes, reintegrating and reorganizing individual and family concerns, and isolation resulting from either external circumstances or self-imposed withdrawal. These issues indicate a need for developing and implementing active emotion-oriented coping strategies, re-examining life values, beliefs and priorities and restoring the balance between dependence on the support of others and interdependence, or reciprocal sharing of support. (Allen, 2013).

Emotional support, problem solving, examining and changing thinking styles, teaching social and other skills – these are some of the basic needs of depressed patients that are effectively met via counselling, including music and other arts therapies. The creative nature of these therapies is unique as it 1) facilitates the establishment of rapport, comfort and trust; 2) allows for less threatening disclosure of the issues that are not easily verbalized; 3) provides a platform for the communication of dysfunctional thoughts that then become the material for discussion, cognitive reframing and the creation of new perspectives; and 4) is engaging thereby encouraging physical participation and activity as well as providing a variety of sensory experiences that reduce tension and offer alternative channels of expression (Malchiodi, 2005; Hultquist, 1995; Bork, 2010 as cited in Fernandez et al., 2014).

The Expressive Therapies Continuum (ETC) was conceptualized in reference to visual expression and is based on the concepts of art educator Victor Lowenfield, cognitive psychologist Jerome Bruner, investigator of imagery in psychiatry Mardi Horowitz, neuroscientist Joaquin Fuster as well as several pioneers of the arts therapies (Hinz, 2009, as cited in Mārtinsone et al., 2013). It provides a framework for understanding how people interact with a variety of experiential and creative activities, and it offers a hierarchy of information-processing and creative expression. In the therapy setting, the ETC can become a guide for assessment, revealing the strengths and difficulties of the client/patient, thus providing a guideline for the therapist when defining the starting point, pathways and goals in art therapy. Initially designed for application in art therapy, the concepts of the ETC are being expanded to other arts' modalities, and one of the aims of this article is to illustrate the first attempt at applying this model to music therapy.

Music therapy for cancer patients with depression

Music interventions both for adult and paediatric cancer patients have been widely used for years. Applications include decreasing anxiety prior to or during surgical procedures, lessening treatment side effects, enhancing pain management, improving immune system functioning and decreasing stress during chemotherapy or radiation therapy (Bradt et al., 2016). Results of a recent systematic review, published by the Cochrane Collaboration in 2016, based on 52 studies with 3731 patients, conducted by Joke Bradt and her colleagues, confirm that music interventions may also have beneficial effects on mental health and emotional functioning of the cancer patients. Although insufficient quality of evidence makes it unclear what impact music interventions may have on depression, the review points out its clear positive impact on anxiety and mood measurements, as well as quality of life in people with cancer. Quality of life includes various psychological aspects such as autonomy, optimal coping and feeling useful, which are characteristic of vital living, as opposed to states of low mood and aversion to activity which are key characteristics of depression.

There are inherent elements of music, such as rhythm and tempo, mode, pitch, timbre, melody and harmony, which are known to influence physiological and psycho-emotional responses in humans. For example, music has been found to arouse memory and association, stimulate imagery, evoke emotions, facilitate social interaction and promote relaxation and distraction (Dileo, 2006). In order to address the predominant biopsychosocial and spiritual issues, symptoms and needs of cancer patients, music therapists use a variety of interventions. The most common include the use of songs (singing, song writing and lyric analysis); music improvisation (instrumental and vocal), music and imagery, music-based reminiscence and life review, chanting and toning, music-based relaxation and instrumental participation (O'Callaghan, 2015 as cited in Bradt et al., 2016). Music therapists adapt and modify music interventions to address symptoms and areas of difficulty based on patient preferences and assessment outcomes. They employ musical and verbal strategies to provide opportunities for expression and communication, reminiscence, processing of thoughts and emotions and improvement of symptom management. Therapist-supported music therapy environments often provide the space and time through which patients and families may experience social connection, improve self-fulfilment and acquire effective coping strategies (Magill, 2011 as cited in Bradt et al., 2016).

The expressive therapies continuum

Overview and perspectives for assessment and planning of therapy

The (ETC) posits (Figure 15.1) that expression and the application of media and techniques in the arts therapies can be seen as taking place on three different levels – kinesthetic/sensory, perceptual/affective or cognitive/symbolic (Lusebrink, 1990, 1992). These levels represent diverse types of information processing, ranging from spontaneous reaction to expression of thoughts and feelings, and they appear to reflect different functions and structures in the brain that process visual and affective information (Lusebrink, 2004, 2010). Each level of the ETC is described as a continuum between two opposite poles. The extreme pole of each level represents psychopathological variations, and the sequence of the levels reflects the mental and graphical development in progression from simple to more complex levels of information processing. The three levels are regarded as different from each other, yet they form interconnected systems, and the expression on a particular level of the ETC incorporates the characteristics of a systems present in lower levels (Lusebrink, 1990). The fourth, creative level, or vertical axis, intersects the horizontal levels, can occur at any single level of the ETC, and represents the integration of functioning from all levels. It is considered as the synthesis, or whole-brain level, and supports the idea of integration as wellness (Fernandez et al., 2014).

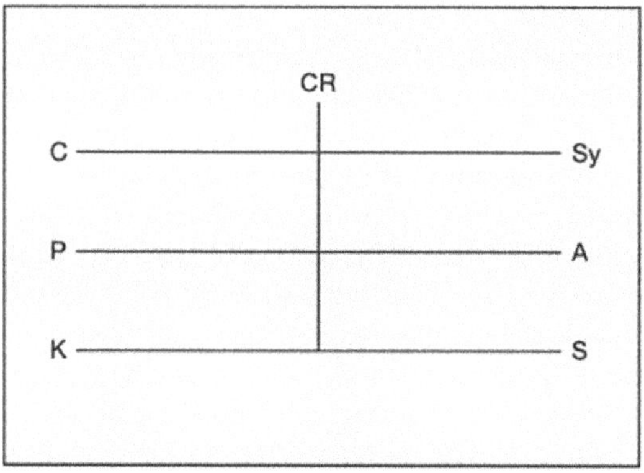

Figure 15.1 Schematic representation of the expressive therapies continuum (K/S – kinesthetic/sensory, P/A – perceptual/affective, C/Sy – cognitive/symbolic, CR – creative) (Lusebrink, 1990).

According to Lusebrink (2004, 2010), the sequence of the first three levels reflects mental and graphical development in progression from simple to more complex levels of information processing as a person develops throughout life. The kinesthetic/sensory level is related to the preverbal experience where gathering of information does not require words. This is an important basic level, as kinesthetic/sensory input and expression forms the basis of many experiences at the foundation of who we are and how we perceive the outer world. The perceptual/affective level corresponds to school-age children and formal and affective aspects of information processing. This may include the creation of formed images, as well as expression of emotion. For people of all ages, this level is helpful in understanding the structural and formal aspects of representational diversity, which involves identifying emotions and discovering the appropriate ways to express them. The cognitive/symbolic level requires planning and complex cognitive action, and, for clients/patients of all ages, helps make connections to their inner experiences (Hinz, 2009 as cited in Vende et al., 2015).

Lusebrink also proposed the possible concomitants of brain areas to the different levels of expression in expressive therapies based on Fuster's classification of sensory information processes on three hierarchical levels (Fuster, 2003, in Lusebrink, 2004, 2010). These levels are defined as: 1) elementary sensory features are analysed by the primary sensory cortices; 2) associated features in a given modality (art, music, movement, etc.) are processed respectively in the unimodal association cortex; and 3) processing across several sensory and non-sensory modalities occurs in the transmodal or multi-modal association cortex in the parietal lobe and in a *bottom-up* direction (Lusebrink, 2010). The multi-modal association cortex processes this information and then forwards it to the prefrontal cortex, which coordinates the processes that are associated with attention, emotion, cognition and action (Fuster, 2003, in Lusebrink, 2010).

Although ETC is not a psychometric test, the criteria provided within the framework can become a guide for assessment (Mārtinsone et al., 2013) as they facilitate identification of one or more predominant levels of sensory information processing. This process is based on the way specific formal elements are presented in the artwork that has been created. Moreover, artistic expressions not only reflect the predominant level of the ETC but also reveal the client's/patient's strengths or difficulties at a particular level. Area of strength indicates a lack of difficulty (and of pathology) as well as provides an entry point or a secure base from which to explore other areas that may be challenging or represent psychopathology. Identifying these allows the therapist to build on the strengths of the patient as well as address missing links in the sequence of information processing (Lusebrink, 2010). According to Lusebrink (2004, 2010), planning of treatment can include and identify either stepwise bottom-up or top-down transitions between the ETC levels or horizontal transformations within each level, depending on the needs, characteristics of information processing and psychopathology of the client/patient.

Levels of ETC and its application in music therapy

Even though the ECT was originally designed for use within the visual art setting, the model can be applied to other art modalities, for both assessment and therapy planning purposes (Lusebrink, 1992).

Kinesthetic/sensory level

On the kinesthetic/sensory level, art media are used for simple motor expressions manifested as sensory and kinesthetic phenomena. If the client/patient focuses on kinesthetic activities, their awareness of the sensory component in therapy decreases, and vice versa. Psychopathological expressions of this component might be characterized by agitated actions, disregard of boundaries and limits, destructive activities or marked lack of energy (Lusebrink, 2010; Mārtinsone et al., 2013). Regarding the sensory component, attention is focused on sensory exploration of surfaces and textures. Psychopathological variations of this component are manifested in an over-absorption in the sensory experience, extreme sensory sensitivity and marked deceleration of movement (Lusebrink, 2010).

Music therapy techniques in the kinesthetic pole of the kinesthetic/sensory level facilitate freedom and authentic energy, and they mostly deal with tempo and effort, e.g. beating, slapping or touching the instrument directly by hand or beater, whereas the sensory pole accentuates not only auditory reaction to sound, but also the tactile and sensory responses while playing or singing, e.g. sensing one's voice vibrating within the body or passing throughout the airwaves. Activities on the kinesthetic pole, especially rhythmic beating, can be utilized both to release energy and subsequently to calm the client/patient down. By contrast, activities on the sensory pole encourage a *here and now* attitude and integration of mindfulness elements such as being in the present moment, curiosity, openness, acceptance and kindness.

Perceptual/affective level

The perceptual component focuses on the details and differentiation of forms. Psychopathological variations of the perceptual component manifest as incomplete forms, figure and ground reversal and either an overemphasis on, or lack of, details (Lusebrink, 2010). The affective component is characterized by increased involvement in the expression of affect and affective modification of forms. The presence, differentiation and change of affect are indicated by the increased use of artistic media, e.g. excessive amount of paint, bright or overwhelming colors, loud or (unnecessarily) large number of instruments. Psychopathological variations of the affective component are marked by unintegrated or incomplete forms, application of artistic means inappropriate to the subject matter, interpenetration of the forms and/or merging of figure and ground, and especially, indiscriminate mixing of artistic means (Lusebrink, 2010).

The musical requisites of the perceptual/affective level on the perceptual pole of the continuum are rhythmic precision and shape (melody, repeating pattern, developing and completed motifs, relationship between the melody and the accompaniment). On the other hand of the spectrum emotional, or affective, expression focuses on the process of experiencing feelings rather than the result. The choice of activities in this level may be challenging, yet highly rewarding. This is because this level of the ETC allows for experimentation between the experience of overwhelming emotions on the one hand and focusing on activities that allow for development of control over intense emotions and – gradually – over the situation. It is quite common in music therapy that inexperienced patients get confused and self-critical with *playing* and need guidance and support from the therapist. This level, especially at the perceptive pole, requires therapist interventions aimed at holding, containing, offering boundaries and encouragement. When starting to trust one's inner musical child by discovering a rhythmic organization for randomly produced sounds or by collecting series of sounds, patients do develop ability to utilize the instruments to meet their needs, either for expression or regulation.

Cognitive/symbolic level

The cognitive/symbolic component emphasizes cognitive operations. This component allows cognitive integration of expression that lead to categorizations, concept formation, problem solving, spatial differentiation and integration, abstractions, word inclusion and differentiation of meaning (Lusebrink,

2010; Fernandez et al., 2014). Psychopathological variations of the cognitive component are characterized by illogical relations between forms and loss of conceptual meaning. The symbolic component, on the other hand, stresses global intuitive processing and involves input from sensory and affective sources, autobiographic processing and symbolic expression. This component is characterized by symbolic relationships, the meaning of affective images, symbolic use of artistic means, symbolic abstractions and intuitive integrative concept formation. Psychopathological variations of the symbolic component occur when obscure or idiosyncratic meaning is ascribed to symbols, or when there is over-identification with symbols, symbolic manifestations of defenses (Lusebrink, 2010; Mārtinsone et al., 2013) and a loss of reflective distance (Lusebrink, 1990, 2010).

When entering the cognitive/symbolic hierarchical level in music therapy, the focus of attention at the cognitive end is on logical, linear thinking and the ability to plan one's actions, whereas at the symbolic pole of this continuum, the creation of intuitive concepts is emphasized. The cognitive component involves work with mental images and verbal expression, be it re-writing song lyrics or composing a melody for the favourite poem, arranging the instruments for a group improvisation or conducting. Activities on the symbolic pole, by contrast, are more intuitive, created on the spot and derived mainly from sensory, affective and autobiographic sources, focused on personal symbolic identification with music, being multi-dimensional and touching the deepest strings of one's soul, which cannot be expressed in words (Lusebrink, 1992 as cited in Mārtinsone et al., 2013). Improvisation is one of the most potent activities for invoking multi-layered and multi-dimensional symbols that can be characterized using kinesthetic, sensory, emotional and subjective or universal aspects of meaning (Vende et al., 2015). The use of the affective pole can especially be promoted via props, evocative poems and stories and elements of reminiscence therapy.

Creative level

The creative level is important part of expressive therapies. In music as therapy it refers to the individual's synthesizing and self-actualizing tendencies as the creative component arises from the capacity to fully utilize his or her potential and desire to improve oneself (Fernandez et al., 2014). Thus, with the use of the ETC, there is an attempt to view the individual as organized, whole, unique and integrated – a self-actualized individual. Creative information processing occurs at any level and with any component process (Hinz, 2009). An individual's functioning can also take place within all component processes in a single event or in a series of experiences. Through arts therapies, the person grows because of integrative encounters, opportunities to submerse himself or herself in creative potential and doing this without fear. On a similar note, through the therapeutic process, the person explores, acknowledges and challenges demands, or stereotypical expectations placed upon them by their environment, which can lead to a realizing their full potential. If the demands are too overwhelming for an individual to handle, then perhaps he or she may take the risk in exploring it in the safety of the therapeutic process (Lowenfeld, 1952).

In music therapy, therapeutic work on the creative level can provide means for the individual to discover and develop different and/or novel ways to organize information. The use of diverse art media, use of recorded, live and sung music, and props and elements from other arts therapies foster curiosity as well as perceptual openness and receptiveness to environmental stimuli with all the senses. This supports the development of spontaneity, expansiveness, openness to inner stimuli and self-acceptance (Lusebrink, 1992).

Case example of an ETC used for assessment and therapy for a patient with cancer-related depression

Anna (pseudonym) is a 65-year-old breast cancer survivor who was visited weekly by a music therapist for ten sessions at a residential care home. Her presenting problems was depressed mood and anxiety that had begun six months earlier when she was diagnosed with stage one breast cancer. She was rushed through the medical necessities, including full mastectomy of her left breast and adjuvant therapy, leading to severe fatigue and nausea. However, at the end of the treatment the news was good – her suffering was not in vain and there was no obvious risk for recurrence. By the time music therapy started, Anna was already taking medication (a selective serotonin reuptake inhibitor) for her mental health problems which appeared to be partially effective, as the anxiety had disappeared. However, the dysthymia, characterized by emotional withdrawal, indifference to either negative or positive stimuli, marked lack of energy resulting in symptoms resembling motor retardation, sleepiness, isolation and even occasional thoughts of suicide, seemed there to stay.

Anna was relatively well looked after by her daughter who paid regular visits once every two weeks and phoned in between. According to standardised measurements, Anna was quite well physically, but seemed being too dependent on her daughter's visits and tended to fall into a cocoon-like condition – both physically and emotionally – demonstrating grief, reluctance to interact with others and increased isolation as she suspended her participation in the recreative music group activities, opting instead to stay in bed staring into space.

Information in Anna's file referred to some musical experience in folk music ensemble in her forties and this was one of the reasons she was offered music therapy. It was decided that one-to-one work would be more suited to her needs. She did not show much enthusiasm, but she was promised that music therapy would be a gentle, non-directive experience. It was explained to her that she was free to choose music therapy whenever she felt ready and, after discussing it with her daughter, she gave her consent.

The first sessions were focused on completing the assessment, creating a therapeutic alliance and setting the goals for therapy – both in general and within the framework of the ETC. The music therapy room was equipped with a variety of instruments, including a piano and electronic keyboard, a guitar, a lute, a set of djembes, a tambourine, a metallophone, a xylophone, hand bells, wind chimes, hangdrum, a singing bowl, a variety of small percussions and a Hi-Fi system with a selection of prerecorded music. There was also a box of basic stationery – A4 size paper, felt markers and glue stick – as well as a selection of magazines for prospective making of collages available.

Although many and varied music therapy techniques were applied during the therapy process, the focus here is on selected episodes that are the most suitable to illustrate the application of the ETC.

Assessment in music therapy revealed slightly decreased social and markedly decreased emotional functioning, and Anna's activities appeared to fall into combination of two ETC components – cognitive and kinesthetic. The cognitive component manifested as a desire to stick to a verbal mode of therapy – providing a detailed description of her life situation and thus revealing her negative perceptions of herself – her loneliness, worthlessness, being inadequate and unable to be in charge of her life, and her future, finding herself in the world that is hostile and ignoring her needs. The kinesthetic component was demonstrated via a preference for atonal percussions – such as djembe and shaker, playing them softly, quietly, insecurely, rather stiffly, physically and mechanically, with emotional and sensory detachment and no rhythmic pattern.

Following the initial assessment, the music therapist and Anna agreed about the aims for treatment. These included increasing wellbeing, identifying Anna's resources and developing an internal locus of control. It was considered that these aims would contribute to the reduction of such depressive symptoms as helplessness and hopelessness. Musically process started from the safe point consisting of kinesthetic activities whilst retaining some cognitive (verbal) elements. Gradually, the client/patient was led towards exploration of all the ETC levels and their poles to gain a variety of experience and flexibility. The stepwise transitions between the different levels and poles of the ETC were facilitated through therapist-directed changes in the mode of musical activity (playing, listening and singing), thus avoiding perseveration on a particular level or pole of the ETC.

The therapeutic process began with the music therapist offering the patient a djembe duet, with the aim of developing the kinesthetic/sensory level, especially at the sensory pole. This intervention provided an introduction to the musical instruments and, in Anna's own words, a way of becoming comfortable with "the noise we were making". It also served as an initial point of contact, leading to the establishment of a therapeutic alliance and sense of security. Firstly, with the help and encouragement of the therapist, Anna explored and shared the ways the djembe can be played: softly or loudly, standing or sitting, with one or two hands, with fingers or a flat hand, playing bass, open, slapping sounds. This was followed by identifying differences in the sound produced and paying attention to the physical sensations experienced while playing with different parts of the hand. Anna enthusiastically explored the sensory pole of this activity and the therapist then encouraged her to pay attention to differences while being between the two poles. As she did this, she was able to demonstrate flexibility, gradually gaining an optimal balance between the beating and feeling the beat. Having successfully experienced a brand new, yet safe activity, Anna proposed this as an opening ritual for future sessions.

In order to address the perceptual/affective level, mainly focusing on the perceptual pole, the music therapist offered Anna a variation of the djembe duet characterized by a stable, set rhythmic form differentiated from the ground. In order to start from a safe place, Anna first provided a bass line, playing a repetitive motif on the djembe whilst the therapist, playing metallophone, provided a 13-note finished form. This consisted of the melody of a well-known children's lullaby with a clear beginning and end, and a stable, specific rhythmic form providing structure and what Lusebrink (1990) refers to as a clear or good "Gestalt", namely, a simple basic structural configuration (of sounds) supporting homeostatic tendencies.

As they played, the therapist rapidly changed the dynamics and tempo, expecting Anna to adjust her part in the performance so to retain the function of the ground. They then switched roles, with Anna playing the solo and therapist the ground. Anna recognized the lullaby, and this initiated a gradual shift to the affective pole, culminating in Anna being willing to sing the song and to share a story from her childhood. She was the soloist again, using her voice as an instrument, while the therapist provided an empathetic ground on the djembe. This singing activity, performing a lullaby whose lyrics contain a strong metaphor of children as bear cubs who were hushed to sleep while their parents take care of their lives, led Anna toward the symbolic end of the cognitive/symbolic pole.

The song and its resolution brought rather strong emotions to the surface. It also offered an opportunity to introduce some cognitive work in the sessions through discussing Anna's family issues and exploring potential ways in which she could independently achieve experiences of wellbeing. Anna turned out to be a good storyteller, and the therapist urged her to consider the idea of developing a family tree by going through photos, documenting memories and calling her mother, aunts and cousins in order to clarify missing information and foster communication that has been lost in recent years. The therapist also suggested that she involve her grandchildren in computerizing this information by scanning photos, using desktop publishing, making a video or developing a simple web page. Anna left the session in an elevated mood, having a plan and a *legitimate reason* to re-establish lapsed contacts. The use of the lullaby as an affective component helped her to make a transition to the next session which involved cognitive level activity utilizing the lullaby material.

Further development of the topic of family ties, with Anna proactively taking responsibility for maintaining contact with her daughter, grandchildren and other relatives, led to the cognitive component clearly taking center stage during music therapy sessions. Characterized by problem solving, sequential activities and planning, the cognitive component of the ETC can be easily observed and developed through song-writing activities. It demands a high level of attention and (if the patient does not have a background in music) some comprehension of the unfamiliar language of notation. Developing the work with the well-received lullaby, Anna was offered the opportunity to personalize the lyrics of the song, making them relevant to her own family. The therapist prepared an easy-to-use notation material and did not interfere with regard to the mood of the song. The task appeared to be quite difficult and Anna struggled with both the technical and affective aspects of the task, writing and erasing, alternating between the hopelessness and clear conviction for a resolution – the best that was possible in her situation. As the session ended, Anna was not ready to share the work she had done; it was probably emotionally too intense for her, too soon, too personal. She said she wanted to revisit it in solitude, to rethink it thoroughly and maybe then to share it. This activity required clear integration of several components of the ETC. First, 1) cognitive, but also 2) affective, 3) some symbolic as the song clearly depicted her circumstances and struggle for resolution, and clearly 4) creative aspect, as this was a new composition rather than reworking of a well-known song.

The last part of the music therapy work for this client/patient came from further development of the symbolic level introduced by the therapist in the following way. Considering the intensity experienced during the session that involved personalizing the song, the therapist chose a neutral topic which contained only one word: "Nature". Be it summer or winter, Latvia or China, meadow, storm or sea – this all was up to Anna, who was asked to pick four different musical instruments, two for her and two for the therapist. The only requirement was that she gave the name to the improvisation beforehand. She was also asked to attribute specific roles or characters to each of the instruments. She wanted to play the *Summer evening in the country house* and was clear that wind chimes, played by herself, would represent cheerful baby birds, the hang drum would represent the intense scent of wild roses, metallophone, played by therapist, would symbolize rising stars and the djembe would represent the rhythmic noise of an empty swing swaying on an old oak tree.

Anna was hesitant to start playing; it seemed that there was some introductory story or poem or picture missing that would help her to immerse in the *summer feeling*. When the play finally started, it was quite clear that Anna had some problems musically attributing the *scent of roses* as this is a symbol usually not that clearly connected with the world of sound. Eventually, the *roses* were gradually introduced, played very softly, lightly and dreamily with long pauses. The therapist provided a bass line with the djembe (the empty swing). Soon after the sound of the of the djembe (empty swing) became quite prominent and rhythmic, Anna stopped the improvisation, saying she wanted to change the role of the wind chimes and to play a girl in the swing instead of birds. As the playing progressed, Anna closed her eyes and rocked her body in the rhythm of djembe. It was apparent, and later revealed in verbal feedback, that had been carried away to a particular period of time in a particular summer house with particular memories, emotions and bodily sensations. The improvisation brought her back to childhood days when Anna, being then the only child in the family, hand no choice but to spend her days in solitude, finding ways to experience small joys within the limits of her circumstances.

Overview of music therapy sessions and discussion

A review of Anna's process and progress in music therapy indicates that transitions, changes, or moments of integration in Anna's behaviour, mood or thinking patterns appeared to be concomitant with the changes in the components or levels of the ETC in music therapy. The framework of the ETC established Anna's comfort zone in music therapy on the kinesthetic and cognitive components, both of which manifested in ways typical for patients with depression, including low energy and negative cognitive thinking. Her music therapy goals aimed to address her markedly decreased emotional functioning on the affective component, with its associated behaviour, through the introduction and experience of all levels of the ETC.

The exploration of Anna's strength facilitated a transition to, and an integration of, the sensory component of the kinesthetic/sensory level and development of the ability to switch between *beating* and *feeling the beat*. Mastering of this *skill* encouraged Anna to engage in further exploration, addressing several aspects in therapy of cancer patients suffering from depression (Allen, 2013). The change from being a background performer in music therapy to becoming the soloist appeared to help Anna to reinforce her internal locus of control at the perceptive component of the perceptive/affective level. This experience in turn enhanced her transition to the affective component, where she became able to express strong feelings, and then to face the transition to the cognitive component, leading to the ability to control, analyze and take charge of her life. This transition marked another important and difficult step for Anna in that she needed time to resolve the struggle between her negative feelings and positive outlook, reflecting the ambiguity of feelings as pointed out by Allen (2013). Music therapy interventions and healing nature imagery brought Anna into meditative state and supported her transition to the symbolic component of the cognitive/symbolic level. It also contributed to the development of Anna's own creativity in that she transformed the sound of the noise of an empty swing to recalling herself swinging as a child. Thus, music-based reminiscence and imagery (O'Callaghan & Magill, 2015) helped to mediate the healing power of integrating the different levels of the ETC by internalizing a healing image.

The multiple changes Anna experienced in her internal mental processes and expressed during the therapeutic process reflected and/or were enhanced by different aspects of music therapy.

Conclusions

Following her work with the music therapist, Anna's indifferent, depressed position receded, and she reported having a definite plan (of doing a family biography) over the following months. The music therapy activities, implemented via the framework of the ETC, helped her to find a more proactive position in the formation of relationships with people both from the past and the present, and to actively seek out fulfilling and lively experiences. Anna's psychiatrist and daughter confirmed the improvement and, having experienced some music therapy, Anna decided to join the recreative music group, thus re-establishing contact with neighbours from her residential home. The framework of the ETC facilitated identification of Anna's weakness and strong points, the setting of therapeutic goals, and it marked some important turning points in therapy.

ETC-based therapy, as presented in this case study, provided a multi-layered and multi-modal experience leading to fuller and more varied functioning of a depressed client/patient, offering perspectives for integration of her experience and a positive outlook for the future. Hence, music therapy can be an effective means of addressing cancer-related depression and the ETC offers a way to conceptualize and individualize the work, providing a framework for assessment, planning and structuring of treatment as well as serving as an explanatory model for the creative transitions as the client/patient goes through therapy. Through kinesthetic/sensory activity, the client/patient can be gently immersed in sensation and achieve an appropriate release of tension through vigorous action. Working on the perceptual/affective level facilitates initial steps toward expression and containment of emotion. Cognitive/symbolic work offers opportunities for active problem solving and highlights personal strengths so that new "out of box" solutions and new aspects of identity can emerge. Finally, creative work provides the challenge and mastery that can induce flow experiences leading to growth.

References

Allen, J. (2013). *Guidelines for music therapy practice in adult medical care*. New Braunfels: Barcelona Publishers.

Bradt, J., Dileo, C., Magill, L., & Teague, A. (2016). Music interventions for improving psychological and physical outcomes in cancer patients. *Cochrane Database of Systematic Reviews*, 2016(8), CD006911.

Dileo, C. (2006). Effects of music and music therapy on medical patients: A meta-analysis of the research and implications for the future. *Journal of the Society for Integrative Oncology*, 4(2), 67–70.

Fernandez, K. T., Serrano, K. C. M., & Tongson, M. C. (2014). An intervention in treating selective mutism using the expressive therapies continuum framework. *Journal of Creativity in Mental Health*, 9, 19–32.

Gomez-Campelo, P., Bragado-Alvarez, C., & Hernandez-Lloreda, M. J. (2014). Psychological distress in women with breast and gynecological cancer treated with radical surgery. *Psycho-oncology*, 23(4), 459–466.

Hinz, L. D. (2009). *Expressive therapies continuum: A framework for using art in therapy*. New York, NY: Routledge.

Hultquist, A. M. (1995). Selective mutism: causes and interventions. *Journal of Emotional and Behavioral Disorders*, 3(2), 100–107.

Irving, G., & Lloyd-Williams, M. (2010). Depression in advanced cancer. *European Journal of Oncology Nursing*, 14(5), 395–399.

Lowenfeld, V. (1952). *Creative and mental growth* (2nd ed.). New York, NY: Macmillan.

Lusebrink, V. B. (1990). *Imagery and visual expression in therapy*. New York: Plenum Press.

Lusebrink, V. B. (1992). A systems oriented approach to the expressive therapies: The expressive therapies continuum. *The Arts in Psychotherapy*, 18(5).

Lusebrink, V. B. (2004). Art therapy and the brain: An attempt to understand the underlying processes of art expression in therapy. *Art Therapy: Journal of the American Art Therapy Association*, 21(3).

Lusebrink, V. B. (2010). Assessment and therapeutic application of the expressive therapies continuum: Implications for brain structures and functions. *Art Therapy: Journal of American Art Therapy Association*, 27(4).

Malchiodi, C. A. (2005). Expressive theories: history, theory, and practice. In C.A. Malchiodi (Ed.), *Expressive therapies*. New York: Guilford Press.

Mārtinsone, K., Šilova, I., Lusebrink, V. B., & Veide-Nedviga, L. (2013). The expressive therapies continuum: An integrative systemic approach to visual expression and its historical background. *Медицинскаяпсихология в России*, 5, 22.

Montgomery, G. H., & Bovbjerg, D. H. (2000). Pre-infusion expectations predict post-treatment nausea during repeated adjuvant chemotherapy infusion for breast cancer. *British Journal of Health Psychology*, 5(2), 105–119.

O'Callaghan, C., & Magill, L. (2015). Music therapy with adults diagnosed with cancer and their families. In J. Edwards. (Ed.), *Oxford handbook of music therapy*. Oxford University Press.

Phillips, K. A., Osborne, R. H., Giles, G. G., Dite, G. S., Apicella, C., Hopper, J. L., & Milne, R. L. (2008). Psychosocial factors and survival of young women with breast cancer: A population-based prospective cohort study. *Journal of Clinical Oncology*, 26(28), 4666–4671.

Schubart, J. R., Emerich, M., Farnan, M., Stanley Smith, J., Kauffman, G. L., & Kass, R. B. (2014). Screening for psychological distress in surgical breast cancer patients. *Annals of Surgical Oncology*, 21(10), 3348–3353.

Vende, K., Orinska, S., Majore-Dūšele, I., Upmale, A. (2015). Dance movement therapy for patients with eating disorders: Model of expressive therapies continuum. In A. Heiderscheit (Ed.), *Creative arts therapies in eating disorder treatment*. Philadelphia: Jessica Kinsgsley Publishing.

Index

For Product Safety Concerns and Information please contact our EU representative GPSR@taylorandfrancis.com
Taylor & Francis Verlag GmbH, Kaufingerstraße 24, 80331 München, Germany

www.ingramcontent.com/pod-product-compliance
Ingram Content Group UK Ltd.
Pitfield, Milton Keynes, MK11 3LW, UK
UKHW010958180926
475701UK00004B/437

* 9 7 8 0 3 6 7 4 8 7 8 4 3 *